BRIAN W. BOYLES

NEW ORLEANS
BOOM & BLACKOUT

ONE HUNDRED DAYS IN AMERICA'S COOLEST HOT SPOT

Published by The History Press
Charleston, SC 29403
www.historypress.net

Copyright © 2015 by Brian W. Boyles
All rights reserved

First published 2015

Front cover: San Francisco 49ers cheerleaders perform during a power outage at the Superdome in the second half of the NFL Super Bowl XLVII football game between the 49ers and the Baltimore Ravens, Sunday, February 3, 2013, in New Orleans. *AP Photo/Evan Vucci.*

Manufactured in the United States

ISBN 978.1.62619.860.9

Library of Congress Control Number: 2014953385

Notice: The information in this book is true and complete to the best of our knowledge. It is offered without guarantee on the part of the author or The History Press. The author and The History Press disclaim all liability in connection with the use of this book.

All rights reserved. No part of this book may be reproduced or transmitted in any form whatsoever without prior written permission from the publisher except in the case of brief quotations embodied in critical articles and reviews.

For Kimberly

CONTENTS

Acknowledgements	7
Introduction. How's New Orleans Doing?	9
1. October 25, 2012: "He Will Shoot You Down"	13
2. November 3, 2012: "Let Them See Me Now"	25
3. November 29, 2012: Parade of Progress	41
4. December 8, 2012: Paths to Progress	55
5. December 17, 2012: The Highway to Baton Rouge	69
6. January 7, 2013: "The Sheriff Has a Gun to the City's Head"	79
7. January 13, 2013: Hack	91
8. January 16, 2013: Music Business	103
9. January 19, 2013: "Be Nice or Leave"	113
10. January 24, 2013: Birds	125
11. January 26, 2013: The Clean Zone of Tombstone	139
12. January 28, 2013: "What It Looks Like to Win"	151
13. January 29, 2013: "We're Not Living in a Commercial"	157
14. January 30, 2013: Residual Effects	163
15. January 31, 2013: "The Green Stuff"	171
16. February 1, 2013: Demand Space	175
17. February 2, 2013: "I Am Your Great Time"	183
18. February 3, 2013: Power	193

CONTENTS

Epilogue. February 8, 2013: Relay Misoperation	199
Notes	203
Index	217
About the Author	224

ACKNOWLEDGEMENTS

My sincere thanks goes out to the many people who paused in their days to speak with me on the streets, in countless loud rooms and through various channels. There are quite a few whose names I never caught but whose humor and insights helped me better understand my subject and course.

Christen Thompson made me feel comfortable about this project from the outset of our fortifying—and, I hope, continuing—dialogue. She was quick on the uptake, carefully incisive with her advice and supportive of the directions and misdirections I chose to follow.

Benjamin Morris put me in touch with Christen and provided early browbeating about the need to proceed. Thanks, sir.

Zack Smith is an artist and a true professional, and I owe him.

Among those who made themselves available for interviews: Delores Washington, Monroe Coleman, Frances Swigart, Meg Lousteau, Askiel, Luna Nola, Edward Jackson and the TBC Brass Band, John Amos, Curtis Williams, Tara Jill Ciccarone, Mike the tarot card reader, Bill Curl, Romaine Stitelet, Lieutenant Governor Jay Dardenne, Mark Romig, Iftikhar Ahmad, Crawford Comeaux, Warren Bell, Marlo Barrea, Paul Timfoney, Naomi Martin, John Cosentino, Marshall Faulk, Gary Johnson, Alex Wommack, Tanner, Gertrude Sigel and Quint Davis.

Along with my first-person observations, this book relies on numerous journalists working in New Orleans. In a trying time for local media, we're fortunate to have many talented people chasing important stories. I read and often quoted reporters Charles Maldonado, David Hammer,

ACKNOWLEDGEMENTS

Jaquetta White, Alex Rawls, Michael Patrick Welch, Allen Powell, Jessica Williams, Jason Brad Berry, Jimmy Smith, Jeff Duncan and Lee Zurik. Among the authors I read to prepare and guide the narrative: Ed Haas, Mark Souther, Richard Campanella, Tom Scocca, Oliver Houck, Matt Sakakeeny and A.J. Liebling.

Several generous editors and publications gave platforms for portions of this content: Rodger Hodge and the *Oxford American*, Jan Ramsey and *Offbeat* and Ben Osborne and Abe Schwadron at *SLAM*/TD Daily.

Thanks to the audiences of the Louisiana Humanities Center for teaching me to listen and to all the people who've participated in our programs. Were it not for all of you, this book would be approximately three pages long.

Deepest fealty expressed to Justin Micaroni, Patrick White and the entire Handsome Willy's family. Thanks to Jarret Lofstead, in whose studio this idea—and numerous others—first germinated, the staff of Rick's Saloon, the staff of Mena's Palace, the supporters of the People Say Project, John B. White, Miranda Restovic, John Richie, Lang Whitaker, Matt Bucher, Will Collicott, Michael Sartisky and Mike Reese, Rachel Leifer, Bart Everson, Ryan Edwards, John Whalen, Andre Perry, Steve Cannon and Melville J. Wohlgemuth III.

Thank you to Jeffrey Boyles, Melissa Boyles and David Boyles for being decent, kind and loving people with whom to grow up.

Ultimately, my deepest thanks go to my teammate Kimberly VanWagner, for every morning, afternoon and night, and to Ivan Ward Boyles, for coming along at just the right time.

INTRODUCTION
HOW'S NEW ORLEANS DOING?

If you live here, you're accustomed to the question. Curious strangers, concerned family members, close associates from other coasts—people care about New Orleans. They want to know if it's as good, as bad or as different as they've heard. *How's the food? What about the levees? Can you get shot? Is it the heat or the humidity?* As a resident, someone who deals monthly with the Sewage and Water Board, you have permission and, it sometimes seems, an obligation to sum up the conditions of 340,000 or so people, not to mention the ghosts, cockroaches and politicians who prosper within the boundaries of Orleans Parish. *How is it down there, anyway?*

The real answer: *When and for whom?* Like any city, New Orleans is better and worse than it was ten, one hundred or one thousand years ago, depending on whose porch you sit and at what time. The point, it seems to me, is to sit on as many porches as possible in as many neighborhoods as possible for as long as possible. That's where you can find answers—and other things, too.

In recent years, however, a strain of answers coalesced into an emerging, adaptable brand: the new New Orleans. In November 2010, *Travel & Leisure* magazine published "Exploring the New New Orleans," a feature by Thomas Beller that encouraged travelers to discover "the eclectic characters, strange beauty, and authentic local experience." The city was "gorgeous and cheap," Beller wrote, with a booming "Hollywood South" film scene and a "sort of improvised communal happiness."[1] The brand was not reserved for passing travelers. The *Wall Street Journal* ranked New Orleans as its most improved city for business in 2011. In January 2012, Inc.com urged readers looking for

INTRODUCTION

a "supportive start-up community in which to launch your venture" to hurry to New Orleans before it was too late. Fueled by a curious national media and an engaged tourism industry, the brand gained traction. The outside world began to take note: no longer was this a recovery story. New Orleans was hot.[2]

The 2013 Super Bowl offered a prism for understanding the brand and its means of distribution. The game, we heard, was a time for New Orleans to shine. I accepted the premise expressed by the mayor and others that the Super Bowl would show the world how far we'd come since the 2005 federal levee failures. Like the world, I wanted to know the answer. I also wanted to know who would provide answers.

Other questions arose as the game approached. If the post-Katrina era was finally over, I wanted to understand the decades prior to Katrina, particularly the evolution of the city's postwar economy and politics. Who had articulated earlier visions for the city's future? Their successes and failures might help us evaluate the promises of the new New Orleans.

Tourism has played a fundamental force in the development of New Orleans since the nineteenth century; indeed, as a river town, it never didn't have visitors. Today, the tourism industry appears particularly robust and more sophisticated; the pace of its successes seemed to quicken in recent years. What changed? How do tourism and politics intersect?

The intersection of tourism and sports also interested me. Between December 2011 and March 2012, New Orleans hosted the New Orleans Bowl, the Sugar Bowl, the BCS College Football Championship, a Saints playoff game and the NCAA Men's Final Four, an unprecedented succession of major sporting events for one city. Now came Super Bowl XLVII, with promises of more than $400 million in economic impact. Professional sports and big games are vital to the local economy, but their history and operations remain opaque. What were the origins of the venues, teams and politics? Who made money off the games?

Finally, I continue to believe that service industry workers know more about the city's byways and conflicts than most politicians and visiting journalists. Behind every nationally televised event, refurbished hotel and photographed second-line parade, there are people who support their families and habits by driving cabs, pouring daiquiris and changing linens. I wanted to know what they thought about the Super Bowl and the new New Orleans.

One thing I know: the minute you think you've figured this place out, your car will be stolen. In this Creole city, never let anyone tell you something is simply black and white; the solidest of truths can vanish into the lake. By

INTRODUCTION

focusing on the one hundred days before Super Bowl XLVII, I hoped to show how, even within this narrow sample, New Orleans continues to be a complex, protean landscape that resists the very generalizations it so often attracts. During a period of heightened visibility, I wondered what contrasts would emerge. To maintain this focus, I set some parameters.

Wherever possible, I included only the information that was available at or before 11:59 p.m. CST on Super Bowl Sunday 2013. When, for example, I saw David Hammer's April 2014 WWL-TV coverage of the Loyola Avenue streetcar line, I did not insert those revelations into this history. I wanted a record of the things people said during those one hundred days, a diary of this brief period that drew from the city's past. Substantial new facts emerged in the months following the game, but for the most part, I've used only what was known in late 2012 and early 2013.

Second, I concentrated on a specific area of the city. From my office in the Central Business District, I've traversed the territory of this book—Calliope to Elysian Fields, North Claiborne to the river—for almost eight years, marveling at the diversity of the commercial structures and their mutating usages. Within these borders are city hall, the Superdome, the French Quarter and the Ernest N. Morial Convention Center, the main linchpins of the Super Bowl period. Many other neighborhoods are equally important, but this was my postage stamp of land.

I'm confident that any stretch of randomly selected one hundred days in this town contains uncountable stories. Pick three months and see what happens. The conflicts in the new New Orleans were visible before October 25, 2012, and after February 3, 2013, from consent decrees to Bourbon Street. Still, I'm glad I paid attention during the approach of Super Bowl XLVII, a tumultuous, exciting time when so many people sought to answer that question: *How's New Orleans doing?* Not for the first time, I heard the city answer: *Listen.*

CHAPTER 1
OCTOBER 25, 2012
(101 DAYS TO SUPER BOWL XLVII)

"HE WILL SHOOT YOU DOWN"

In front of the Superdome sat a black hearse carrying an empty coffin. A stout black woman in a mourning dress, hat and veil smiled broadly next to the open passenger door as another woman snapped a picture and people convened to laugh. "We Shall Not Rest in Peace Mayor Mitch," read the sign taped to the hearse's window. Behind the hearse, a line of at least one hundred taxicabs, in every shape and size, ran down Poydras Street: black-and-white minivans, yellow station wagons, red Suburbans, brown sedans.

The crowd gathered near the Superdome was also strikingly diverse, if largely male; this stretch of five hundred feet likely contained a wider range of nationalities than any other swath of the city. Skullcaps and baseball caps, arguments and jokes in various tongues—for one overcast morning, the Superdome sidewalk looked more like Queens than New Orleans. In a city forever debating the relationship between blacks and whites, the taxi industry offered a complex palette.

On October 25, 2012, we waited for what the cab drivers were calling a "motorcade," their rolling protest against new regulations proposed by Mayor Mitch Landrieu and approved by the city council in April. By January 1, every taxi was required to be equipped with a surveillance camera, credit card machine and GPS unit. No car older than ten years—seven, by the end of 2013—would be granted a renewed certificate of public necessity and convenience, or CPNC, required for cab owners. All drivers would be

A protestor awaits the start of the October 25, 2012 taxicab motorcade. *Photo by author*.

subjected to background checks, and new procedures would standardize the process of inspection and renewal and the maintenance of trip logs.

"Our unique culture, music, cuisine and architecture makes us an enviable place to live, work and visit, but for more than a generation, our taxicabs have been substandard," Landrieu said when the regulations passed. "This is not an assault on the thousands of taxicab and for-hire drivers who serve as important frontline ambassadors for our city and region, but the quality of cabs need dramatic improvement."[3]

As I waited to speak with one of the motorcade's organizers, a man approached me with a box of Mardi Gras beads he was selling to raise money for the family of a fallen comrade, a cabbie who was fatally stabbed a few weeks back. The motorcade protesters had adopted the man as their collective symbol, hence the coffin and hearse. I apologized to the donation taker—unfortunately, I had no cash. Nearby drivers cracked up when he assured me that he had a credit card machine in his car. Another man showed me a photocopy of a money order made out to the City of New Orleans, with a scrawled message: "Payment Received, Call Customer Pick-Up." He offered this as proof that he paid for his CPNC renewal in January but still had not received his new permit. He shrugged his shoulders and shook his head in annoyance.

Other conversations along the sidewalk echoed the same complaints: the city demanded the taxicab industry get its house in order, but the city didn't hold up its end of the bargain. Corruption at the inspection office, incompetence in the permitting process and the employment of a single, rapacious vendor to install new equipment—what was a cabbie supposed to do? Several drivers told me the new taxicab bureau chief, Malachi Hull, was a crook who was run out of similar positions in other cities. The purportedly business-friendly reforms weren't accompanied by training programs to ensure that cabbies got their paperwork in order—to teach them, for example, how to set aside money to pay taxes and how to register for and renew permits—and properly account for the new credit card machines. Worst of all, they said, was the short timeline. The Landrieu administration wanted a reformed system in place for this year's Super Bowl, scheduled for February 3 at the Superdome. During an earlier protest march, drivers chanted, "If you want a cab for the Super Bowl, Malachi must go!"

Over a megaphone, a voice called "all drivers" to meet at the concrete entrance ramp to the Superdome's Gate A. Atop the ramp stood protest spokesman Monroe Coleman, in an outback hat, sunglasses and a red golf shirt emblazoned with the logo of his Coleman Company. He appealed to the crowd for donations to cover the $2,400 permit fee for another motorcade in November.

"The permit is going to cost us more money because it's Saturday, and we're going to have more cabs in the motorcade. Now, are we in agreement that we're going to continue this effort until the city comes to the bargaining table?" The crowd roared its approval.

"The theme of this motorcade is the wrongful death of the taxicab driver. The administration is killing us slowly but surely." He denounced the background checks that penalized longtime drivers for youthful infractions.

"We are not going to stand by and let [the mayor] take the liberty from each of us. He will shoot you down, one by one! They're trying to get the independents out of this cab business. So are we together or not?"

Roar!

"Are we together?"

Roar!

A woman took the megaphone and asked for donations for "our fallen comrade," the stabbing victim. Then a preacher offered a prayer, punctuated by a collective "amen" from this international, likely interdenominational assembly. Coleman returned for one last announcement. "I need those pallbearers right now."

As the crowd dispersed, protest co-organizer Delores Washington led me to Monroe Coleman's black Escalade. It was driven that day by Dina, Coleman's longtime accountant, who invited me to wedge myself between the boxes of Mardi Gras beads that filled the backseat. We were near the front of the motorcade, ahead of the hearse and behind four bikers wearing leather vests emblazoned with "Nubian Kruzers" and "My Brother's Keeper." Two motorcycle cops waited at the head of the procession.

A little before 11:00 a.m., six pallbearers took the casket out of the hearse, and the motorcade began to move down Poydras to the corner of Loyola Avenue. On our left, we passed city hall, where Mayor Landrieu had begun a press conference to mark the one-hundred-day countdown to Super Bowl XLVII. Surrounded by his deputy mayors, Landrieu declared the city "well on our way to being 100 percent ready," with all planned projects on schedule. He explained:

> *The idea is to make sure that New Orleans shines its brightest light at this particular time when we are on the world's stage. The idea is, from the moment a tourist steps into the city of New Orleans, or a customer from anywhere, that they have a wonderful experience. When they come in on the plane, they walk into a concourse that is newly renovated. If they have to use the facilities, they walk into a beautiful restroom facility. If they want to eat food and they're hungry, they walk into a newly constructed restaurant. When they walk outside, they're greeted by somebody who has*

ONE HUNDRED DAYS IN AMERICA'S COOLEST HOT SPOT

customer service at the forefront of their mind. They get into a cab that is clean and safe.

The mayor was compact, maybe five feet, eight inches tall, with an athletic build, shaved head, watery blue eyes and a dimpled jaw. He spoke with a white New Orleanian's accent of broad *a*'s and soft *r*'s. The son of a former mayor and, at one time, an aspiring actor, Landrieu took podiums with relish. The press conference marked the start of regular addresses outlining the importance of the Super Bowl to the revitalized New Orleans.

He listed the $340 million improvements to the Superdome, the reopened Hyatt on Loyola Avenue and the game's expected $400 million economic impact for the state and city, all part of a civic "redemption and resurrection" story. "As I like to say, New Orleans has become the coolest hotspot in America."

America, said Landrieu, could also look to New Orleans as a model of progress, with its reformed schools, the reconstruction of its healthcare system, the reorganization of city government, the revitalization of transportation and its emergence as a national focal point for sports and entertainment. "New Orleans is on the rise," he said. "It's been noted by the *Wall Street Journal*, it's been noted by *Forbes* magazine…I want to show the world what the best looks like." It was a bold statement from the leader of a city renowned for its systemic, multiple dysfunctions, but Landrieu was committed to changing that image.

For details, the mayor introduced a carousel of city officials, each of them assuring the media that the improvements promised for the game were on schedule. Deputy Mayor Cedric Grant predicted the January completion of all infrastructure repairs in the "Hospitality Zone," the section of the city encompassing the French Quarter, Central Business District (CBD) and Superdome. Among the most visible projects was the new Loyola Avenue streetcar line, which ran past city hall.

"Yes, we are ready," said Regional Transit Authority director Justin Augustine. "That iconic project that's going on right outside these doors will be completed by January 13." Repairs to the St. Charles Avenue line would halt so that Mardi Gras parades could run unimpeded. The Super Bowl fell in the middle of the 2013 Carnival, forcing the city to schedule the first parades a week earlier than usual, break for the game and then resume the celebrations, culminating with Fat Tuesday on February 12.

Dina navigated through the streetcar construction at Loyola and Poydras, where a man helmed a large saw that whined fiercely into the concrete. Hundreds of car horns blared as we crept through the CBD, past officeworkers on early lunch breaks, puzzled tourists and two boys on bicycles. The tourists made me curious about the situation at the airport: if all the cabs were here, who picked up the incoming visitors? Dina said that during last week's protest, Monroe's company had received 170 calls in two hours from people desperate for a cab, a sharp uptick that reflected the power of drivers to shut down transportation in the city.

The day's route traced the border of the Hospitality Zone mentioned by Deputy Mayor Grant. We turned up Convention Center Boulevard, which was quiet, save for a few kids holding "Cruise Ship Parking" placards. When the motorcade reached I-10 near the last hall of the New Orleans Ernest M. Morial Convention Center, the police made a U-turn and led us back toward the French Quarter. On the way, Dina picked up Coleman, who waited on the median, known in New Orleans as "the neutral ground." He climbed into the passenger seat and asked me to hand him his black-and-gold beads. I dug through the boxes and boxes of colored beads in the rear of the Escalade until I found them. Beads in hand, Coleman stood up through the open sunroof so that all I could see were his black pants and "C" belt buckle, and he tossed beads to pedestrians like a Carnival float veteran.

We stopped in front of the Harrah's Casino on Canal Street. A police officer approached us. "Y'all keep stopping, and we're going to cut it off," she said. "Supposed to be 150 cars out here…there's 500. You're killing us." We continued down North Peters Street into the French Quarter.

At city hall, Landrieu maintained the stiff-necked manner of a train conductor, calling forward each speaker to provide updates on his specific tasks. Iftikhar Ahmad, director of the Louis Armstrong International Airport, reported that 90 percent of planned projects were complete, including a new rental car facility, improved furniture and concessions and landscaping. Upgraded food and beverage services would debut on January 15, and each gate would feature a television in time for the game. "We feel good and ready for the Super Bowl, thank you very much," said Ahmad.

Deputy Mayor of Operations Michelle Thomas described "sweeping taxicab reforms," scheduled to be in place by the end of January, that would "give our residents and guests the type of ground transportation experience they deserve and that one would expect from a world-class tourism city…To date, we have more than 400 of our 1,551 vehicles in compliance."

Scott Hutcheson from the mayor's Office of Cultural Economy introduced a new poster for the "Don't Trash Dat" anti-litter campaign. The phrase was a play on the "Who Dat?" phrase used by Saints fans, three of whom appeared on the poster under a speech bubble containing, "Oh no YOU didn't."

ONE HUNDRED DAYS IN AMERICA'S COOLEST HOT SPOT

The mayor repeated that line with a tight smile and reminded everyone that the Super Bowl was a national security event. Police Superintendent Ronal Serpas told reporters, "We feel really good right now. We're ready to make this the best Super Bowl ever." Serpas was tall with wide hips, a boyish haircut and an easy manner. He mentioned the many big events hosted by the city in the last fifteen months, including the Men's Final Four, the BCS College Football Championship and the Sugar Bowl. "Our police department continues to prove that when it comes to this particular task, we're the best in the world."

After the last report, Landrieu emphasized the unprecedented run of scheduled events. "We have Mardi Gras, we have three Hornets games, we have a Justin Bieber concert, we have the Super Bowl and then we have Mardi Gras again." Behind him the group giggled, and the mayor praised their commitment and focus.

"As we reinvest into making New Orleans what it always wanted to be," he declared, "it's quite a magnificent opportunity. [When New Orleans acts as] one team, one fight, one voice, one city—that's when New Orleans shines." After plugging the city's candidacy for the 2018 Super Bowl, just in time for New Orleans' 300th anniversary, he welcomed questions. The first reporter asked about the "line of taxis" outside. Would the city have sufficient ground transportation in one hundred days?

"We spent a very long time working with the industry," Landrieu answered. The majority of drivers and owners were in compliance.

"I think there are two hundred people outside. I guess my message to them would be, 'I'm sorry that you feel disgruntled, but we feel like the rules and regulations designed in partnership with the industry make a lot of sense.'" Another reporter asked about the short timeline, and the mayor observed, "Sometimes my brothers and sisters in New Orleans wait until the last minute to do something." The cabbies, he promised, had more than enough time. "As it relates to everything in New Orleans, I'll quote my friend Sam Cooke. 'Change is gonna come.'"[4]

The motorcade turned heads as we passed Jackson Square and the French Market, where several vendors raised their hands to catch beads. At Elysian Fields and Dauphine, along the eastern border of the Quarter, we stopped, and Coleman made a call.

"Otis, how many pallbearers we got?" Apparently, the casket would travel again by foot when we returned to Canal Street. We turned up S. Rampart Street and drove the length of the Quarter. Outside the Best Western across from Armstrong Park, tourists boarded an airport shuttle, while other tourists passed in a lavender horse-drawn carriage. Throughout our trip, I saw no one waiting for a cab. I wondered how the drivers protesting that day made a living, and Monroe told me that the average taxi driver took home between $100 to $150 for a twelve- to fifteen-hour shift, after paying for lunch and gas. Drivers who owned their own cars but rented their CPNCs from permit owners paid $430 a week, meaning a driver might take home anywhere from $300 to $700 weekly, depending on the season and special events. Most drivers, he said, were semi-retired or part-time students, meaning they didn't drive seven days a week. He cited the lighter workload as an argument against the vehicle age limit: cabs weren't operated equally, and a 2000 model might have less wear than a 2007 model, depending on the operator. The city was attacking the small businessmen it was supposed to protect.

"Where's the educational component of reform? You're teaching the people to be angry at you. You're teaching people to talk about you like the dogs that you were. You doggin' me, so I'm gonna dog you to the people coming for business. We the ambassadors. If I'm telling people, 'The city's a dog, don't come here, don't do business with them,' who do you think they're going to believe? You know taxicab drivers know. We the first and the last."[5]

At the corner of Rampart and Canal, we hit more streetcar construction—stacks of rail lines, giant drills, dust-caked utility tracks and piles of copper piping. When we reached North Claiborne Avenue, Coleman said to us from the sunroof, "They still got cabs on Elysian Fields two miles away." Another cop approached the Escalade to speak to Coleman, and I heard him say, "Not my decision. I'm just a soldier."

"Whose decision is it?" Coleman asked.

"The superintendent's."

"Who?"

"Serpas."

"Then I'm going to apply for my refund."

The police chief had made the call: the protest was too large and must return to the Dome. "We really need cameras, now," Dina said "We paid for a route, and they cut it."

Later that afternoon, Mayor Landrieu and Superintendent Serpas appeared before another audience. The doors were closed, media were not invited and no cameras recorded their remarks, but both men appeared afterward to recap the conversation. Like the Super Bowl press conference, this second speaking engagement projected the image of an administration that tackled its challenges with bold action and innovative strategies.

ONE HUNDRED DAYS IN AMERICA'S COOLEST HOT SPOT

In a courtroom at the Orleans Parish Criminal District Court building, Serpas and Landrieu were joined by District Attorney Leon Cannizaro, U.S. attorney Jim Letten and a reported forty special guests: probationers and convicts, called in by probation officers or "invited" by law enforcement, who were identified by the administration as "high-risk" individuals, "a statistical zone of people you'd expect either to shoot or be shot by somebody," Landrieu said. When the session ended, the mayor assured reporters that the assembled guests had received a stern message. He repeated the warning spelled out on two large video screens placed in the courtroom: "We know who you are. We know who your friends are. We know where you go. We know everything about you."[6]

The presentation was part of the mayor's "NOLA for Life" anti-crime initiative, a comprehensive strategy to "end murder and violence in the city." Introduced at Landrieu's State of the City address in July, NOLA for Life included a public awareness campaign crafted by director Spike Lee's advertising firm. This fall, billboards popped up across the city with block letters spelling out crime reports. "BLACK MALE RETURNS WITH GUN AND TAKES VICTIM'S LIFE AROUND 2:45 PM" featured the words "BLACK," "TURNS" and "LIFE AROUND" in bold font, an example of the campaign's "Flip the Script" theme.

According to the *Times-Picayune*, sheriff's deputies guarded the courtroom doors as Serpas, Letten, Cannizzaro, Orleans Parish sheriff Marlin Gusman and NOPD commander Henry Dean "flexed some criminal justice muscle." Criminologist and consultant David Kennedy of Harvard University, a consultant in the development of NOLA for Life, was on hand for the implementation of his anti-gang approach. "Sometimes you see an impact right away," he told the *Times-Picayune*. "Sometimes you have to make it clear you mean it."

Upon taking office in 2010, Landrieu invited the U.S. Justice Department to assess the NOPD and the city's criminal justice system. In a letter to U.S. attorney general Eric Holder, the mayor wrote, "It is clear that nothing short of a complete transformation is necessary and essential to ensure safety for the citizens of New Orleans." A day later, he named his superintendent: the New Orleans–born Serpas, a twenty-year NOPD veteran who left town in 2001. As Nashville's police chief since 2004, Serpas had earned a reputation "as a reformer, kind of a zero-tolerance guy," an advocate of traffic stops and statistics who rarely shied from the spotlight. "He has very high visibility, more so than any police chief," said Nashville district attorney Troy Johnson. "He is a change agent, which is why he was selected to come to Nashville and shake up the department. He has done that in a big way."[7] At Serpas's swearing-in ceremony, Landrieu compared him to the Saints' quarterback. "Now we have the Drew Brees of police chiefs. We didn't get the best police chief in New Orleans. We got the best police chief in the country."[8]

Serpas made his intentions clear that day. "Violent crime is our number-one issue, and we're going to be on it like a dog on a bone," he declared at Gallier Hall, the Greek Revivalist former city hall used for official occasions.[9]

Despite his familiarity with the department, Serpas stumbled out of the gate. His first year included an investigation into "paid details," the moonlighting by off-duty, in-uniform officers at private locations for supplemental pay. Serpas's friend and NOPD captain Ed Hosli formed a company staffed by off-duty officers that contracted with the city to review traffic camera tapes; essentially, the city paid the company to employ its off-duty policemen. Serpas claimed no knowledge of Hosli's apparent conflict of interest and suspended his friend. A subsequent controversy focused on the chief's questionable handling of his own pension fund. Hopes that the smooth-talking Serpas would instill renewed trust in a wary population gave way to frustration over business-as-usual.

Along with internal reform, the city's murder rate remained the most urgent challenge for the NOPD. In a March 2011 "business plan," Serpas promised the mayor a 5 percent reduction in the murder rate, a target that former mayoral candidate James Perry called "listless and uninspiring" in the *Huffington Post*. In fact, it was overly ambitious: murder increased by 14 percent in 2011. The rate of homicide in New Orleans was 58 for every 100,000 residents, down from 73 in 2007 but up from 2009's 51. In March 2011, the Justice Department announced its findings in a scathing report that questioned the NOPD's training methods, use of force and community relations. Landrieu accepted the report's findings and, after more than a year of negotiations, signed a consent decree in July 2012. The agreement stipulated changes to the department's training, organization and paid detail policies that, once implemented, would transform the troubled police force. Holder joined the mayor for a signing ceremony at Gallier Hall.

"The consent decree filed today is the most extensive and far-reaching in this nation's history," said Landrieu. "The people of this city should rest assured that together with the Department of Justice, we will fundamentally change the culture of the NOPD once and for all."[10]

Three months later at the courthouse, Landrieu delivered tough talk to the offenders. It was his unique position as mayor to spend one part of the day preparing the city for the approaching national spotlight and the other promising criminals that he had his eye on them. Landrieu believed in a new New Orleans, a reformed city that welcomed the world with shining facilities, robust culture and a well-organized government. When he faced the men in the dim courtroom at Tulane and Broad, the mayor saw the products of another city, where generations of poverty, corruption and crime threatened to dash the excitement and hope symbolized by the Super Bowl. In a city known for its contrasts, these two versions of New Orleans continued to intersect over the next one hundred days.

For the next seventeen days, no one was murdered in New Orleans.

That evening, I walked with my father through the French Quarter. We maintained a tradition of celebrating Halloween together in New Orleans, and a mutual favorite, Neil Young, was set to take the stage the next day for the Voodoo Festival in City Park. Before I moved here for college in 1995, my father had traveled to the city multiple times for Mardi Gras and Jazz Fest, visiting an old friend who'd relocated in the 1970s from our hometown, Pittsburgh. This night he asked me, "What the hell is happening to the French Quarter?"

One hundred days before Super Bowl XLVII, change was afoot in the historic neighborhood. Orange plastic fences encircled gaping holes in the asphalt. Bulky equipment sat along the curbs. As we made our way down Royal Street, we passed sidewalks stripped of the iconic tile street signs and men in fluorescent vests leaning against bulldozers. Scraped clean of its top layer, the street famed for its antique stores was grooved and dusty. The construction felt careless, far from complete and, most of all, unlikely. Change was not what you expected in the French Quarter, where, despite the proliferation of T-shirt shops and daiquiri outlets, the physical landscape remained an old-world time capsule of recessed courtyards and mysterious balconies, many of its barrooms still smoky and dim. Change happened in the Quarter because of decay or disaster, not progress or deadlines.

We stopped at a hole. In a recent article for the Preservation Resource Center, Tulane geographer Richard Campanella remarked on the educational byproducts of the current French Quarter construction. "Soft red river bricks and hard clay lake bricks, rangia and oyster shells, a layer of ancient paving stones, an occasional rough-hewn wooden board recycled from a barge of flatboat, and more recent strata of concrete and asphalt" were among the visible materials in these holes, all employed to turn marshland into a city.[11] One could read the history of the city, Campanella wrote, in the layers revealed by this latest upheaval. My father and I stared down into the muddy square.

New Orleans, I told him, was changing. And they had better finish this job before the Super Bowl.

CHAPTER 2
NOVEMBER 3, 2012
(NINETY-TWO DAYS TO GO)

"LET THEM SEE ME NOW"

Tad Gormley Stadium sat at the western edge of City Park, where a palm-lined sidewalk led from Marconi Drive to a worn brick booth that waited like a tired sentry. When I reached the bars of the ticket window that afternoon, the middle-aged woman inside croaked, "Five dollars."

Two Catholic high schools' football teams were set to face off under a spotless sky. Both Brother Martin and Archbishop Rummel wore red-and-white uniforms, so followers from each side drifted through the main gates in red sweatshirts, red letterman jackets and red skirts. The crowd was almost all white, and if you didn't know the candidates in the day's presidential election, you might be convinced a portal had opened up and thrust you back to a crisp afternoon in 1959.

I found a seat on an aluminum bleacher three rows back from the field. A group of Brother Martin boys sat next to me—all pimples, cargo pants and nerves. On the rubbery track that circled the field, cheerleaders painted crimson crosses on their cheeks. The drums of the marching band rumbled around the horseshoe-shaped stadium. On the field, players ran through drills, returned short kicks and shoved one another. The visitors' bleachers on the opposite side of the field were only half full. After a few minutes, applause began from both sides.

New Orleans Saints owner Tom Benson and his wife, Gayle, appeared in the end zone to my left. The eighty-five-year-old Benson crossed the track gingerly, his hand pinned to his wife's elbow. Twenty-two years his junior,

Mrs. Benson wore a queenly straw hat with a red bow, a red blouse and gold pants, while her husband looked more gentleman farmer than tycoon in red suspenders over a red shirt and a black baseball cap. The cheers built as the couple sat down on the Brother Martin bench, directly in front of me. Groups of men came to pay their respects as a state trooper stood watch. Benson rose several times to introduce his wife. Two photographers trained their lenses on the couple as the teams clustered at opposite ends of the field for final pre-game huddles.

A brief ceremony honored the year's graduating Brother Martin seniors, each of whom stepped forward to be recognized with their parents. When the ceremony ended, two trainers picked up framed, number 1 Brother Martin jerseys from the sidelines, one stitched with "T. Benson" and the other "G. Benson." The PA announcer directed everyone's attention to midfield, where the trainers joined the Bensons and other school officials.

"Mr. Benson is a 1944 graduate of St. Aloysius High School [the original name of Brother Martin] and was named the alumnus of the year in 1986," the PA announcer tells us. "Mr. and Mrs. Benson have pledged a gift of $10 million to establish the Brother Nicholas endowment at Brother Martin High School. This afternoon, the Bensons will be presenting the first installment of $1 million to Brother Martin. In their honor, the student hall, the center of activity on the Brother Martin campus, will be named the Tom and Gayle Benson Hall. Thank you, Mr. and Mrs. Benson for your continued support of Brother Martin High School and the brothers of the sacred heart." The band resumed, and everyone began to clap in unison, including Benson. He tipped his cap to each side of the field and then made his way back to the sideline to pose for pictures. Both Bensons returned to midfield with the team captains for the coin toss, which Brother Martin won.

The afternoon was another warm moment in the autumn of a very successful life. In the following weeks, NFL officials, fellow team owners and local and national media praised Benson's steady hand and civic pride as key forces in the selection of New Orleans for Super Bowl XLVII. His story seemed to reflect that of his fellow citizens: a resilient, if eccentric, people dedicated to their hometown and unwilling to abandon it after disaster.

Born in 1927, the year of a great flood, Benson grew up on North Johnson Street in the St. Roch neighborhood, back when German and Irish working-class families still populated that part of the Seventh Ward and whites were the decided majority in the city. The family was not well off, and at fifteen, he took a job as a car washer at a dealership on the 300 block of North Rampart Street. When his father fell ill, Benson approached the dealer, Mike Persia,

ONE HUNDRED DAYS IN AMERICA'S COOLEST HOT SPOT

Tom and Gayle Benson at Tad Gormley Stadium. *Photo courtesy of Brother Martin High School.*

to ask if he might pick up more work. Persia appreciated the boy's ambition and made him a counteroffer: Benson could work a full-time schedule, but Persia would send him to St. Aloysius High School, whose Catholic brothers had their cars prepped at the dealership. Over the next four years, Benson worked evenings and weekends while earning good grades at St. Aloysius. Upon graduation, he told Persia that he was ready to sell cars, but again Persia set a higher goal. The brothers at Loyola University had cars prepped at the lot, too, and besides, Benson was too smart for sales. With his aptitude for numbers and fervent Catholicism, Benson cruised through his courses at Loyola, graduating in 1948 with an accounting degree after a stint in the navy. Persia had a dealer friend in San Antonio, Stanley Rosenberg, who wanted to retire from the business but was afraid to leave the lot to his bungling children. Persia offered him Benson, with the understanding that the young man could have free reign for six months, none of the Rosenberg children on the lot. If Benson turned things around, Rosenberg would sell him half the business.

Benson succeeded, and Rosenberg was good on his word, even teaching the New Orleanian how to buy his own dealerships. Finance was much more interesting to the young numbers man than cars, and Benson began to explore new options. During the 1970s and '80s, he purchased several community banks around San Antonio and built Benson Financial, with Rosenberg's son as his lawyer and trusted advisor. The makings of an empire were in place. Benson eventually sold the financial firm to Wells Fargo for $440 million in 1996.

Sitting on the sidelines at Tad Gormley Stadium, twenty-six years after purchasing the Saints, Tom Benson was arguably the most powerful man in New Orleans, with an estimated worth of $1.3 billion. His philanthropic gifts and business acumen were roundly praised and publicized. As the owner of a professional football team, he was an undisputed success. A loyal fan base regularly packed the Superdome for home games, wrapped itself in team merchandise and still reveled in the afterglow of the Saints' 2009–10 championship season. Yet like the relationship between the NFL and New Orleans, the history of Tom Benson and his hometown was marked by numerous unlikely turns, instances of good fortune, public disgrace and triumph. As the city prepared for Super Bowl XLVII, Benson enjoyed a period of unprecedented wealth and influence in a town where he and the NFL were synonymous for almost thirty years. To understand just how surprising this was, we must return to the dawn of professional football in New Orleans. From Tad Gormley Stadium, we must travel to earlier games and past ceremonies.

But let's start on Bourbon Street.

Ernie Warlick had big hands. Combined with his six-foot-three, 235-pound frame, Warlick's hands made him the greatest tight end in Buffalo Bills history and earned him a simple nickname: "Hands." A four-time American Football League (AFL) All-Star, Warlick helped lead the Bills to victory in the AFL championship game on December 26, 1964. But two weeks later in New Orleans, Hands Warlick couldn't catch a cab.

He and his fellow players were in town for the annual AFL All-Star game, scheduled for the following day at Tulane Stadium. The game was a big deal for football fans in a city without a professional team, and promoters expected to sell fifty thousand tickets. The AFL was a short-lived but important rival to the NFL, eventually merging with the older league in 1969. A strong turnout for the All-Star game might raise New Orleans' odds for securing a team of its own. On Saturday, January 9, 1965, Warlick stood outside the Fontainebleau Motor Hotel on Tulane Avenue, hoping to hail a ride to the French Quarter. But as an African American male in the segregated South, Warlick's odds of catching a taxi were decidedly long.

"Several cab drivers outside the Fontainebleau refused to take me," he told reporters later. Other black All-Stars had similar experiences.

"We decided to relax in the French Quarter Saturday night," said halfback Clem Daniels of the Oakland Raiders, "and tried to catch a cab in front of the Roosevelt [Hotel, just off Canal Street]. Finally, we stood in the middle of the street, and a cab stopped rather than run us down." When Warlick, Davis and others eventually reached Bourbon Street, they were greeted with hostility.

"Doors were shut in our faces as we attempted to enter several establishments, and some people hurled insults at us," said Dick Westmoreland of the San Diego Chargers. "Employees of some nightspots milled around us as we walked down the street." Back at their hotels, other players relayed similar experiences. A decision was made: the African American players would boycott the All-Star game. Warlick spoke to AFL commissioner Joe Foss, who said the league would back the boycott. Foss then informed local promoter Dave Dixon that the game would move to Houston. Primed for the big leagues, New Orleans appeared backward and inhospitable, a southern city where the ugly realities of segregation made its world-famous street off limits to black customers.[12]

National columnists chided New Orleans, with one *Boston Globe* writer asking why black players should "slink around town as second class citizens while their presence in the game's line-up brings profit to the cabbies and the other white promoters?"[13] As local segregationists accused the players of plotting the boycott ahead of time, Mayor Victor Schiro objected that the players "should have rolled with the punch." The *Times-Picayune* described Dixon as "struggling to pick up the pieces of a shattered dream." The rare combination of antiques dealer and sports fanatic, Dixon had dedicated years of his life to bringing professional football to the city, staging several exhibition and pre-season games since 1962, featuring both NFL and AFL teams at Tulane Stadium and City Park Stadium. He was particularly familiar with the intersection of race and football. To increase attendance, Dixon partnered with local civil rights lawyers in 1964 to defeat a state law requiring segregated seating for sporting events. The AFL debacle stung him.

"You can imagine what this will do to our efforts to bring professional football to New Orleans," Dixon said in a statement. "I'm heartsick."

He was not, however, without friends.

In 1964, Dixon promoted an exhibition game between Green Bay and St. Louis. At a pre-game reception at the New Orleans Country Club, Governor John McKeithen whispered into Dixon's ear that he was an "enormous" football fan. Dixon saw his opening and secured a meeting with the governor to reveal his grandest dream: a domed stadium. Along with an NFL team, this "Ultradome" or "Superdome" could host trade shows, conventions and even a baseball team. Then Dixon delivered a pitch to McKeithen's wheelhouse. "I pitched him the idea that this would be a chance for Louisiana to pass Houston."[14] State politicians and businessmen were eternally envious of the progress in other New South cities like Atlanta, Houston and Dallas. The governor stood up and banged his fist on his desk. "My God, that would be the greatest building in the history of mankind! We'll build that sucker!"[15]

To begin the sucker, the governor needed more money and more power. In 1966, he sponsored two constitutional amendments: Amendment #1, granting Louisiana governors the right to a second consecutive term, and Amendment #10, approving the use of state funds to create the Louisiana Sports and Entertainment District. The district would manage the construction of a proposed fifty-thousand-seat stadium at a cost of $35 million financed by state bonds and a new hotel tax. The amendments required a statewide referendum. Across Louisiana, opposition rose swiftly to the increase in terms and to the heavy expenditure in New Orleans, a city ever at odds with its state. But McKeithen had the wind at his back.

In June 1966, the NFL and AFL agreed to a merger scheduled for the 1970 season, a transaction often cited as the birth of the modern NFL. In the meantime, the leagues sought to host joint drafts of college players and, most importantly, negotiate for lucrative television rights as one entity. In essence, this partnership monopolized professional football. Congressional approval was needed for an anti-trust exemption that, in the words of *Atlantic* columnist Gregg Easterbrook, gave the new league "a license to print money" and enabled the NFL's reclassification as a nonprofit organization.[16] At Dixon's suggestion, two Louisiana congressmen, House majority whip Hale Boggs and Senate Finance Committee chair Russell Long, served as legislative midwives for the exemption. Boggs was particularly interested in supporting the cause of professional football in New Orleans: the prior year, the congressman had supported the 1965 Voting Rights Act, and his popularity took a palpable hit. He needed something to win back white New Orleans voters. According to a 2010 *New York Times* article, Boggs made clear his demands before the start of a committee hearing in October 1966:

> As Rozelle and Boggs walked to the Capitol Rotunda, Rozelle said he did not know how to thank Boggs.
> "What do you mean you don't know how to thank me?" Boggs said. "New Orleans gets an immediate franchise in the N.F.L."
> Rozelle waffled ever so little, saying he would do everything he could.

ONE HUNDRED DAYS IN AMERICA'S COOLEST HOT SPOT

"Well, we can always call off the vote while you—" Boggs said.
"It's a deal, Congressman," Rozelle said. *"You'll get your franchise."*[17]

Thus began the long and curious relationship of the New Orleans Saints and the NFL, a partnership that included not a few favors and a sufficient number of conflicts. Congress approved the exemption on October 21, 1966. Less than two years after the AFL All-Star game boycott, on November 1—All Saint's Day in Catholic Louisiana—the NFL announced that New Orleans would receive a team. A week later, McKeithen's Amendment #1 garnered 86 percent of the vote, clearing the way for his second term in office. Amendment #10, which allocated funding for construction of the Louisiana Superdome, was slightly less popular but no less successful: it received 76 percent. "That sucker" was born.

After the Saints' arrival in 1967, local politicians and business interests set their sights on securing the Super Bowl. With years of college football's Sugar Bowls under their belt, organizers were eager for the national limelight provided by the increasingly popular (and recently expanded) NFL. The first Super Bowl was held in Los Angeles in 1967, followed the next year by Miami. New Orleans made its initial attempt to attract the 1969 game through a bidding process conducted in 1968. In the early years of the selection process, the mayors of competing cities made final presentations to the league. Apparently, the league didn't notify the losing mayors before announcing its decision.

"You mean there's nothing we can do?" asked Mayor Schiro when reporters notified him of Miami's victory.[18] Earlier that morning, Schiro had argued on behalf of his city for ten minutes in front of league officials. "When the owners didn't ask me any questions at this morning's meeting, I thought we had it. But we must keep trying for the game." The *Times Picayune* labeled the miss a "$5 Million Setback," citing Miami mayor Stephen Clark's figure for the 1968 game's impact on his city. "The city will have to sit down and see what went wrong," wrote columnist Bob Roesler. "If we want the game, the time to get working on it is now. If not, let's forget about the Super Bowl once and for all."[19] A month later, Schiro named the paper's editor, George Healy, and trumpeter Al Hirt as co-chairs of a "Super Bowl Task Force 1970" campaign. Dave Dixon also joined the committee.

On March 19, 1969, the NFL announced the decision to play Super Bowl IV at Tulane Stadium in New Orleans on January 11, 1970. Compared to the two-year head start for the 2013 game, the ten months allocated for preparation reflected the smaller scale of the event. Nonetheless, the *Times*

Picayune praised the selection victory as "an example of what can be done" and an opportunity for civic advancement:

> [T]*he outcome in this instance should stir some community get-up-and-go for various planned but dragging or hung-up projects to get the city, area and port moving. It seems to us that there is nothing in the critical surveys, inflation troubles and public revenue problems that unity of action under good leadership cannot overcome. The bowl game effort and results seems to show that achievement is possible and that now is a good time to say that for this community "the thrust is forward," beginning now.*[20]

From its first incarnation in New Orleans, the Super Bowl was viewed as both a catalyst for overdue change and a stamp of approval for a city often unsure of its esteem in national circles. "If you don't think New Orleans is a magic name," reported the *Times Picayune*'s Roesler from the owners' meetings, "you should have seen the way many West Coast newspapers treated the announcement."[21] Tourism advocates were ecstatic. "Obtaining the Super Bowl and the long-range economic possibilities it represents will affect all Orleanians,"[22] said Robert Rhoden, former president of the New Orleans Restaurant Association. There was "no limit to the tremendous possibilities" for tourism. Rhoden projected $50 million in economic impact, a steep increase over Miami's $5 million from two years prior. To prepare, the city needed to clear its streets of abandoned automobiles. In December 1969, the city council unanimously approved a resolution to "take emergency measures" to remove these "unsightly hulks" before the "extensive national television and press exposure which our city will receive from the aforementioned events."[23]

The council also took action to avoid a repeat of the 1965 AFL All-Star debacle. Council president and mayoral nominee Moon Landrieu crafted an ordinance banning racial and religious discrimination in "facilities of public accommodations, resort or amusement." Mayor Schiro's human relations director, John Pecoul, assured reporters that the law would impact only the central business district and major thoroughfares, with little effect on neighborhood bars. The hotel-motel association and the New Orleans Convention and Visitors Bureau (NOCVB) voiced their support. After a 7–0 favorable vote in the council, Schiro signed the ordinance; it went into effect on January 1, just in time for the Sugar Bowl.[24] Dave Dixon wrote a letter to the editor praising the *Times Picayune* for its "splendid job in helping" garner public approval.[25]

Still, local interest in the Super Bowl was mixed. As part of its efforts to secure the game, the task force had successfully lobbied city council to waive the 5 percent amusement tax on tickets. If the move helped unleash "the untold millions of dollars [the game] will pump into the city and state economy," it did not ensure a sellout.[26] As early as November, lower-than-expected ticket sales raised the specter of a television blackout. Los Angeles viewers suffered such a fate during the first Super Bowl, and the league reminded New Orleanians that the rule "will not be lifted under any circumstances."[27] Classified ads suggested the fifteen-dollar tickets were in competition with other entertainment options. "2 Super Bowl tickets, sidelines for 1 shotgun, automatic or pump," ran one notice. Other offers included "6 Super Bowl tickets for new console colored TV or used car in good shape"; "2 Super Bowl tickets for flute, sax or what have you"; "2 Super Bowl tickets for liquor or what?"; and "4 Super Bowl tickets for what?" Outboard motors, horse trailers, movie projectors and drums were among the preferred prospects for ticketholders. A tally of the exchanged goods was likely not part of the post-game economic impact figures. The game failed to sell out, and the league kept its word: the Super Bowl was blacked out locally.

The week of the game brought excitement and anxiety. A Tuesday editorial reminded readers of the "special responsibility on many local businessmen and on law enforcement" to make sure visitors were shielded from price gouging and poor service. If the city put its best foot forward, "New Orleans will have added to its reputation in a way that can be a matter of commercial success as well as for community pride."[28] Soon the French Quarter filled with fans of the Minnesota Vikings and Kansas City Chiefs. Upscale restaurants like Antoine's were booked up, while Charity Hospital reported "no great influx" of injured visitors, and the NOPD dealt with just a few rowdies. On Saturday, the Fair Grounds held a race, a $16,000 Super Bowl Handicap attended by Ed McMahon, Toots Shor and other visiting celebrities. The players' union honored the Apollo 12 astronauts at a game-day luncheon. Cabbies and barkeeps reported brisk business; now, according to the *Times Picayune*, experts forecasted $6 million in game-related revenue.

New Orleans' first Super Bowl Sunday began with rain and windy conditions that complicated the pre-game "Great Balloon Race," which pitted two hot-air balloons representing the Vikings and the Chiefs. Prophetically, the Vikings balloon had barely lifted off when it crashed into the stands, somehow failing to injure any spectators. Backed by *Tonight Show* bandleader Doc Severinson and the Southern University band, actor Pat O'Brien recited the words of the national anthem.

New Orleans was the star for the halftime show, and the city received more than its share of free advertising. Under the theme "Way Down Yonder," the entertainment included selection committee chair Al Hirt jamming with jazz great Lionel Hampton; Carol Channing butchering "When the Saints"; a re-creation of the Battle of New Orleans, complete with muskets and cannons; twenty-four "southern belles" on a riverboat-shaped float; the Onward and Olympia brass bands in a second-line parade with members of local social aid and pleasure clubs; and, finally, a brief Mardi Gras parade. By comparison, the 1969 game in Miami featured a long performance by the Florida A&M University marching band. For its first Super Bowl, New Orleans took advantage of the spotlight to showcase a potent mix of national celebrities and local culture that set the tone for future halftime shows.

The game stoked new ambitions for New Orleans. "[The] happiest man—outside of those rooting for [the victorious] Kansas City—had to be Mayor Victor Schiro," said the *Times-Picayune*.[29] Indeed, the mayor crowed that the weather might've been unseasonably cold, but "I heard Miami had 40 degrees and rain this afternoon." In an editorial titled "Super Bowl Lesson: Promote Tourism," the paper quoted mayor-nominee Landrieu: "Yesterday was a great day for New Orleans, and we want many more like it." Schiro and Landrieu also announced plans for a new task force to attract the 1971 game. The paper had even greater hopes. "New Orleans, if it will invest more money and effort in promotion, could be, in a sense, an all-year Super Bowl, with 'extra' millions regularly going into circulation."[30] If the city took it seriously, tourism was the future.

The next step for tourism was the Superdome, but the path to the stadium's opening was riddled with political, legal and managerial potholes. Originally budgeted at $35 million, construction costs eventually totaled more than $163 million. By March 1975, former governor McKeithen lamented the controversies and politicization of his "sucker." What began as a state-directed project became a magnet for New Orleans interests. "There is no other city on god's green earth," he told the *Times-Picayune*, with forces "trying to make a fast buck" from a public project. "Everybody is trying to get in on something."[31] Despite the myriad disputes that plagued the final months of construction, most observers were awed by the sheer size of the building. At the public unveiling on August 3, 1975, the Dome's giant scoreboards greeted visitors with optimism: "The Louisiana Superdome Welcomes You to Tomorrow." A video on the history of stadiums began with the Roman coliseum and ended with the Superdome, "man's monument to his own imagination." Lieutenant Governor James Fitzmorris proclaimed, "In the future, it will be recognized that in 1975, the people of Louisiana lived not only for today, but much more importantly, for tomorrow."

McKeithen's successor, Edwin Edwards, reminded the audience of the state's efforts. "Louisiana money, Louisiana planning and Louisiana workmen made it possible, and let's not forget that," said Edwards. State bonds and revenue from a new hotel-motel tax funded the construction, which began in 1971, the year of Edwards's election. In succeeding years, he'd weathered the backbiting, lawsuits and escalating bills. Once the doors opened, the storm intensified, and Edwards soon went looking for more Louisiana money. In the first six months of operations, the Dome ran a $4.6 million deficit. Seeking a "bailout" from the legislature, the governor told the *State Times Advocate* that "he was not required to defend the stadium or to justify it, only to keep it operating."[32] The money pit was plagued by inadequate security, poor sanitation conditions and a flawed ticket system. In the Dome's first month, a state legislator claimed his son was mugged on the way to buy popcorn, and the Allman Brothers Band sued over undercounted ticket sales for an August 31 concert. By November 1976, Dixon declared, "The Superdome is headed to be a disaster for the state, rather than the great thing it should be, and was designed to be."[33] Much of the ire centered on Superdome Services Inc. (SSI), a minority contractor led by Sherman Copelin, a former staffer of Mayor Moon Landrieu. Charged with accepting bribes while with the city, Copelin had little experience in event management, much less the janitorial, security and ticket services for a monument to man's imagination. For many white politicians, locally and around the state, Copelin seemed to represent the loss of power resulting from demographic changes in New Orleans. SSI provided a scapegoat, too, for the poor planning by the state's commission, which appeared to under budget operation costs as it rushed to open the stadium. In 1977, operations were turned over to the Hyatt Management Corporation, which eventually gave way to SMG, the national corporation that still manages the Dome today. The troubled first years of "tomorrow" soon faded.

"We're here today to witness a major miracle," Governor Edwards announced at a press conference on June 3, 1985. "I can't tell you how many times it took just another little miracle to keep the deal afloat."[34] The governor rarely shied from hyperbole, but he had a point: after seventeen losing seasons under original owner John Mecom, the woeful Saints were rescued by a native son. Mecom was a rich man's son, an unpopular Texan whose family owned oil wells and chemical plants. His Saints never finished with a winning record, going a combined 83-187-5 and driving fans to don paper bags over their heads in shame. Some predicted the franchise would relocate. Instead, Tom Benson returned to purchase his hometown team. He entered the bidding as an underdog: the NFL required an owner to purchase 51 percent to officially hold a controlling stake in the team. Unable to hit the percentage on his own, Benson lobbied successfully for special approval by league owners to be declared the principal owner among a group of ten investors. Once again, the Saints found themselves on the positive side of a rule change. Together with Edwards, Benson wrestled a new Superdome lease and a sales-tax waiver on concessions from a skeptical state legislature. On May 31, 1985, the sale was approved. "I want everybody to know who I am," Benson reportedly told his lawyer. "Everybody is saying, 'He's just a used car dealer.' Let them see me now."[35]

In his first victory as Saints owner, the kid from the Seventh Ward grabbed a parasol and led his own sideline parade. The "Benson Boogie" replaced the paper bag as the prominent image of the Saints for national television audiences. In 1987, the team finished 12-3 and went to its first playoff game.

Succeeding years brought peaks and valleys, occasional trips to the playoffs and a combined 151-152 record from 1986 to 2004. In the 1990s, the team failed to sell out the Superdome for many home games, resulting in TV blackouts locally. There was talk that Benson might move the team to his base in San Antonio, but mostly there was frustration and mediocrity.

The low point for Benson came in the months following Katrina and the federal levee breaks, a hellacious period when thousands of citizens faced personal and financial crises. For Benson, as it did for so many New Orleanians, hell looked a lot like Baton Rouge.

On October 30, 2005, the displaced Saints returned to Louisiana to play the Miami Dolphins at Tiger Stadium in Baton Rouge. Two weeks earlier, Benson had fired his confidant and Saints VP Arnold Fielkow. Alarmed by in-house relocation discussions—including a strategy to drum up and leverage interest from San Antonio, Albuquerque and Mississippi—Fielkow broke ranks to alert a state legislator. Benson was irate, and Saints fans were panicked. Would the team ever return? Was San Antonio—with its unused Alamodome, corporate sponsors and football-crazed Texans, not to mention the offices of Benson's business operations—where the owner wanted to be?

"Tom Benson Wants to Return to New Orleans" ran the headline on a full-page advertisement in the October 26, 2005 *Times-Picayune*. According to a letter below the headline, "No decision has been made on the future of the team because no decision has been made about the future of New Orleans." The second part of that sentence could be read as a poke at Mayor

Ray Nagin, who, days before, had told the public he was appalled at talk of relocation. It also displayed a noncommittal attitude during a time of high passions. As a party line, the advertisement did little to salve the wounds.

Four days later, Benson met with NFL commissioner Tagliabue, Louisiana governor Kathleen Blanco and state and city officials at the Governor's Mansion before the Tiger Stadium game. Joining Tagliabue was NFL chief operating officer and future commissioner Roger Goodell. The two men questioned Benson about his recent negotiations to determine both a temporary and permanent home for his team, his plans to vacate the Saints' suburban practice facility and the long-term viability of the city. Sensitive to the perception that the NFL might abandon the city, Tagliabue promised all present that "a friend in need is a friend in deed." The league also asked Louisiana officials to refrain from public attacks on Benson. "[T]he tactic of vilifying the owner is shortsighted and will ultimately not lead them to their objective," wrote Goodell in an e-mail recap of the meeting.[36] Though later reports cited the meeting as a turning point, Benson remained on edge. Hours later, he took a swing at a cameraman.

As the final minutes ticked away on a 21–6 Saints loss, Benson and his party moved toward the exit. The atmosphere was unpleasant throughout the evening as fans booed the owner and heckled him for flirting with other cities. The fed-up seventy-seven-year-old lunged at a WWL-TV news camera, knocking it down. His grandson at his side, Benson also engaged in a verbal confrontation with a spectator. The team and the old man looked to be two more casualties of Katrina, unable to adjust to new surroundings and challenges. In the days that followed, national and local media outlets questioned Benson's fitness to lead. ESPN personality Skip Bayless titled a column "Benson Should Say Good-Bye."[37] Longtime *Times-Picayune* columnist Peter Finney asked, if Benson "loves Louisiana, why doesn't he step aside?"[38] T-shirts reading "Fuck Benson" appeared in New Orleans.

In an e-mail to NFL commissioner Paul Tagliabue and two other league officials, Benson described his trip to Baton Rouge as "a total disaster":

> *As my wife and the rest of my party left the suite, well before the end of the game, we were attacked by a number of hecklers who shouted obscenities at me and my party and put my wife and family in danger. Security was inadequate and nonexistent, and we were led out through a hostile crowd on a very long route. If it had not been for my grandson and his friend, we could have all been severely injured or killed...After this traumatic experience, I will not return to Baton Rouge for any reason.*[39]

The impression was that of an owner at war with his team's displaced fan base. In the context of his recent actions, the letter was about as popular in New Orleans as President Bush's helicopter flyover of the flooded city.

A week after the incident, Tagliabue and Goodell staged another intervention. Together with a group of respected team owners, they toured the city and held a news conference to offer conditional support for a return. When the season ended, Tagliabue announced that Benson's team would come home. "We think it can, but it's not a slam-dunk."[40] Wide gashes remained in the roof of the Superdome, and the facility would require substantial repairs. According to Blanco, Tagliabue guaranteed that if the state could fix the stadium, the Saints would stay in town. Ensuing negotiations brought all parties together, with the still-reeling state contributing $121 million, the Federal Emergency Management Agency directing $56 million in recovery funds to the project, the NFL chipping in $15 million and the Louisiana State Exposition District (LSED) providing $44 million, a figure that eventually tripled through financing costs, according to Bloomberg News.[41] Buoyed by public funding, Tom Benson recommitted to New Orleans.

The team's return to the Superdome on September 25, 2006, marked the beginning of the popular narrative that combined the on-field success of the Saints with the recovery of New Orleans. U2 and Green Day kicked off the festivities with a rousing, Katrina-tailored version of an old punk song. Less than two minutes into the nationally televised game, special teams player Steve Gleason blocked a punt by the rival Atlanta Falcons, resulting in a New Orleans touchdown. The Dome crowd exploded, the Saints prevailed 23–3 and a storybook season was underway. Political consultant and Louisiana native James Carville called the Atlanta game "one of the most significant regular-season games in any sport anywhere."[42] Newly named NFL commissioner Goodell observed, "Tonight is obviously more than just a game. This means more to this community and more to this region…[it is] an opportunity to show the world the human spirit that exists here."[43] Led by new coach Sean Payton and new quarterback Drew Brees, the Saints finished 10-6 and won their division before losing in the second round of the playoffs. The team was not just back; it was better.

When he sat down with the state in February 2009 to negotiate a new lease for the Saints, Tom Benson went long and emerged with more power. The franchise was more popular than ever, but the cash-strapped state wanted to renegotiate what had been a very beneficial arrangement for Benson. Under the previous lease, Louisiana paid subsidies to the Saints, with the team receiving $23.5 million annually just to play in the Dome; instead of paying rent, Benson earned substantial revenue to remain a tenant. The team's state-appointed landlord, LSED, forecasted a $27.5 million deficit in the 2009 fiscal year. With budget crunches an annual concern, Louisiana needed a change. The resulting seventeen-year extension was based on a sliding scale of payments to the team, with an annual cap of $6 million. Atop the $210 million in renovations recently done to the Superdome after Katrina, the state committed to another $85 million upgrade, with the Saints earning the revenue from new luxury boxes. In return, Benson agreed to buy and renovate a shuttered office tower adjacent to the Dome and then rent the majority of its office space back to the state. Formerly home to the New Orleans Centre mall, the building was later re-christened Benson Tower. A neighboring parcel would be transformed into a public plaza, eventually named Champions Square, owned by Benson but rented back to LSED to handle events and concessions during pre-game celebrations. As a final cherry, Benson received ownership of naming rights for the Dome, with the first $1 million of any sale going to him and the balance split with the state.

Everybody, it seemed, was happy. The Jindal administration predicted a total savings of $281 million. Formerly skeptical of the city's viability, Benson was now a player in the recovery. "Our community is coming back slowly, and I think this is going to be a shot in the arm that's going to keep it goin' in that direction." He also praised Governor Bobby Jindal, a sharp contrast to his clashes with Jindal's predecessor. "He's not easy to negotiate with, but he's very intelligent," Benson said. "He sees both sides of the fence. They've reached some, and we've reached a lot."[44] Jindal's intelligence might have saved the state money, but Tom Benson walked away from Katrina's aftermath with his kingdom intact and, indeed, expanded. The owner had a renovated stadium, paid for by the state, the federal government and the NFL, with luxury boxes and naming rights at his disposal; an office tower in a prime location to be rented out back to the state; and a new park for future celebrations of his suddenly relevant team. The ugly events at Tiger Stadium were buried.

On May 19, 2009, less than a month after the lease was signed, the NFL awarded Super Bowl XLVII to New Orleans. The selection marked the tenth time the NFL chose the city for the championship game, tying New Orleans with Miami for most Super Bowls hosted. The new Superdome agreement was cited as a crucial factor, proof that the Saints and the city had regained stability after the initial post-Katrina struggles. In his concession remarks, Dolphins owner Stephen Ross pointed toward another factor. "People have a lot of respect for Tom Benson," said Ross.

"And Tom delivered for New Orleans. He's been there, and people respect what he's done over the years. He's stayed steadfast behind New Orleans even in the worst of times, and that kind of swayed a lot of owners."[45] As New Orleans continued to recover from disaster, Benson was recast as the august leader of the city's most visible symbol.

At Tad Gormley, a security guard escorted the Bensons down the track to two chairs set up in the shade. I finished my pizza as Rummell kicked off, the ball hurtling through the glorious sky like countless others had for more than a century in America. The game quickly went downhill. As sometimes happens in high school football, a clear size advantage prevailed on the field, and today Brother Martin was on the smaller squad. Rummel scored on its first two drives, and the Bensons slipped out with their team down 14–0 at the end of the first quarter. I stayed for another Rommel score and then made my way to the exit.

CHAPTER 3
NOVEMBER 29, 2012
(SEVENTY-FIVE DAYS TO GO)

PARADE OF PROGRESS

"It was worse yesterday."

The salesman smiled and continued to set his table. A rack of incense bottles, stacks of paperbacks, bracelets, knitted hats—he ducked into the side door of a white conversion van and emerged with more items. He didn't seem to mind the noise, and he shrugged when I asked if it was always this bad. People greeted him as they sauntered down the sidewalk, and the salesman responded with blessings and nods of recognition; he'd worked this corner for years.

All around him, however, the landscape was changing. Construction on the new Loyola Avenue streetcar line had reached the intersection with Canal Street, where the track would join the existing line that ran from the Mid City cemeteries to the Mississippi River. On this day, the first block of Loyola was a field of mud. The piercing report of a jackhammer filled the area as men in reflective vests climbed into a small cavern to dig deeper. A mechanical shovel broke off remaining chunks of concrete and then flipped them back into the mud. River-bound traffic crept down Canal, narrowed to one lane by plastic jersey barriers. It had rained earlier. The clouds hung low, and every car, person, machine and building appeared to sag toward the mud. The new streetcar line was scheduled to open on January 28, the Monday before the Super Bowl. With seventy-five days remaining until the game, progress appeared slow.

Still, the progress was unmistakable. Despite the disruption in his turf, the sidewalk salesman, Askiel, admitted, "We know there's a pot of gold at the end of the rainbow." The Loyola Avenue line would bring more customers past his table, but more importantly, it would rejuvenate this crumbling section of Canal. Just four blocks from the foot of Bourbon Street, the corner was an unmarked border for tourists, who encountered a "real New Orleans" traditionally excluded from advertisements for the city. Several city bus lines stopped here; the Wall of China takeout joint and numerous urban wear retailers attracted kids from the nearby Iberville housing project along with off-duty French Quarter service workers. Drug dealing was common and barely concealed. "They get bolder after dark," Askiel said when I asked why he didn't work at night. If the Quarter welcomed tourists with to-go drinks, joke T-shirts and street performers, this end of Canal showed them the city unmasked and, for the most part, unconcerned with their presence.

Askiel's table stood on the curb in front of the shuttered Loew's State Palace Theater. When I moved back to New Orleans in 2006, the theater's marquee bore two lines of promise: "Lil Wayne" and "Thanksgiving." The native New Orleanian and self-described "best rapper alive" never performed that night because the State Palace never reopened. But the letters remained on the marquee for a few years, the sort of forgotten signage that haunted placards, billboards and fast-food joints during that period of slow recovery. Now the marquee was blank. Cracks spread across its plaster underside, and wiring dangled from the dead light sockets above the boarded-up ticket booth. Askiel and I noted a weathered "For Sale" sign slumped against the main entrance. The State Palace showed no hints of progress.

A look through the day's fog, though, and a vision emerged. Across the mud pit was the reopened Joy Theater, its iconic neon sign relit at a December 2011 ceremony in which Mayor Landrieu danced in the street with soul legend Irma Thomas. On the downtown side of Canal, work continued at the four-thousand-seat Saenger Theater, scheduled for reopening sometime next summer, after $53 million in repairs. From the corner of Basin—Loyola incarnate after crossing Canal—the "1201 Canal" condominium complex beckoned new residents, its rooftop beach chairs visible from the street. A Crown Royal billboard mounted atop the Saenger read, "Never stood a chance," but for the first time in years, this intersection had prospects. The new streetcar line triggered revitalization. In February 2010, the U.S. Department of Transportation awarded a $45 million Tiger Grant to the Regional Transit Authority (RTA) to cover the entire cost of the project. Part of the Obama administration's stimulus package, the funding was intended to connect pre-existing transit hubs, in this case linking the Canal Street line to the Union Passenger Terminal bus and Amtrak station at the

Elk Place under construction. *Photo by author.*

edge of the Central Business District (CBD). Such an investment in nine blocks of track—with a parallel St. Charles line only four blocks—might seem misdirected in a poor city with insufficient mass transit. Clearly, the project wasn't designed to transport the maximum number of citizens, but to spur development along a dilapidated section of the CBD. In a statement issued for the June 2011 groundbreaking, the RTA said, "The benefits of a streetcar line are not lost on investors."[46]

The original grant agreement called for the completion of the Loyola line by June 2012. Almost six months later, I walked the length of the still in-progress project. Along this frontier of urban development, the only thing certain was that the Super Bowl would be here in ten weeks. Now the game itself was a deadline for a federally funded project intended to reignite downtown New Orleans. For those nine blocks, I watched for the changes sparked by the streetcar. I listened for echoes of Loyola Avenue's past, a history filled with stunted dreams of civic rebirth and promises of a new New Orleans.

I said goodbye to Askiel and crossed Loyola, pausing to look at the statue of "Molly Marine" now stranded in the mud field that was Elk Place.

Binoculars at the ready, Molly stared over the chaos of Canal to a larger statue of Simon Bolivar at the foot of Basin Street. Both figures served as reminders of New Orleans' internationalist past, when World War II boats were constructed here, when foreign exiles plotted revolutions from taverns in the Quarter, when the city was commercially, and not just culturally, the northernmost outpost of the Caribbean. I reached the Joy sidewalk as a double-decker tour bus rumbled over the rutted Canal Street, followed by a bread truck.

A block up from Canal was the first streetcar stop, at the intersection of Loyola and Tulane Avenue. Looking down Tulane, I could see the top of Charity Hospital, still shuttered seven years after Katrina. Opened in 1937, the massive complex was once the second-largest hospital in the nation, a dilapidated fortress serving the poor and indigent. After Katrina, the hospital was the center of ongoing uncertainty when the state decided it was no longer salvageable, despite assessments to the contrary just months after the storm. Instead, the Jindal administration began construction of a new hospital six blocks away on Tulane Avenue, part of a $2 billion, sixty-seven-acre project that included a new Veterans Administration facility. Scheduled for completion in 2015, the so-called Biomedical District was cited regularly as a future source of jobs and a magnet for new residents of renovated buildings in the downtown neighborhood.

Meanwhile, Charity's prospects remained unclear. In his August 2012 public budget meetings, Mayor Landrieu floated the idea of moving city hall and the district courts to the old hospital. "City Hall is fifty years old, the elevators don't always run and we need to get out of there," he said.[47] With the neighborhood's predicted renaissance, a sale could generate much-needed revenue. It was a creative idea but ripe with irony for anyone familiar with the history of Loyola Avenue.

On the uptown side of Tulane and Loyola stood the New Orleans Public Library Main Branch, a modernist three-story rectangle of concrete, aluminum and glass. The next block was Duncan Plaza, a public park that sat between the library and city hall on Perdido Street. On New Year's Eve 1913, just a block from the library site, Louis Armstrong, a twelve-year-old native of the "Black Storyville" neighborhood, fired a pistol in the air, leading to his arrest and his induction into the Home for Colored Waifs, the school where he eventually took up the trumpet. In the 1950s, the area was cleared to make way for a series of public projects that were the vision of Mayor deLesseps "Chep" Morrison, who served four terms from 1946 to 1961. Today's Loyola Avenue was his legacy, and if any mayor served as a model for Mitch Landrieu's ambitions and rhetoric, it was Morrison. The remains of his new New Orleans lined the street.

A handsome World War II veteran who favored white suits, Morrison led the city as its population peaked and its footprint extended to Lake Ponchartrain and into the Lower Ninth Ward. Known in some circles as "the walking man" for his ubiquitous presence around town, he promised the long-awaited arrival of modernity to the city through the reorganization of government and a focus on international trade. In 1958, he graced the cover of *Time* amid the flags of Latin American countries and later kept company with starlet Zsa Zsa Gabor.[48] Morrison's power crested in 1954, when a new city charter allowed him to run for a third term and to secure backing for the civic center complex along present-day Loyola Avenue. A new city hall, the public library, an expanded airport, the Union Passenger Terminal rail station and a bridge to the west bank of the Mississippi were among the capital projects set in motion that year. "These achievements, plus many others, testify to the fact that New Orleans can stand proudly before the nation and before the world as a dynamic city which makes its dreams come true," said Morrison.[49]

On May 6, 1957, Morrison's vision culminated in the "Parade of Progress," an hour-long procession featuring marching bands, convertibles carrying foreign diplomats from forty-two nations, new construction equipment, color guards and "10 floats depicting the progress of New Orleans."[50] The floats depicted the new city hall and civic center, the union passenger terminal, the new Mississippi bridge, oil industry progress, industrial development, tourism, international trade and commerce, cultural progress, the airport and other aspects of the city's advancement. The parade began on Canal Street, with the dedication of the Simon Bolivar statue, and ended at the new city hall, which Morrison opened with a ceremonial sword.

A new era for New Orleans was at hand, but it was not the one Morrison celebrated. Larger forces began to overshadow the ambitions of the mayor and his city. The Democrat's three failed runs for governor were marred by accusations that he was "soft" on race. Morrison was a relative moderate in the Deep South, but when integration arrived in New Orleans with the November 1960 school crisis, he held back as white mobs rioted outside city hall and terrorized black students at two schools. Still clinging to his gubernatorial hopes, the mayor hesitated. As a result, his attempts to craft a cosmopolitan image of New Orleans were replaced by Norman Rockwell's painting of six-year-old Ruby Bridges entering her elementary school with four National Guardsmen. The crisis marked the beginning of the end for

Morrison's new New Orleans, as ensuing white flight drained the city's tax base and altered its political power structure. In June 1961, he stepped down as mayor to accept President Kennedy's appointment as the first head of the Organization of American States. He and his seven-year-old son perished in a 1964 plane crash over Mexico.

As I passed through Duncan Plaza, I paused at an obelisk that bore JFK's eulogy for Morrison, along with a bust of the mayor and a list of his accomplishments. It was interesting to compare the current occupant of city hall with "the walking man." Chep Morrison and Mitch Landrieu each saw himself as an agent of change who could wrest the city from the mud of corruption. Each wore the mantle of reform despite deep connections in local politics, and both were unafraid to bruise feelings while consolidating power. Morrison's dream ran aground when he proved unable to lead during a crucial moment in the city's history. Despite high approval ratings, Landrieu's destiny remained unclear; issues of race and ambition were inseparable in his quest to remake the city. In coming weeks, he repeatedly hailed the Super Bowl as a moment of unity and affirmation, proof of a new New Orleans and a new type of leader.

Against a field of political neophytes, Landrieu won the 2010 election in a landslide, a satisfying reversal of his 2006 loss to incumbent Ray Nagin. He'd served sixteen years as a state legislator and was in the middle of his second term as Louisiana's lieutenant governor, but in many ways, he remained in the shadow of his father and sister. As mayor from 1970 to 1978, Maurice "Moon" Landrieu was a transitional figure, an ardent opponent of segregation elected with 90 percent of the African American vote and 40 percent of the white. Demographic changes allowed him to rebuke the white political class and, in many ways, to sew the seeds of its demise. As white families fled the city and its integrated public schools, the elder Landrieu played a pivotal role in the rise of black political groups, opening city hall to African Americans and hiring many activists as staffers. Faced with a dwindling tax base, his administration took advantage of increased federal support for U.S. cities. Federal funds as part of the city's budget grew from 3 percent, or $2.4 million, in 1970, to a peak of 39 percent, or $66.6 million, in 1976. Across the city, new organizations sprouted to provide federally funded social services in poor neighborhoods. New black political leaders rose through the ranks of these groups as the city became mostly African American during the 1970s. Leaving office in 1978, Moon Landrieu was the city's last white mayor until the election of his son in 2010. The family's legacy of integration received credit for Mitch's victory, as well as the unlikely 2008 reelection of his sister Mary, a Democratic U.S. senator in a deeply red state.

The mayoral campaign of 2010 was uncharacteristically dull for a politics-obsessed city, but the shabby field of candidates could accept only partial blame for public disinterest. For the first time in modern memory, there was something in New Orleans more important than politics, Mardi Gras and disaster: the Saints were going to the Super Bowl. The fever that began in 2006 was a citywide condition by the middle of the 2009–10 season. Big plays and mounting victories became weekly rebukes of the confusion and uncertainty of the recovery. Finally, New Orleanians knew something for sure: the Saints were going all the way.

Inside the Superdome on January 24, 2010, the team won its first NFC Championship and the right to face the Indianapolis Colts in Super Bowl XLIV in Miami. For the next two weeks, nothing else seemed to matter. On February 6, the front page of the *Times-Picayune* included a column headlined "Today's Election Day in N.O., Too." Landrieu won 67 percent of the vote, avoiding a run-off in an unprecedented victory for a non-incumbent. Some political analysts—especially veterans of the black organizations—grumbled about low turnout, but Landrieu's closest opponent, African American businessman Troy Henry, put it succinctly after his concession: "I think Mitch was the leading black candidate."[51] At his victory party, Landrieu took the podium to the Saints' fan chant of "Who Dat!"[52]

"We decided that we were going to stick the pole in the ground and strike a blow for unity, strike a blow for a city that decided to be unified rather than divided," he said that night. "We took a huge leap forward into the future today. The city of New Orleans showed America what it takes to rebuild a great place. We're all going together, and we're not leaving anybody behind."[53] The emphasis on unity was part Landrieu family branding, part rebuke of his predecessor, who was seen as increasingly divisive during his second term. His own mayoralty as a defining moment of the recovery and the first step into the future—these were themes Landrieu returned to in subsequent speeches and interviews; the city was back and better than ever, he repeated, and his policies catalyzed that progress. Three years later, as Super Bowl XLVII approached, the mayor rarely missed an opportunity to cast himself as the steward of the new New Orleans, a rebuilt, unified city that was an example for America.

I passed city hall and stood at the intersection of Loyola and Poydras Street. Officeworkers on their lunch breaks strolled the sidewalks beneath the shadows of the city's skyscrapers, which clustered along Poydras from the Superdome to the river. Forty years ago, this was an economic frontier during an earlier moment when New Orleans believed it had turned the corner toward modernity and prosperity. In the 1970s, developers referred to the six-lane street as "the Park Avenue of the South," as office towers rose to meet the boom in the petroleum industry. Sparked by the OPEC crisis of 1973, oil prices soared and battered the U.S. economy but enriched Shell, Mobil, Amoco and other industry giants, which doubled down on offshore drilling in the Gulf of Mexico. Jobs poured into Louisiana, and Poydras Street became home to numerous corporate headquarters. Locals often talk of New Orleans being ten to fifteen years behind the rest of the nation. In the 1970s, as the national economy suffered through inflation and recession, New Orleans was flush with petrodollars.

The boom bred a shortsighted confidence in the city's long-term economic future. Real estate developers ran wild on Poydras Street, sure that prosperity was here to stay and in desperate need of new digs. Local media echoed the bright forecasts. Announcing a new Amoco headquarters, a 1976 *Times-Picayune* article declared, "This building will give form to an urban complex that can have far-reaching economic and artistic consequences on the downtown scene."[54] With the Superdome as its origin, the titans along the Park Avenue of the South would reinvent the city, slay the rivals in Houston and Atlanta and drag the city back to national prominence.

"The year 1982 will go down in history as the year the *new* New Orleans was built—or at least begun," predicted reporter Lettice Stuart in the 1983 New Year's Day edition of the *Times Picayune*. "And it will long be remembered as the year New Orleans caught up with the rest of the country and began its move ahead into the 21st century—for better or worse."[55] In fact, signs of a bust were already evident. Increased fuel efficiency and overproduction by the oil giants on Poydras sent prices plummeting. The bottom fell out in 1985, and Louisiana followed suit. Soon the optimistic developers of Poydras Street faced a glut of empty offices. By 1986, the state led the nation with a 12 percent unemployment rate. To keep state government functioning, the cash-strapped Edwards administration withheld tax refunds and child support payments.[56] If the 1980s symbolized greed and economic high times for much of the nation, they were remembered in New Orleans for vanishing jobs, vacant buildings and a sense that the city's best days were, yet again, behind it.

Stuart's 1982 year-in-review is a useful capsule for another change that took place in the 1980s. As she breezed past pending disaster, Stuart noted the completion of new hotels along Canal Street, the start of construction on the convention center along the river and the seeds of the 1984 World's Fair, a "$2 billion event." These projects were part of a fundamental transformation of the city's economy. The international metropolis of Chep Morrison's dreams and the brief petroleum heyday were replaced by the rise of a focused tourism industry supported by city government and marketed through new festivals and slogans. With the emergence of containerized cargo, New Orleans fell behind in the shipping industry, and fallow wharfs in the French Quarter gave way to tourist magnets like the Riverwalk, the Aquarium of the Americas and the convention center. In a 1987 *Atlantic Monthly* piece, New Orleans–born columnist Nicholas Lemann warned of the perils of overdependence on tourism:

> *Tourism can enrich a small group of local entrepreneurs, including real-estate developers and concessionaires; some of these come from groups, like the black middle class, that were previously shut out of the business life of the city. New entry-level jobs in hotels are cold comfort for unemployed longshoremen, but they are a real help to poor blacks working as domestics or not working at all. Still, tourism is cyclical, and it's dominated by national chains whose profits go out of town. And if New Orleans is primarily in the business of selling itself rather than its raw materials and its dock facilities, then being a city that satisfies its own requirements but not the outside world's might not work anymore.*[57]

From the corner of Poydras and Loyola, I could see the once-celebrated Amoco building, no longer occupied by Amoco. In May 1989, the company moved its headquarters and more than one thousand jobs to Houston. Now the tower housed a hodgepodge of law firms and government agencies, including the Orleans Parish District Attorney's office. A sports memorabilia shop occupied one corner of the first floor, selling jerseys and hats during Saints games. On my left was the Little Gem Saloon, scheduled to reopen that month. Long vacant, the former nightclub had been a favorite of early jazz legends Buddy Bolden, Freddie Keppard and Jelly Roll Morton. New owners had recently renovated the building, installing a restaurant and second-floor lounge for live music. The Little Gem and neighboring restaurants were part of another reinvention of Poydras Street, this one banking on the streetcar, the big events at the Superdome and the potential of the latest new New Orleans.

The Hyatt Regency occupied the middle of the next block of Loyola. Originally opened in 1976, a year after the adjacent Superdome, the hotel served as a refuge for city government and several media outlets during Katrina. In a memoir self-published after he left office, Nagin recounted a strange incident at the hotel just days after the storm. On the evening of August 30, twenty men "dressed in black combat outfits and adorned in bulletproof vests, rifles, and leg straps holding at least two very large handguns each" appeared on the fourth floor and announced, "We're here to protect the mayor. Everybody else get out." Fearful of repercussions for his infamous post-storm rants against the federal government, Nagin believed the men were Blackwater contractors sent "to plant bugging devices" in his twenty-seventh-floor suite; his staff, the mayor recalled, eventually convinced the men to withdraw. Like Nagin's psyche, the Hyatt suffered substantial damage from the storm, which blew out all the windows on the Poydras side of the building.

The hotel remained closed for six years, its battered face a symbol of the slow recovery. New owners purchased it in 2009, and after $275 million in repairs, the Hyatt reopened in October 2011. A new entrance ushered visitors into a redesigned interior featuring nearly 1,200 rooms, three new restaurants, 100,000 additional square feet of convention space and eight hundred new jobs. Now out of office, Nagin attended the ribbon cutting and commented, "We had to revive it, so it's nice to see this comeback. It's another great step forward for the city of New Orleans." His successor found more meaning in the occasion. "This is another stake in the ground that the people of New Orleans have dug really deeply," Landrieu declared. "It is also a symbol to the rest of America—not just that we're back, but that we can be better. It shows that the rest of the country can find a way to make it work."[58]

Landrieu's words echoed Chep Morrison's promises of a New Orleans "that makes its dreams come true." Mayoral hyperbole at ribbon cuttings was predictable, but these champions of Loyola Avenue shared a deeper faith in the city's unlocked potential. Since election night 2010, Landrieu repeatedly tied new projects—the streetcar, the new theaters on Canal, the opening of the Hyatt, the coming Super Bowl—into a narrative about the new New Orleans. The city was no longer in recovery—it was back. A hotel wasn't a hotel but a "stake in the ground" for the public to celebrate. There was a key difference, though, between Landrieu and "the walking man" and between the cities they sought to shape. Morrison's sword opened new public facilities on Loyola Avenue—libraries, post offices, railway terminals—that were tied to government and trade, in particular the port. Landrieu invoked the dreams of all citizens, but his backdrops were more often private investments—hotels, sporting events, entertainment venues—that served tourists. The vocabulary and geography might be similar, but these were different versions of Loyola Avenue.

After the Hyatt, I crossed Girod Street and passed the main post office, another piece of the civic center. Next door was the Union Passenger Terminal, where, less than seventy-five days from now, the new streetcar line would begin its inaugural trip. A circular driveway fronted the station, with a peeling sculpture and a grove of palms in its center. The station's name hung above the entrance in an Art Deco font; signs for Greyhound and Amtrak perched atop rusting poles. Dilapidated and slightly tropical, the grounds of the station were a ghostly expression of Chep Morrison's unrealized dream.

Progress was in swing, though. A construction crew worked on a shelter for the streetcar platform. Like a sail laid horizontally, metal beams supported a greenish Plexiglas roof. There were maybe twenty workers in all, plus an official-looking contingent in suits. After the muddy mess on Canal Street, the scene here was encouraging.

Inside, the station appeared as it usually did: oversized and nearly empty. "On the move since 1954" was printed on the doormats in the lobby, where a plaque commemorated Morrison and the railroad commission. The main terminal was built too late, designed for the railroad era but opened at the dawn of the automobile age. I counted ten people in the waiting room, not including two bored clerks at the Amtrak desk and a sheriff's deputy, who nudged at a sleeping woman. "You can't sleep here, ma'am." I sat down near a television to watch news of the crisis in Libya. I couldn't really hear because every few moments, a saw whined from behind a plywood wall that blocked one gate. Next to the wall, a man stood atop a hydraulic lift and brushed white paint onto the ceiling while another man waited in silence below. Besides this activity, the station felt nothing like a vibrant transportation hub ready to link up with a new streetcar line for a big game—today was just another afternoon in a tired southern terminal. A woman waited for her train in the snack bar; a guy talked on a payphone. One clock read 9:15 a.m., another 11:25 a.m.; the real time was 12:08 p.m.

Above the gates, though, was the most remarkable part of Union Passenger Terminal. A four-paneled mural ran the length of the station, two panels on each facing side, totaling more than two thousand square feet. Completed by painter Conrad Albrizio in 1954 for the terminal's opening and restored in 2006, the panels depicted the history of Louisiana. Shapes and symbols were crowded together in a style reminiscent of Diego Rivera yet more feverishly layered and colored. Louisiana history was divided into four periods: the

Age of Struggle

Detail from Conrad Albrizio's *Age of Struggle* mural in Union Passenger Terminal. *Courtesy of Louisiana Cultural Vistas* magazine.

Age of Exploration, the *Age of Colonization*, the *Age of Struggle* and the *Modern Age*. Masked natives in loincloths gave way to monarchs in curly wigs, while soldiers leveled rifles at colonists and slaves tilled fields next to scientists

Modern Age

Detail from Conrad Albrizio's *Modern Age* mural in Union Passenger Terminal. *Courtesy of Louisiana Cultural Vistas magazine.*

hovering over microscopes. There were riverboats and playing cards, Union soldiers stealing silver from a southern belle, an olive-green figure in a gas mask, a hooded Klansman and an angel. In its riotous disorder, the mural depicted something essential about Louisiana, a terrain marked by disaster and perpetual change.

Albrizio was a New Yorker who moved to New Orleans in 1920, eventually teaching at LSU and contributing several WPA-commissioned frescoes to public buildings, including the state capitol. He called the terminal in New Orleans his most important work. As the final stop on my tour of Loyola Avenue, Albrizio's mural reinforced my sense that, no matter how soaring the descriptions of the present moment in New Orleans, there were messy complications underneath the sheen, past conflicts that resisted tidy resolutions.

CHAPTER 4
DECEMBER 8, 2012
(FIFTY-SEVEN DAYS TO GO)

PATHS TO PROGRESS

If you had to make the case for the unique charms of the French Quarter, the 900 block of Royal Street would be a great place to start. On a bright Saturday morning, the street seemed like a postcard come to life. Narrow doorways offered glimpses of recessed courtyards, and wrought-iron balconies held planters overfilled with ferns and flowers. People drifted in and out of art galleries, gazed into a wig store window or emerged from a coffee shop slightly less drowsy. Here was the Vieux Carré in its ideal form, balanced between careful preservation and carefree pace.

The contrast with the rest of the neighborhood was stronger now because so much of the Quarter was under construction. Particularly on the blocks closer to Canal Street, workers and machinery disrupted the landscape with noisy repairs and clouds of dust. Along with streetscape projects in New Orleans East, the Ninth Ward and Jefferson Parish, the French Quarter work was directed by Paths to Progress. Described on its website as a $90 million "collaborative effort between the Federal Highway Administration, Louisiana Department of Transportation and Development, New Orleans Regional Planning Commission and City of New Orleans," Paths to Progress drew 80 percent of its funding from the federal government. In the French Quarter, Paths to Progress would repave the ever-troublesome streets, bring the curbs of the district up to ADA safety codes and replace sidewalks. Street repairs were ongoing throughout the city, but like the Loyola streetcar line, the French Quarter efforts were now under pressure to meet the Super Bowl deadline.

NEW ORLEANS BOOM & BLACKOUT

Frances Swigart. *Photo by Zack Smith Photography.*

Construction was complete on the 800, 900 and 1000 blocks of Royal, where a new layer of black asphalt covered the street. I'd heard there were problems, though, and they didn't take long to detect this morning. Asphalt lapped unevenly against the curb, cresting and falling in waves. In some sections, the blacktop was flush with the curb, so that the street and the sidewalk were on the same level. Royal appeared humped, so that if you stood in the middle of the street, your feet were higher than the pedestrians on the sidewalk. The closer I looked, the more slapdash the work appeared. Along this iconic stretch of the city's most famous neighborhood, progress had arrived in a hurried, almost crude fashion.

The shoddy work had consequences. Yellow caution tape hung between two poles supporting the balcony of 1014 Royal. Here, the street was an inch higher than the building's narrow driveway and even with the curb. I called through a small window into the courtyard, where a woman sat at a round iron table.

Frances Swigart grew up visiting this three-story house built in 1835, and she moved here in 2001 to care for an ailing aunt. The French Quarter is the oldest part of the city and sits on relatively high ground near the river. This block, she assured me, had no history of street flooding, not during Hurricane Betsy in 1964 and not during Katrina in 2005. Things changed with the October 2012 repaving by Paths of Progress. "It became apparent, absolutely apparent just by sight, that the elevation of the street was higher," she told me. We sipped coffee in the courtyard amid hanging plants and the bubbling of a fountain; this was the French Quarter from the travel magazines. When the construction crew left at the end of October, Swigart turned her garden hose onto the sidewalk. Water pooled in front of her building and ran into the courtyard. She was worried. When the forecast called for a thunderstorm on November 4, Swigart asked her neighbors to document the effects of the repaving.

"It turned out to be an afternoon thunderstorm," she said. "It did not last very long. [Water] came up to the edge of my building; it did not come in, as best I know. Across the street, it went down the alleyway, filled the patio and then receded, leaving a pond in the patio, so that the people living in the far back part of the house had to wade through water for an entire day to get to the street. Severe flooding occurred at St. Philip and Royal."

For the first time in living memory, Royal became a flood plain. On the 900 block, waves caused by passing trucks splashed into the beloved courtyard of Café Amelie and against the sculpted wrought-iron fence of the Cornstalk Hotel. Swigart sent photos and a video to the mayor's office and her councilwoman. The Friday before we met, she had received a visit from Paths to Progress's spokesperson Alexandra Wommack and Lieutenant Colonel Mark Jernigan, the city's director of the Department of Public Works. Swigart was told that the original sidewalks were the issue but that the balcony poles in front of many properties prevented repairs. Paths to Progress would not tear up the repaving and begin again.

"I said, 'Well, you are responsible for damaging my building and my neighbor's building with a road that's improperly done. And I need you to fix it.'" Wommack and Jernigan explained their solution: a twelve-inch-long, two-inch-deep trench in front of Swigart's building, carrying water to a larger-capacity drain two doors away. Swigart considered the offer an attempt at placation rather than a long-term solution.

"I said, 'What will happen after you dig the trench and we have a hurricane and my house floods?' And [Jernigan] said, 'Well, we can't predict the future.' I said, 'If you're going to build a road in New Orleans, in the oldest neighborhood in the country, you better be able to predict what's going to happen in a hurricane or you better leave the road alone.'"

Meg Lousteau confirmed Swigart's version of events. "They're going to build a trench," she deadpanned. As director of Vieux Carré Property Owners, Residents and Associates (VCPORA), Lousteau relied on a dry sense

Paths to Progress notice outside Frances Swigart's house. *Photo by author.*

of humor to mask the frustrations that came with her job. The organization was founded in 1938 to preserve the Quarter as both national treasure and living neighborhood, two admirable goals that grew increasingly at odds as tourism deposited more revelers outside historic homes with ample property values. Multiple organizations claimed to represent the neighborhood, and Lousteau's job was part diplomat, part investigative journalist. According to her measurements, the crown of the street was now seven inches higher than the sidewalk on the 800 to 1000 blocks. Unsatisfied with the response from Paths to Progress, she made a public records request to the city for the original repaving plans. The response arrived at her Rampart Street office just before I did, and it was shocking: the Landrieu administration claimed it had never received any such plans. Lousteau smirked slightly and raised her eyebrows. The crown jewel of the city was under construction, but no one at city hall had the blueprints?

Yet there was a plan—for Royal Street, the French Quarter and New Orleans. The Super Bowl was part of the plan, a manifold initiative designed by consultants and adopted by powerful interests. If Paths to Progress and street flooding weren't part of the original vision, they were telltale signs of the difficulties of applying well-designed strategies to the unique political and economic landscapes of New Orleans. Just as holes dug in the French Quarter streets revealed a centuries-long struggle against water, the misshapen pavement on Royal Street reflected the pressures and ambitions of the new New Orleans. The tourism industry had a plan.

In January 2010, the Boston Consulting Group (BCG) released "Celebrate Our History, Invest in Our Future: Reinvigorating Tourism in New Orleans," a tourism master plan commissioned by then-Lieutenant Governor Mitch Landrieu, whose office included the Department of Culture, Recreation and Tourism. BCG developed the plan with the New Orleans Strategic Hospitality Task Force, a Landrieu-appointed group that included the heads of the Morial Convention Center (MCC), Harrah's Casino and the Superdome; hotel general managers; restaurant owners; and tourism marketers. The report provided a rare capsule of the aspirations of some of the city's most powerful interests. Bar graphs and marketing buzzwords mingled with images of horse-drawn carriages and street parades in a twenty-four-page expression of the industry's vision.

The plan's executive summary declared, "Tourism: It's Our Future." Post-Katrina New Orleans was "not maximizing the opportunities tourism offers—opportunities for job creation, tax generation and cultural renewal." The industry should use the upcoming fifth anniversary of the storm, the NCAA Final Four in 2012 and the 2013 Super Bowl as opportunities to renew the world's faith in local hospitality, with each event marked as another step toward the biggest milestone: the city's 300th anniversary in 2018. The task force set a goal of 13.7 million visitors for that year, an increase of 6 million from 2008. It was an aggressive target, the plan's authors admitted, but New Orleans faced a choice: "reinvigorate the city's tourism economy or accept the consequences of a further decline in tourism, including stagnation and weak economic development across all sectors." In other words, as tourism goes, so goes New Orleans.

Challenges were legion. "Nonleisure" travel (i.e., business meetings and conventions) was declining in New Orleans and across the nation, so the city needed to dedicate itself to attracting leisure travelers. According to BCG surveys, potential visitors saw the city as "fun for adults" and "authentic," with a reputation for good food and live music, but added that "crime and Katrina are barriers to success." New Orleans visitors were older than average compared to peer cities like Chicago, Las Vegas and Miami; Canal Street was struggling; and the airport was "problematic." The French Quarter remained the "crown jewel," but safety, code enforcement and cleanliness were all concerns. The city didn't spend enough on marketing, and the industry lacked coordination. Change was urgently needed to keep New Orleans competitive. "In addition to preserving and enhancing existing assets…New Orleans must adopt new ideas and approaches."

None of these laments was particularly original, but the assumptions, comparisons and data behind them were revealing. The public—which funded the lieutenant governor's office and thus the report—was only privy to the executive summary until May 2012. After her public records request was denied, blogger Luna Nola obtained a link through City Councilwoman Kristen Giselson Palmer's office to 119 PowerPoint slides from a September 1, 2009 meeting of the hospitality task force. Leading the discussion was John Lindquist, a BCG senior advisor specializing in tourism on a global basis and, according to *Business Week*, an advisor to the World Bank since 2004. The vocabulary and granular analysis of the slides left little doubt: BCG approached New Orleans as a product in need of repositioning. Katrina was no different than other PR nightmares like Mattel's 2007 recall of toys tainted by lead paint or the deaths from cyanide-laced Tylenol. In each case, companies responded with aggressive spending on ad campaigns, repackaging and media outreach. "Celebrations and special events draw young visitors," a key demographic, and the 2018 tricentennial had a model: the fiftieth anniversary of Disneyland's castle, celebrated with $150 million in marketing and a 6 percent increase in attendance. "People have a thirst for nostalgia," read one slide. To attract tourists, New York fought crime, Chicago tore down public housing and Miami rebranded South Beach. New Orleans could look to countless examples in cities that committed to a focused, well-funded strategy.

The consultants understood the funding challenges faced by the industry. The city invested far less on tourism marketing (about $20 million annually) than Las Vegas and Orlando, and though its 13 percent hotel tax was comparable to peer cities like Chicago and Nashville, higher rates for hotel rooms in those cities generated greater revenue. In other cities, a unified agency directed all tourism efforts, but in New Orleans, various entities received funding through the hotel tax, with the largest portion routed to the state. The biggest share went to the Louisiana State Exposition District (LSED), the state-controlled administrator of the Superdome (31 percent) and the Morial Convention Center (24 percent), while the marketing professionals at the New Orleans Convention and Visitors Bureau (NOCVB) and the New Orleans Tourism Marketing Corporation (NOTMC) were left with 7 percent and 3 percent, respectively, to compete against Disney and Las Vegas for coveted leisure tourists.

In place of the two-headed leadership of NOCVB and NOMTC, the master plan's Priority A called for a single body to direct the industry efforts. The unified industry would fight for increased funding to market the city nationally and "protect the city's core assets," which were the target of Priority B: "Aggressively focus on basics to revitalize core assets and address weaknesses." Initiatives included a crime prevention campaign in the Quarter, CBD and Superdome district; improved airline access through more direct flights; enhanced "arrival experience" and reformed taxi service; and "Initiative 4: French Quarter":

> *Reinvigorate and revitalize the city's crown jewel, including Bourbon, Royal, and Canal streets. Efforts should include preserving the historic architecture while repairing and maintaining sidewalks and other infrastructure, adding lighting and patrols to make the areas safe, and ensuring that zoning laws consistent with the desired New Orleans image are established and enforced.*

While the other priorities targeted better branding, training for tourism workers and transformative changes to the riverfront, Priorities A and B precluded any future plans. Unified leadership, more money and dependable infrastructure made everything else possible. Perhaps unsurprisingly, the executive summary emphasized the dreams of 2018 and job creation (targeted for thirty-three thousand new jobs, with average salaries of $33,300 by 2018) and left the funding issue to its final pages, where the task force identified seven options for raising funds. These options, the report said, "would require citizen and/or government approval." Bonds, grants, loans and public-private partnerships would cover one-time investments of up to $405 million, including $330 million in capital projects along the riverfront, Canal Street and in the Quarter. Ongoing "tourism-focused taxes" and a "business and tourism improvement district" would support marketing and operating expenses. The executive summary concluded with a plea for the public's commitment: "We have the leadership, expertise, and vision to make it happen. All we need is the will."

The will proved elusive. The slide show emphasized the need for "stakeholder management" to implement the entire plan successfully, in particular to support requests for new funding sources. Lists of primary and secondary stakeholders included members of city council, state legislators, hoteliers, museum directors, musicians and the head of United Cab Company. A flow chart detailed tactics for aligning "stakeholders, community leaders and citizens for execution." Yet in a plan compiled in late 2009 for a city marked by increasingly powerful neighborhood organizations, resident groups were curiously absent. The omission proved costly. In May 2012, the hospitality industry approached the legislature with a package to address the ongoing funding needs and desired upgrades for the French Quarter. Despite the meticulous analysis in the BCG plan, the industry walked into a public relations firefight. The fiercest resistance came from residents of the "crown jewel."

On May 17, 2012, the Louisiana Senate's local affairs committee met to consider Senate Bill 573, a proposal to create a "Hospitality Zone" tax district. Authored by Senator Edwin Murray of New Orleans and supported by the Landrieu administration, the bill created a new board consisting of tourism industry leaders, two city council members and mayoral appointees to oversee spending of revenue raised by increased hotel taxes and new taxes on restaurants, bars and parking lots in a new "Hospitality Zone." The zone covered not just the French Quarter and CBD but also the Tremé, Faubourg Marigny and Seventh Ward neighborhoods. The NOCVB and NOTMC would receive two-thirds of the total revenue for use in marketing efforts, with remaining funds directed toward infrastructure. To sweeten the deal, the convention center offered a one-time, $30 million pledge for upgrades and repairs to French Quarter streets, sidewalks and streetlamps. If the bill was approved, the work would wrap up prior to the Super Bowl, meaning a rebuffed, safer French Quarter would greet visitors in late January 2013.

In its original version, the Hospitality Zone legislation was a pure expression of the BCG master plan: a united tourism industry overseeing increased public funding to rebrand and promote the city. In an e-mail to his members, NOCVB president Stephen Perry called the meeting "the most important vote in the history of New Orleans' hospitality industry."[59] An estimated 150 supporters, wearing red T-shirts emblazoned with "Tourism Matters," packed into buses to Baton Rouge.[60] They were not alone on the road that morning. Chanting, "We are a community, not a commodity," twenty-five French Quarter activists, including Lousteau and Luna Nola, arrived prior to the industry contingent. Their timing meant the small chamber was split between supporters and opponents of the bill. Senator Karen Carter Peterson, who once represented the French Quarter, chaired the committee. After a brief introduction, Peterson cut to the chase. Why, she asked Landrieu's deputy mayor, Andy Kopplin, was the convention center's $30 million presented as a "quid pro quo."[61] "If [French Quarter upgrades are] a priority for the Super Bowl, which I agree with you, I think it is, why would it be tied to anything else but the infrastructure?"[62] Kopplin replied that MCC wanted to know that any investment would be sustained by the city. MCC chairman Melvin Rodrigue confirmed the offer, explaining that the $30 million was surplus money from the center's own hotel tax share. Katrina delayed a planned expansion upriver, Rodrigue said, so the convention center had cash to address another "dissatisfier," the streets, signage and lighting of the Quarter. The center's mission was to generate economic development for the region via tourism, so an investment in the Quarter made business sense.

Rodrigue's largesse revealed a blind spot. The master plan's list of stakeholders neglected leaders from other parts of Louisiana, a crucial mistake given the perpetual animus between state and city. Senator Page Cortez of Lafayette reminded Rodrigue that the legislature had recently cut $20 million from MCC's state funding. Would that reduction affect the offer? Rodrigue was unfazed. "I can live with it. We want to help." Senator Greg Tarver of Shreveport joked that, as Finance Committee chair, he wondered how much MCC had to give away and whether he could get a little.[63] The audience laughed, but Rodrigue's testimony was a poor argument for increasing taxes.[64]

After a brief disappearance during testimony from two hospitality workers in "Tourism Matters" shirts, Senator Peterson returned with several amendments to the bill: a ten-year sunset clause for the tax district; the elimination of the independent board and the redirection of funding decisions to the city council; the removal of Faubourg Marigny from the zone (Tremé and the Seventh Ward had been removed prior to the meeting); and a revised distribution plan for the tax revenue, with 50 percent dedicated to infrastructure and 50 percent to marketing, to be divided among NOCVB and NOTMC (each receiving 20 percent, down from 33.3 percent) and the minority-owned Multi Cultural Tourism Network (10 percent; the network was excluded from the bill). Expenditures of these funds by all entities were now subject to public disclosure and accounting. Instead of an industry-driven, industry-overseen revenue generator for tourism marketing, the amended Hospitality Zone was a government-controlled tax district, split evenly between marketing and city-directed infrastructure upkeep. The hearing continued, but for all intents and purposes, the tourism industry walked out.

Four days later, the tourism coalition issued a statement withdrawing support of the bill. "We are extremely sad that this very unselfish effort to tax ourselves and generate significant dollars for marketing, job creation and revenue growth for our businesses and the city has come to an end."[65]

The original legislation was a "once-in-a lifetime opportunity to improve downtown and French Quarter infrastructure, gain $11 million in additional marketing funds, create thousands of new jobs and elevate our national reputation before we host the Super Bowl." The convention center's $30 million was off the table. MCC's Rodrigue remained open to partnering with the city but said the amendments "have effectively killed this very important marketing and infrastructure initiative for the time-being."

Why? The revised bill still generated new income for marketing and street repairs, both master plan priorities. Deputy Mayor Kopplin mentioned the instability created by the sunset clause, but the infrastructure upgrades funded by MCC's $30 million upgrades to the Quarter would likely need revisiting after ten years, regardless of the law. The industry's concession statement emphasized the reduction in marketing dollars. "We cannot support the amendments and the drastically reduced marketing in the new version of the bill," said NOCVB chair Fred Sawyer.

Whatever the source of the industry's abrupt withdrawal, the failure to engage certain stakeholders—legislators, French Quarter residents—toppled the master plan's central funding initiative. In a way, this was the latest incarnation of a persistent conflict. Most everyone agreed that the French Quarter was the "crown jewel," the primary reason visitors flocked to New Orleans. But how to increase the number of tourists while preserving the unique quality of the neighborhood—that was a question the hospitality industry couldn't address on its own. The master plan aimed to turn New Orleans into a tourism juggernaut for the city's greater economic good. It did not address the ways such changes would impact New Orleanians who lived in this upgraded landscape and therefore paid for the changes. But despite the abandonment of the Hospitality Zone legislation, change arrived in the French Quarter.

"We have no control; we're just being walked all over just so they can get it done by the Super Bowl," said Tanner, a painter and gallery owner. Five days after I spoke with Francis Swigart, Tanner and I stared out the window of his gallery at 830 Royal. The workers and earthmovers had arrived the day before and began tearing up the sidewalks and curbs of the resurfaced 800 and 900 blocks. Now three men in fluorescent jackets dug into the mud where the sidewalk once stood. Shop entrances were marooned above a mix of old brick and new concrete. The original curbs were still in place, propped up by metal rods. Wood planks offered passage from the dusty street to a slab of newly laid sidewalk. A few non-workers wandered about like confused extras on a film set. Another shopkeeper

ONE HUNDRED DAYS IN AMERICA'S COOLEST HOT SPOT

The 800 block of Royal Street, December 9, 2012. *Photo by author.*

called out to Tanner; she was closing for the afternoon. Who wanted to come down Royal Street in these conditions?

The convention center's $30 million pledge evaporated with the Hospitality Zone's defeat. Now the French Quarter received the upgrades through the federally funded Paths to Progress. Street repairs were urgent throughout the city, but the crown jewel had a deadline.

"Business doesn't slow down for this; it stops," said Tanner. "There's no use in us being open, and it's the week before Christmas." A linebacker-sized man with a shaved head and warm eyes, he opened the gallery three years ago to sell his psychedelic bayou landscapes. The original Paths to Progress construction decimated sales during the week of Halloween, the gallery's busiest time of year. Now this.

I called Paths spokesperson Alexandra Wommack and asked if the new work was the result of the poor paving. No, she said, these were part of the original plans, "but throughout construction, they had to be skipped over at the time because of the safety concerns with shallow electrical conduits." Nothing was wrong with the repaving. "We removed two inches of asphalt and replaced two inches of asphalt," Wommack said, but the contractors couldn't remove sidewalks under balconies, thus the flooding at Frances

Swigart's house. Today, workers would cut a gutter ("I hate calling it a gutter, but that's the best way I can describe it on the phone") to redirect rainwater, which was now a problem for the first time in centuries. But wasn't the middle of Christmas shopping season an inopportune time to shut down these blocks? I asked. "We do understand that it was inconvenient and the timing was inconvenient, but the city wanted to take full advantage of the available funding—and the fact that the contractor was on site—to go ahead and move these improvements forward right now." The majority of Paths projects in the region were 100 percent federally funded, but for the Quarter, Wommack said, the city contributed 20 percent of the costs, or about $2 million. I wondered where the money came from. Wommack said she couldn't speak for the city, but she believed "they had money they wanted to contribute to improvements in the French Quarter." Paths to Progress targeted a total of sixty street segments in the metro area for repair; the French Quarter stage would wrap by the end of December.

The refurbishment of the neighborhood came at a cost for merchants like Tanner and residents like Frances Swigart. The Quarter was the focus of a concerted effort, led by the mayor and a determined tourism sector, to make New Orleans more hospitable for large crowds like those attracted by the Super Bowl. As represented by the mess on Royal Street and the failure of the Hospitality Zone, those efforts suffered from the sense that residents weren't at the forefront of tourism's big-league plans.

A pile of gravel three feet high stood in front of Sigle's Antiques at 935 Royal. When I tried to enter, the door was locked. I rang the bell and then stepped into the street and looked up to the balcony, where an older man unfurled a German flag hung from a pole. A moment later, the front door opened, and Gertrude Sigel greeted me. I stepped into the cramped shop, where ceramic frogs, brass angels and assorted chandeliers filled the shelves in two adjoining rooms.

Gertrude Sigle and her husband moved to New Orleans from Stuttgart in 1957. They bought the building when the Quarter still brimmed with immigrant families, mostly Italians but also a cluster of Germans. The neighborhood was different now, Mrs. Sigel told me in accented English. "The uniqueness is gone." Business had changed, too. After 9/11, tourists no longer took larger items home on the plane, and anyway, the crowds for bowl games weren't interested in antiques. Yes, that was her husband on the balcony. The balcony had saved her sidewalk from the repairs, and she avoided flooding because her entrance was a step up. She sympathized with her neighbors, but she doubted anything would come from their protests. "If you go to the city, they say you're a complainer." Now, though, the pile of gravel blocked her entrance, and she was indignant. Why didn't the workers ask before essentially closing her business for a day or more? Her husband told her it was no use. "He says, 'Trudi, we only have a few years left.'" With his heart condition, why get agitated over things they couldn't control?

We talked about the defeat of the Riverfront Expressway, a landmark preservationist victory that galvanized French Quarter residents in the 1960s. Powerful interests lobbied for a highway along the Mississippi as a crucial infrastructural measure if New Orleans had any hope of keeping up with Houston, Atlanta, etc. The state and the Schiro administration agreed; federal funding seemed imminent. The highway would run between Jackson Square and the river, creating a noisy eyesore through the district and blocking the view of the water. It was difficult to imagine today, but big business and the political establishment almost sacrificed the crown jewel's tranquility in the name of a Robert Moses–designed vision of progress. Mrs. Sigle remembered well the relentless efforts of residents to save the Quarter from those careless ambitions. The mess outside her door was more of the same.

"They say we are always griping, griping, in the French Quarter. If we didn't gripe, there would be no French Quarter!"

CHAPTER 5
DECEMBER 17, 2012 (FORTY-EIGHT DAYS TO GO)

THE HIGHWAY TO BATON ROUGE

Heading west on Interstate 10, you immediately felt the isolation of New Orleans. The highway elevated after the exit for Louis Armstrong Airport, carrying traffic forty miles across the swampy edges of Lake Ponchartrain and then Lake Maurepas before resettling on solid land near Sorrento. You rode close to the water and parallel to the long lake horizon, tracked by the occasional pelican or boat. The view was often spectacular, sometimes foreboding and even, unexpectedly, inspiring—an appropriate path to the interior of Louisiana.

On this mid-December morning, the water and sky were shades of gray. After the swampland, much of the route to Baton Rouge was indistinguishable from other highways in the South: exits with larger or smaller truck stops, similar fast-food offerings, windowless video-poker casinos. In Baton Rouge, the state government buildings were clustered on the east side of the river in a compact neighborhood of orderly streets, light foot traffic and modern buildings that seemed to renounce the messy conditions in the rest of Louisiana. I parked in front of the capitol and walked across the street to the Capitol Annex, where I had a 9:00 a.m. appointment with Lieutenant Governor Jay Dardenne.

Dardenne greeted me warmly in a well-furnished but modest office, where he leaned back in his chair behind a wide desk. He had dark eyes and thick salt-and-pepper hair. In conservative Louisiana, Dardenne was a centrist Republican, Jewish and a career politician who won a seat in the Baton Rouge city council at age thirty-four. He spent fifteen years in the state senate and served three years as Louisiana's secretary of state prior to winning a special election to succeed Landrieu in 2010. A history buff, he embraced his role as a cultural advocate, but he made clear his gubernatorial ambitions. As head of the Department of Culture, Recreation and Tourism (CRT), Dardenne picked up where Landrieu left off, canvassing the state and traveling abroad as the ambassador for an increasingly popular brand: Louisiana.

The governor and lieutenant governor do not run on the same ticket in Louisiana, and though they shared a party affiliation, Dardenne and Governor Bobby Jindal had a less-than-cordial relationship. While approving the state budget in July 2012, Jindal inflicted ten line-item vetoes, two of which struck money from the lieutenant governor's office. Dardenne viewed the cuts as payback. "I have been critical on [state government] not spending enough money on marketing our state," Dardenne said at the time. "If that's what's provoked the governor to veto these items, it's unfortunate. That's not a rational reason."[66] Five months later, he bemoaned Jindal's disregard for tourism and culture. "One in every ten people in Louisiana works in the hospitality industry. It's big business," he told me. "It's not viewed, it seems to me, as a business by the current administration." That disconnect led to budget reductions for CRT, which forced Dardenne to reduce funding for arts programs, museums and tourism marketing.

Things were different when Dardenne first took office. On April 20, 2010, the *Deepwater Horizon* oil spill shattered the celebratory hangover of the Saints' recent Super Bowl victory. The catastrophe put a halt to offshore drilling and the seafood industry, inflicted untold damage on the Gulf of Mexico and sparked fears that the state might become uninhabitable. As days became weeks, the image of oil bubbling up from the floor of the ocean warned off tourists and emptied beaches. With Landrieu victorious in the February mayor's race, secretary of the Department of Natural Resources Scott Angelle served as lieutenant governor during the crisis. BP successfully cut off the oil on July 15, ending the initial stage of the disaster. There were rushed assurances that the Gulf was safe for visitors; in August, President Obama and his daughter swam off the coast of Panama City, Florida. On November 1, Jindal joined Angelle and representatives from the seafood, restaurant and tourism industries at Acme Oyster House in New Orleans, where he detailed an agreement with BP: the oil company would contribute $48 million for seafood safety and testing efforts, $140 million for coastal restoration and $30 million for tourism. "We saw the Saints win the Super

ONE HUNDRED DAYS IN AMERICA'S COOLEST HOT SPOT

Governor Bobby Jindal (left) and Mayor Mitch Landrieu at Acme Oyster House, November 1, 2010. Jindal announced an agreement from BP including $30 million for Louisiana tourism efforts following *Deepwater Horizon*. *Photo courtesy of Creative Commons.*

Bowl months ago, after years of struggles and setbacks," Jindal told reporters. "It is with that same perseverance and determination that we will emerge victorious over this oil spill."[67] The next day, Dardenne won the special election for lieutenant governor. The $30 million became fuel for tourism efforts in parishes across the state. Festivals, magazines and television shows benefited from the influx, but by late 2012, the BP money was running low.

Even worse for an ambitious politician, Dardenne couldn't exercise total control over his department's spending. The Super Bowl was a great boon for Louisiana tourism, but the game was a budgetary disaster for CRT. As part of the selection process, the New Orleans Super Bowl Host Committee promised $12 million to help market the game, with half of the money covered by the private sector and the other half by state government. Dardenne was surprised to find himself on the hook for the state's $6 million, or more than a quarter of his annual $23 million tourism promotion budget. "The city had hosted nine previous Super Bowls, each more expensive than the last, but in the past, the state general fund or the Department of Economic Development bore the brunt of the monetary commitment that the state had to make," he explained. "This year, for the first time, it's being taken out of the tourism budget." Once a highly respected legislator, he was clearly irked at the limits of his power. "What I argued last year was, let's all belly up to the bar and share in this obligation. Everybody's going to benefit—it shouldn't come entirely out of an advertising budget. But I lost that fight, and it's all coming out of my budget."

In a November speech at the Baton Rouge Press Club, Dardenne proposed the creation of a revolving fund to pay for future events. State tourism efforts were funded through a three-one-hundredths-of-a-penny sales tax. A slight increase could generate $5 to $10 million set aside for the next big game. He assured me he understood the financial restraints the state faced but added that Louisiana was due for more and more spectacles, and each of them had a price. "It's a great problem to have, but it's only going to be a bigger problem."

He'd had a brief discussion with Landrieu about the proposed fund, as well as possible increases to the city's hotel tax, but admitted the mayor "obviously doesn't want to peel off any revenue that would otherwise be coming to the city, so there's always going to be a little tension" between city and state. In fact, the city had aired its complaints two weeks earlier during a meeting to discuss Landrieu's 2013 budget. According to *Gambit*'s Charles Maldonado, Councilwoman Diana Bajoie told administration officials, "I was somewhere yesterday and I was asked the question, 'Why is it the city doesn't have enough money when we have all these big events coming into town?' Super Bowl, Final Four, Mardi Gras, all these things filling up hotel rooms." If the special events business was booming, why was the city still struggling to cover its expenses? Council president Jackie Clarkson, a Landrieu ally, pointed to the hotel tax split detailed in Chapter 4. "We pay everything to the state. We collect all the big monies to the state through tourism—and they send us unfunded mandates."[68]

In Dardenne's office and in the New Orleans council chambers, the arguments were essentially the same—CRT and the city bore substantial burdens for tourism, but neither received its fair share of the tax revenue from events like the Super Bowl. Dardenne agreed with industry supporters in New Orleans: "When it comes to these sporting events, there's no question about the return. Hotels get filled, restaurants are booked, people are buying stuff; national attention is focused on Louisiana. There are any number of benefits, tangible and intangible." Big games were on the rise, but revenues didn't reach the public bodies charged with promoting the big games and attracting future events. The private sector raked in hundreds of millions of dollars, but the state remained poor. If the Super Bowl heralded the new

New Orleans, it was also a reminder that the city was still part of the same old, dysfunctional Louisiana.

Bobby Jindal was supposed to be different. And he was—just not in the ways many had hoped. Now in his second term, the nation's first Indian American governor was unlike any politician in modern Louisiana history. He grew up in Baton Rouge to immigrant parents from Punjab, took on at the age of nine a Westernized first name borrowed from *The Brady Bunch*, covertly embraced Catholicism over his family's Hinduism and excelled in school, landing at Brown University, where he planned to study medicine. While at Brown, Jindal decided policy was a better route if he wanted to improve health conditions for the public. After studying at Oxford as a Rhodes Scholar, he returned to Baton Rouge, where, at the age of twenty-four, he became the state's secretary of the Department of Health and Hospitals under Governor Mike Foster, who declared Jindal "a genius." Inheriting a $400 million deficit, Jindal turned around the state's bankrupt Medicaid program, eventually generating three years of surplus totaling $220 million. In 1999, he took over as the youngest-ever president of the University of Louisiana system, serving until 2001, when George W. Bush appointed him assistant secretary of the U.S. Department of Health and Human Services. In 2003, he ran to become Louisiana's first non-white governor since Reconstruction, in a historic election against Lieutenant Governor Kathleen Blanco, vying to become the state's first female chief executive. Observers called Jindal's race and youth "wild cards," particularly in north Louisiana, where Catholicism was only slightly more popular than Hinduism. Some political observers wondered if Jindal was "too brown." The contest was close, but in the final week, the cagey Blanco hammered her young opponent with questions about his cuts in healthcare. She prevailed, garnering 52 percent of the vote to Jindal's 48 percent. In his concession speech, Jindal told supporters, "We made the case that the American dream is more alive in Louisiana than anywhere else in America. Something special happened here."[69] He rebounded quickly, filling the House seat vacated by David Vitter's 2004 senate victory.

In 2007, Jindal ascended to the governor's mansion with 37 percent more of the vote than his nearest opponent, avoiding a runoff and immediately becoming the darling of Republican circles. He helped his image by attacking the status quo: he called a special session of the legislature to push through an ethics reform package directly aimed at the state's culture of backroom dealings and ingrained corruption. Lobbyists could no longer use pricey meals to woo legislators, who were required to reveal all sources of income and avoid conflicts of interest. "New Louisiana Governor Pierces Brazen Style of Business as Usual," read the *New York Times* headline. "I've talked to C.E.O.'s in New York, even the president of the United States," Jindal told the *Times*, "and when you ask them for more investment, more help on the coast and other areas, their first reaction always is: 'Well, who do you need to know? Who do I have to hire? Is this money going to end up in somebody's pocket?'"[70] He'd risk alienating Baton Rouge to make friends on Wall Street.

"Is Bobby Jindal the GOP's Obama?" asked *Newsweek* in December 2008, suggesting the party, desperate for intellect and diversity after losing the White House, saw the former Rhodes Scholar as a future presidential candidate. But in his first turn in the national spotlight, Jindal failed miserably. Republican leaders selected him to give the party's response to Obama's first state of the union address. If Obama used his momentum to deliver a soaring rallying cry to a nation in the depths of the financial collapse, Jindal seemed to waste his intellectual skills in a folksy critique of the federal stimulus plan. Conservative columnist David Brooks labeled the speech's anti-government tone "a disaster for the Republican Party," while *Fox News* commentator Juan Williams called Jindal's tone "amateurish, and even the tempo in which he spoke was sing-songy. He was telling stories that seemed very simplistic and almost childish." In the ultimate signal of national embarrassment, *Saturday Night Live* dedicated a sketch to lampooning the GOP's would-be star.

Yet Jindal was undaunted, and his ambitions were no laughing matter at home. Adhering to the national party's stance, Jindal refused $98 million from the 2009 stimulus plan and $300 million to build a high-speed rail line connecting New Orleans and Baton Rouge. Tax cuts, tax breaks for private industry and Jindal's strict no-tax pledge left state coffers bare. Days before I visited Dardenne, the administration announced $165.5 million in mid-fiscal year cuts, with the state's Department of Children and Family Services and Department of Health and Hospitals bearing the largest burden. The announcement marked the fifth consecutive year of mid-year budget cuts due to revenue shortfalls.[71] Since 2008, cuts to higher education totaled $426.5 million. In a state ranked at or near the bottom in public health indexes and the percentage of adults with college degrees, the impact of closed hospitals and reduced universities was widely felt. Education reform centered on a voucher program that sent public money to private charter schools, while a full-scale privatization of public hospitals eliminated thousands of jobs and left New Orleans—still recovering from the effects of Katrina—without a mental health facility. For the poor and uninsured, the consequences were dire. Tax orthodoxy might appeal to certain national kingmakers, but the winnowing of government services left Jindal with few options for funding the sort of high-profile initiatives popular among primary voters.

Ironically, Jindal's carefully crafted narrative seemed more concerned with national affairs during a period when the nation was most interested in Louisiana. Reality television, Hollywood and professional sports were more captivated than ever with the state's people and culture, yet Jindal spent less and less time at home. Records showed he traveled outside Louisiana one out of every four days in 2012, mostly to campaign for other candidates and attend fundraisers. Between his outward focus and his repeated revenue shortfalls, it was little surprise that Jindal continued to ignore his lieutenant governor's pleas for more tourism dollars. Culture and tourism might be a growing business for Louisiana, but in the most important office in the state, they took a backseat to national politics.

Back in Baton Rouge, Dardenne told me he hoped to see a full accounting of the Super Bowl's economic impact, predicted to surpass $400 million. Of course, he said, "I don't believe our office has the personnel or the funds" to carry out such a study, but certainly the tourism officials in New Orleans or mayor's office should validate the quoted numbers. "Whether the economists are accurate, who knows, but there have been some good studies I think that confirm what everyone would suspect—that this means big bucks for the GNO area and for the state."

As for his office's plans for the game, the lieutenant governor admitted that advertising during the week was simply too expensive, but opportunities abounded. "We've just confirmed that the folks from [Louisiana-based reality show] *Duck Dynasty*, and I think the folks from *Swamp People*, will be accompanying me on some walkthroughs in the media area during the week because there's so much interest in the reality shows about Louisiana."[72]

We'd talked for an hour, and I left with an impression of Dardenne as frank and levelheaded, an eager ambassador for the state's tourism industry who understood the problematic landscape he faced. On the one hand, the money and attention generated by the Super Bowl were a politician's dream, providing countless photo-ops with celebrities and potential supporters. The whole world tuned in for a week of media coverage, free advertisements for the very attractions he was charged to promote. But he'd turned over a quarter of his annual tourism budget to the game, and the revenue generated from all those visitors slipped through his hands like sand. Instead of capitalizing on the attention, he was handcuffed by budget cuts and a governor who had his eyes on a bigger prize. Ideally, the big game would raise money to attract more big games; in fact, that money ended up in the dwindling general fund. During Super Bowl week, the most the state's second-in-command could hope for was making the rounds with a few reality show stars.

I crossed the street to State Capitol Park, where a statue of Huey Long stared up at the capitol building, a thirty-four-floor monument to Long's impact on the state. Sitting at the base of the statue, it was hard not to compare the all-powerful Kingfish with the men who ruled present-day Louisiana. Imagine Huey Long under the spotlight of the Super Bowl, I thought. No walkthroughs with television personalities for the Kingfish, no one wondering if the state would get its fair share. Long would have a coercive arm around Roger Goodell all week and probably find his way to the ceremonial coin flip on Sunday.

Born in 1893, Long rose from humble beginnings with a preternatural political acumen and a ruthless impatience. For the first time in Louisiana's history, a gifted speaker addressed the state's rural poor in their own vernacular, framing attacks on the wealthy with stories about greedy barbecue guests. The success of his populism depended on forces outside the state: Long's ascent coincided with the nation's growing interest in the exploitation of Louisiana's natural resources. As the combustible engine transformed the country in the first half of the twentieth century, Louisiana ranked among the top ten states in oil and natural gas production. Control of these resources, though, belonged to out-of-state corporations.[73] To crowds demanding he "Rub their noses in it!" Long made and kept promises to levy taxes on extraction of the state's mineral wealth, wrestling free the necessary revenues to pull Louisiana into the modern era.

Like Jindal, Long was in a hurry. He campaigned tirelessly for Franklin Roosevelt's 1932 presidential election, seizing on oratorical opportunities to reach a national audience. The alliance soured quickly, though, with FDR telling intimates that Long "really is one of the two most dangerous men in the country."[74] With his eyes on the White House, Long started his own newspaper to spread his gospel, authored a widely read biography/manifesto and became a popular radio presence. By the time an assassin's bullet mortally wounded Long in the capitol building in 1935, the Kingfish and the president were at war, with Long refusing to accept Louisiana's share of the New Deal and Roosevelt questioning the legitimacy of the state's elections. After his death, accusations of dictatorship persisted in the popular memory of Long, but so, too, did his contributions to the state's infrastructure. Every day, Louisianans crossed bridges, attended schools and drove on highways built during Long's reign.

The current governor shared some similarities with Long. Jindal was a born outsider, a political prodigy and a strident opponent of the federal government who very much wanted to be president. The jury was out on his impact on Louisiana, though certainly no one in Baton Rouge plotted where to erect a statue of Bobby Jindal. The Kingfish and the genius exercised power in very different ways. Long sought to control every aspect of political life in the state; Jindal rarely interacted with legislators. Instead of capital projects, Jindal could point to slashed budgets, elimination of government waste, increased tax breaks for the private sector, and perhaps the defense of the state against the designs of the Obama administration. For New Orleans, the consequences were myriad. The urban poor saw the loss of public hospitals and mental health facilities, while the middle class watched government jobs disappear. The renaissance in New Orleans might depend on tourism and culture, but Baton Rouge didn't seem to care. Under Jindal, the state couldn't afford to reinvest in tourism—unless, of course, there was a disaster in the Gulf. The Super Bowl generated revenues for the state, which was in no position to offer a larger share of those dollars to New Orleans. The money traveled up I-10 and didn't come back.

I headed back in the opposite direction.

CHAPTER 6
JANUARY 7, 2013
(TWENTY-SEVEN DAYS TO GO)

"THE SHERIFF HAS A GUN TO THE CITY'S HEAD"

The speaker's voice echoed down the marble-floored corridor. As I reached the ballroom, his words became clearer. "Our founders sought to lift the spirits of the citizens, stimulate tourism and create an organized celebration on Mardi Gras Day."

Inside Gallier Hall, Carnival season was officially underway. Krewe of Rex member Christy Brown stood on a dais before two hundred guests, including police officers, leaders of Carnival organizations and tourism officials. They were gathered to celebrate Twelfth Night, the traditional start of the festivities leading up to Mardi Gras Day.

"Carnival has become a central celebration to our culture," Brown said, "and millions and millions of happy tourists visit us each year and have accepted [Rex's] invitation and traveled to our Carnival." He read the krewe's official Carnival proclamation. "Rex, King of Carnival, sends greetings and announces with pleasure his intention to visit his capital city of New Orleans. His majesty invites all his subjects to gather from far and near to join in this celebration."

Brown was replaced on the dais by Naaman Stewart, president of Zulu, the major African American krewe. At least a dozen Zulu members sat in the audience wearing their customary mustard-colored jackets and black pants. Stewart acknowledged many of them by name and title, including the Zulu Mayor Man, Witch Doctor, Province Prince and this year's King, who, unlike the King of Rex, is not bound by tradition to keep his identity a secret

Sheriff Marlin Gusman (left) and NOPD superintendent Ronal Serpas (center) ride with Mayor Landrieu in the 2012 Zulu parade. *Photo courtesy of Creative Commons.*

before Fat Tuesday. The krewe emerged in 1909 as an edgy satire that used Mardi Gras as an expression of freedom in a city where such displays were highly dangerous. To mock the racist white elite, Zulu members embraced the blackface and jungle imagery popular at the time. A century later, the krewe was a pillar of Carnival culture.

"I brought a couple gifts today," Stewart said. "I heard the mayor make reference to the Super Bowl in several of his remarks." He mentioned the club's famous hand-painted coconuts, each of them crafted according to the year and the member's particular bent. "However, this year we have something different. Mr. Mayor, it's an honor to present you with a very original rendition of a coconut slash football."

Naaman handed the mayor a ceramic, football-shaped coconut emblazoned with "Super Bowl XLVII." "I accept," said Landrieu to general laughter and applause. With twenty-seven days until the game, the mayor was increasingly in the spotlight, both locally and in the national press. There were benefits and perils to the exposure.

The night before, the television show *60 Minutes* had run a segment on the unfolding drama at the *Times-Picayune*. Veteran reporter Morley Safer introduced his piece with images of second-line parades, street musicians and a series of clichés. "There's no doubt: New Orleans is a city like no other, a wonderful ethnic cocktail, a place that dances to its own rhythm." The first voice heard from this ethnic cocktail belonged to Landrieu. "When you take away a venerable institution like the *Times-Picayune*, you really kind of take away a piece of the soul of a city," said the mayor. "People in this city were worried that it was going to send a message to the rest of the country that we weren't a big-league city because we weren't going to have a daily paper."[75] Landrieu's emphasis on the city's national image may have reflected his own preoccupations. For many New Orleanians, however, external messaging wasn't the problem. The changes at the paper were another instance of outside forces wreaking havoc on their way of life.

David Carr of the *New York Times* broke the story on May 23, 2012: New Orleans would become the first major American city without a daily newspaper. Advance Publications, owner of the *Times-Picayune*, planned to reduce printing to a Wednesday-Friday-Sunday schedule beginning in September and focus its efforts on the paper's online version, NOLA.com. Staff reductions were imminent. The next morning, the city's social media community was aflame with outraged Facebook posts and tweets. Several newspaper staffers confessed that Carr's article was the first they'd heard of their newly established positions as sailors on a punctured ship. Crime reporter Brendan McCarthy tweeted, "Just learned in the *NY Times* that my newspaper, my employer, my morning routine, may cease to exist."[76] The paper's Pulitzer Prize–winning Katrina coverage and a more recent series about the Louisiana penal system were held up as proof: the city needed its paper.

In the *60 Minutes* segment, Safer agreed. "The *Times-Picayune* was one of the few things that worked in a city that generally doesn't." Interviewed by Safer, Carr seconded the sentiment: "Schools aren't great, public housing doesn't go very well, they have problems with their police. They've always had a really great newspaper."[77] Though complimentary to the paper, the assessments by two national reporters reflected New Orleans' long-standing reputation as lazy and dysfunctional, characterizations that Landrieu sought to erase.

"Save the *Times-Picayune!*" The cry echoed across the Internet and appeared on placards posted in front yards. In a column on the investigative journalism website The Lens, former *Times Picayune* city editor Jed Horne appealed to the city's old money elite: "Memo to St. Charles Avenue: How about a Hornets-style 'I'm In' campaign where the ante isn't the cost of a season ticket. Instead it's an investment sufficient to save a local institution at least as important as any other cultural asset or sports franchise."[78] Launched by the NBA, the "I'm In" campaign boosted attendance for New Orleans' NBA team.

The most significant ante came not from Uptown but from a wealthy Seventh Ward native. Tom Benson made his case in two letters to the paper's ownership and at a private meeting. The first letter, dated just days after the initial announcement in May, urged Steven Newhouse to reconsider the cuts. Benson raised the specter of the Super Bowl. "Major-league cities (and rest assured, we are one) have high-visibility entities such as NBA and NFL teams," he wrote. He also mentioned the recent run of big sporting events: "It is hard for me to imagine no *Times-Picayune* on Monday, February 4, 2013, the day after our city hosts Super Bowl XLVII. Cities like ours deserve, and have, at least one daily paper."[79] Copied on the letter were Landrieu, Jindal, Benson's granddaughter and team official Rita Benson Leblanc and several team employees.

Two months later, WWL-TV published a copy of a second letter, which opened with Benson thanking Newhouse for his hospitality during a recent visit to Advance's New York offices. Benson and his wife listened that day as Newhouse laid out his plans and "the complicated business of operating a newspaper."[80] The eighty-four-year-old Benson remained unafraid of such complications. He requested "the opportunity to speak to you about my interest in purchasing the *Times-Picayune*, with others." A handwritten note appeared at the bottom of the letter: "In 1985, the Saints were leaving. I would hate for this to happen with our paper." Could Benson—once a focus of public scorn similar to the Newhouses—save another local institution?

This time Benson never got the chance. Advance's president, Donald Newhouse, told WWL-TV that the company had "no intention of selling The *Times-Picayune*." Once again, New Orleans would serve as a "laboratory," this time for the future of print media. What better place to try out a new distribution model than a "major-league city" in a content-rich region with a national profile and sustained local demand?

"New Orleans is a kind of reporter's delight," Safer told Landrieu at the end of the *60 Minutes* segment. "Of course it is," Landrieu said with a grin. "We tell good stories down here." "There's a lot of hanky-panky that goes on," Safer added. "Yessir," Landrieu replied. Would the public interest suffer without the daily paper? "I hope not," the mayor said. "The more robust press we have, the better everybody is." His appearance on national television as the first and last voice for New Orleans reflected Landrieu's growing stature as the new face of the city. The show's portrayal of the city, however, was not the representation pushed by the mayor in his pre–Super Bowl addresses.

ONE HUNDRED DAYS IN AMERICA'S COOLEST HOT SPOT

At Gallier Hall, Landrieu promised to wrap things up quickly so everyone could get their piece of king cake, the traditional Carnival pastry. He praised the artists who created this year's official Rex and Zulu Carnival paintings, slipping easily into the role he'd played as lieutenant governor. "There's no better example than these two individuals of what the cultural economy really means," he said. "This is a business. We're in the business of entertaining people." In Louisiana, the cultural economy was a big business: 125,000 jobs and a $9 billion annual economic impact. "When you think of the back of the house side of what we do, the people that actually make the floats, the people that paint the floats, the people that put up the Mardi Gras stands—all of you that work in the businesses that actually create the economic impact." He turned toward several men in uniform seated in the rear and said, "I want to just reiterate how thankful I am to Chief Serpas and to the police department, the firemen, EMS—all those folks who are about to get on their feet…and they're not going to sit down for about forty days."

And now, there was cake to eat. The room filled with friendly chatter as krewe members mingled with NOPD officers and city staffers. I stopped next to the Zulu painting to say hello to New Orleans Tourism and Marketing Corporation executive director Mark Romig, who helped put the event together. Genial and trim, Romig was blessed with his father's voice—Jerry Romig was the longtime PA announcer at the Superdome. When we met in October, Romig was already knee deep in the preparations for the Super Bowl. There were corporate partnerships to secure, fan and media guides to produce and a Super Bowl app in development. "Everyday there's a Super Bowl component. Soon it'll be three, four hours a day," he said then. "But the eyes of the world are on New Orleans. In fact, almost every week somewhere along the NFL track, someone says, 'I wonder if this team is going to play into the Super Bowl in New Orleans?' So New Orleans is being mentioned. It's advertising you couldn't buy."

Romig admitted that the public outreach for the Hospitality Zone legislation was insufficient, but the goals remained urgent. "You've got to fix the dissatisfiers," he said. "You've got to deal with the crime issue. You've got to get the taxi cab industry working together, to being where it is in other tourism centers. You've got to fix the litter issue. Gotta fix the streets, gotta build a better infrastructure."

Today, Romig and I wished each other a happy Mardi Gras. I walked into the corridor, where another painting hung near the front entrance. Ray Nagin's official portrait captured the former mayor in a dark suit and red tie. To his left was the faint outline of the Saints' Lombardi Trophy, which struck me as funny. In the ultimate indignity, Nagin found himself without tickets one week before the 2010 Super Bowl. He was shocked, he told the African American–owned radio station WBOK, that he hadn't received complimentary tickets. "I just thought that as mayor of the city, I would go to the [Super Bowl] as a representative of the city and of the Saints and it wouldn't be an issue."[81] During the same show, Nagin and NOPD chief Warren Riley bemoaned the "shadow government," a conspiratorial term for the wealthy white elite that some African Americans felt controlled the city. With the mayoral election approaching, both men warned callers of racist forces that tarred the reputations of black politicians. Asked to name names, Riley demurred: "You know, that's why it's the shadow government, because you're not supposed to know. That's just my opinion." The theory wasn't new, and anyone familiar with it would include the old-money Rex members in a hypothetical roster of shadow government.

Looking at the portrait, I was reminded of the bitterness of Nagin's final months in office. In contrast, Landrieu had made racial unity a key theme in his campaign and in his public persona as mayor, an emphasis reflected by the bubbling crowd of white and black officials in the ballroom today. I stepped back inside and selected a large piece of king cake.

JANUARY 10 (TWENTY-FOUR DAYS TO GO)

Three days later, steady rain fell on Loyola Avenue as I entered the Orleans Parish Civil Courthouse next to city hall. In the lobby, another "back of the house" group awaited its own kickoff to Carnival season. The ceremony featured no king cake, but the Super Bowl and political intrigue were well represented. And if reforms and master plans shaped a new image of government in New Orleans, the proceedings in the courthouse were a throwback to business as usual.

Mardi Gras was the original big New Orleans event. Carnival generated millions of dollars for hundreds of residents who sold goods and services to their fellow citizens and thousands of visitors. According to a 2009 study, Mardi Gras had a $145 million direct impact on the New Orleans economy. After substantial public investment—overtime for police officers, cleanup costs, court proceedings—the city reaped a net fiscal benefit of more than $11 million in revenues.[82] Amid the revelry and chaos, a system of regulations evolved to control and tax the celebration. Today's event, the Mardi Gras Permit Lottery, was a link in the chain between partying and revenue.

The city's municipal code featured a section for Mardi Gras regulations, and a detailed Mardi Gras Vendor guide was available on the city's website, outlining everything from the location of vendors to the types of goods they could sell. The owner of a funnel cake stand applied for a fixed-location permit, while the roving glow-stick salesman was classified as a non-fixed-location vendor, prohibited from operating in the French Quarter and the busiest blocks of Canal Street. Fixed-location vendors incurred higher fees and limits on the size of their vehicles. Neither vendor, the code made clear, could sell "silly string, regardless of its brand name." Stink bombs were also prohibited, as was "peddling novelties, souvenirs and food" near elementary or secondary schools during school hours. "Novelties" were defined as small, inexpensive toys, ornaments and trinkets, "treasured for the memories associated with Mardi Gras." Fixed-location vendors could not set up card tables on sidewalks, while non-fixed-location vendors could stop walking only to conduct a sale.

It was a byzantine code, but its motivations were transparent. The city's job was to collect taxes and ensure public safety; the ways to earn a buck during Carnival were countless, with loopholes and hazards that required additional prohibitions. In 2013, the Super Bowl interruption created challenges for vendors and public officials. To the untrained eye, a weeklong break might seem like a welcome respite, a time to recharge before the grander parades on the final days leading up to Fat Tuesday. But for the men and women who worked in the "back of the house," the delay created multiple headaches and the prospect of diminished profits. In an article on Vice.com, local writer Michael Patrick Welch detailed the problems faced by the krewes that organized and rode in the first weekend of parades, now scheduled a week earlier than usual. Declines in membership, warehouse fees, skyrocketing hotel rates and tight post-holiday budgets were among their complaints. When the 9-11 attacks led to a delayed 2002 Super Bowl in New Orleans, the Mardi Gras schedule was similarly altered, and krewes were compensated. "I was part of that settlement, and it covered our krewe's losses," Krewe of Ponchartrain captain Sam Scandaliato said. "But this year the city didn't want to share the $50 million they got up front from the NFL."[83] It was an anxious season for the krewes.

The people in the Civil Court lobby focused their anxieties on ping-pong balls. Conducted by the Orleans Parish Sheriff's Office, the lottery decided the selection order for fixed locations. Entrants paid a refundable $1,000 tax deposit per application by January 4. Numbers were assigned today and listed on a poster board with the names of ninety-six applicants vying for thirty-three locations. The higher your number was picked, the better spot you could select on the parade route. While her co-workers took names and scrawled numbers onto ping-pong balls, a statuesque young woman in a black dress and pink stilettos watched over a vented brass cylinder where the balls would soon gather. I leaned against a wall etched with a tribute to Chep Morrison and his cabinet.

Another woman took the podium to explain that the sheriff was fighting through the rain but would join us momentarily. I struck up a conversation with a short, silver-haired man in a black leather jacket, who introduced himself as Rock Nelson, owner of Rock-n-Sake, a restaurant in the Warehouse District. He'd been in business fifteen years, but this was his first lottery. Some of these people, he knew, were here every year. The rules stated that each person or business could enter the lottery once, but there were outfits that registered under multiple members and LLCs, thus gaming the odds. "Like the Mitchells," he said, nodding toward the corner where a group of four men and a woman chatted and poked at their cellphones.

Sheriff Marlin Gusman appeared and welcomed everyone in his customary monotone. At fifty-six, he had soft features, a neat mustache, a high forehead and graying hair parted down the middle. Well-coiffed and somber, Gusman looked like the unlikely combination he was: an Ivy League–educated politician who oversaw almost two thousand prisoners at one of the nation's most dangerous jails. Now the city's highest-ranking black official, he rose to prominence as second-in-command under Mayor Marc Morial and then served six years as a city councilman. Despite no previous experience in law enforcement, he was elected in 2006 as Orleans Parish criminal sheriff and then as "super" sheriff when the criminal and civil positions merged in 2010. Cagey and guarded, Gusman arrived at the Mardi Gras lottery suddenly embroiled in the fight of his career.

Fights were nothing new for the Orleans Parish Prison (OPP). In 1969, the American Civil Liberties Union sued OPP for maintaining "cruel and unusual" conditions, a suit that led to the first federal oversight of the jail. Ensuing decades saw more complaints as OPP built a reputation for violence, wonton supervision and prisoner escapes. When its treatment of prisoners during Katrina was widely criticized and litigated, Gusman dismissed the complaining inmates as "crackheads, cowards and criminals."[84] In September 2009, the Justice Department reported that prison conditions "violate[d] the constitutional rights of inmates" and demanded Gusman take action. Citing ongoing reforms, the sheriff called the report "terribly dated" and "fundamentally flawed." Two years later, the department sent a draft of a federal consent decree, which Gusman ignored for months. In April 2012, the Southern Poverty Law Center filed suit in federal court against the sheriff, claiming he operated "a facility where violence and widespread contraband—including knives and drugs—are the norm." His deputies were "poorly trained and supervised, and are often complicit in the abuses suffered by the prisoners," while prisoners with mental illnesses "were held practically naked in overcrowded cells that reeked of human waste."[85] The Justice Department joined the suit in September 2012, forcing Gusman to negotiate a consent decree for reforming the prison. Seemingly cornered, the sheriff once again proved slippery.

When Landrieu and Attorney General Eric Holder signed the NOPD consent decree in July 2012, the mayor estimated $11 million in annual costs associated with the mandated reforms. Succeeding months found the administration focused on budgeting for the reforms, a delicate process in the already cash-strapped city. Presented in October 2012, the proposed 2013 budget requested $7 million in initial costs, including cameras in patrol cars, mobile data terminals, "electronic control weapons," an outside monitor to oversee implementation and new NOPD personnel. As city staff and programs were cut to make room for the decree, city council members protested the expenses. "I think this is a rip-off," said Councilwoman Cynthia Hedge-Morrell, the mother of two police officers. "I'm tired of New Orleans being the subject of somebody's arbitrary and capricious decisions."[86] Asked by *Gambit* reporter Charles Maldonado if events like the Super Bowl would improve revenue estimates, Landrieu pointed to the limited share of hotel and sales taxes. "We can't host our way out of a budget crisis," he said.[87] Despite the run of big games, the price of reform forced new austerity measures on New Orleans. The budget passed on November 30. Councilwomen-at-large Stacey Head and Jackie Clarkson issued a statement: the budget process, "while long and arduous, was well worth it to build a consensus with the City Council and mayor that led to good results that will benefit the entire city of New Orleans."[88] Ten days later, all hell broke loose. Marlin Gusman had cut his own deal.

When the Justice Department announced its proposed consent decree for the prison on December 11, 2012, the Landrieu administration expressed shock. Unfortunately—and fatefully—the city arrived late to the jail consent decree negotiations, apparently failing to send consistent representation to the talks. In its absence, the sheriff agreed to reforms that he didn't need to pay for—the city was responsible for OPP's $22 million annual budget. On top of the $11 million price tag for police reform, the federal government now expected Landrieu to find $14 million to reform the jail. The administration's carefully planned 2013 budget was suddenly insufficient.

In an interview today with the *Times-Picayune*, Landrieu declared that the future of New Orleans was at stake. "I don't want this to catch anyone in the city by surprise. We're headed for a cliff," Landrieu said. "It could threaten in a real way the tremendous progress we've made in the recovery."[89] The sheriff and the Department of Justice had created, he said, the potential for "catastrophic damage" to the city budget. The black hole of the city's justice system imperiled the mayor's vision for a new New Orleans. Landrieu found himself cornered, and he blamed Gusman. The confidence and bonhomie of Twelfth Night were replaced by menace and alarm.

At the lottery, Gusman betrayed no signs of inner turmoil. He explained that the lady in pink stilettos would place the balls into the hopper first while he read out the registered names. He began a steady roll call: "Number eleven, Houston Dix. Number twelve, Merrit 'Speedy' Edwards…" A succession of Mitchells held numbers forty-five (Anthony) through fifty-five (Sandra). "See?" Rock asked me. A similar batch of Stanleys controlled the seventies, and Gusman stopped to joke that the Stanleys and Mitchells were related. When the sheriff finished reading off the ninety-six names, the lady turned the arm of the hopper, and the ping-pong balls tumbled. She stopped, plucked out a ball and handed it to Gusman.

"Number fifty…Ralph Mitchell. Ralph M. Mitchell."

From the family's corner, a tall, young man hollered. Rock and I shook our heads. Of the thirty-three names selected for fixed-location spots, the Mitchells took four and the Stanleys three. Gusman read every name in the same flat voice, one through ninety-six, but the room began to drain around forty, and the conversations grew louder. By that point, uncalled vendors knew their shots at a fixed location this year had passed. The winners would return on Saturday to select their spots on the parade route.

The sheriff finished, and everyone crowded around the white board to write down numbers or take photos. I asked the young guy who whelped if he was Ralph M. Mitchell. "No." He smirked a little. Was he with the Mitchells? "My family," he said and walked away.

Outside, the rain continued. An older man in a knee brace waited for a ride. "How'd you do?" I asked. "Oh, not bad. I got number ten," he replied with a smile. "I'm not sure what we're going to do," he said of the revised parade schedule. He, too, worried about the possible decrease in crowds because of the game and the weak national economy. This year's schedule was a hassle, he said, because fixed-location vendors usually set up on the first Friday, shut down after the Sunday parades and then leave their stands locked in place until the following Thursday, when parades resume. Now, he would need to pack everything up and come back almost two weeks later. A pickup truck made a U-turn on Loyola, and he hobbled to the curb.

Overseen by a controversial jailer, the lottery left a tired aftereffect. The hope of random fortune gave way to the disappointment that, once again, money talked. The Super Bowl disrupted the practices of the "back of the house," themselves divided between those who could purchase the most ping-pong balls. Mardi Gras was big business for New Orleans, but business was still conducted in hallways, subject to the turn of a wheel.

JANUARY 13, 2013 (TWENTY-THREE DAYS TO GO)

A day after the lottery, Federal District Court judge Susie Morgan signed the NOPD consent decree, despite the loud protests of the same city administration that negotiated the agreement. The city was now on the hook for up to $24 million in federally mandated criminal justice reforms in 2013. "What is concerning me is that the relationship the Justice Department has now engaged in with the sheriff has a gun to the city's head," said a despondent Landrieu this morning at a groundbreaking ceremony for a redeveloped hospital in New Orleans East. "I'm not happy with the situation. I want to think about it over the weekend."[90]

As he joined other leaders to bury a shovel into the flood-ravaged earth, the mayor faced the most significant challenge to his vision for a new New Orleans. He began his tenure with a focus on crime and police reform, the issues most important to a long-suffering population. He emphasized racial unity and a tough approach to criminals and errant police officers. He welcomed increased national exposure and federal intervention as historic opportunities for reform. Yet when the rotted core of the criminal justice system came under scrutiny, reform demanded a financial commitment that the still-recovering city could not afford. Landrieu articulated the dream of a New Orleans that worked efficiently, protected its citizens and earned the trust of the federal government; he took meaningful action to realize those goals. In January 2013, the headlines of the city's troubled newspaper offered conflicting diagnoses. The promises of progress strained against the shackles as the spotlight neared. There was a lot to think about over the weekend.

CHAPTER 7
JANUARY 13, 2013 (TWENTY-ONE DAYS TO GO)

HACK

James Carville thanked us for coming. He knew everyone had worked hard and given up their weekends. "Being a New Orleanian," said Carville, "I know what weekend means." We all laughed. "This is not a weekend in Oklahoma City you're giving up." More laughter. Since moving to the city in 2008, Carville had rarely skipped an opportunity to praise his adopted home. Today, he said, was another signal of the vibrancy he'd come to cherish.

"I think it's one of the great stories in the Super Bowl, what you guys are accomplishing today," said Carville. "It's terrific to know that we've got this kind of a technology community in our city. On behalf of the New Orleans Super Bowl Host Committee, thank you from the bottom of my heart." The crowd responded with applause.

Inside the conference room at the headquarters of the Peter Mayer advertising firm, the CODEMKRS Super Challenge "hackathon" approached its zenith. After forty-eight hours of coding, eight teams of sleep-deprived young men—and a few women—awaited their turns to present a new app to Carville; his wife and host committee co-chair, Mary Matalin; other host committee members; and members of the business community and local media. The event was the brainchild of entrepreneur Travis Laurendine, who saw the Super Bowl as a chance to show off the emerging New Orleans tech sector to the world. "We want to show the rest of the country that New Orleans is the place where you can take an idea and turn it into a company," he said.[91]

James Carville speaks at the 2010 Bipartisan Policy Conference at Tulane University. *Photo courtesy of Creative Commons.*

Peter Mayer and the host committee came on board as co-sponsors, and Landrieu press secretary Ryan Berni was among the competition's judges. While Laurendine kept the presentations moving, Carville served as the focal point. Two years into his residency as the city's most famous post-Katrina transplant, he appeared comfortable as a spokesperson for New Orleans and the coming Super Bowl. The hackathon came just two weeks after the *Gambit Weekly* had selected Carville and his wife as the New Orleanians of the Year for 2012. The paper applauded Matalin's advocacy for public education and the local Catholic Charities organization (she converted after the move), and Matalin praised the faith and values of the community. "It's like living in a good society as envisioned by Socrates," she said.[92] The couple's advocacy for the city was widely respected.

"Their proactive messaging about New Orleans' uniqueness and authenticity is heard across the nation each and every day," said NOTMC's Mark Romig. "Their leadership work as co-chairs of the Host Committee for the Super Bowl has raised the bar for such events in the future."[93] As he often did, Carville provided positive sound bites about his adopted hometown: "New Orleans has more culture than most countries. People in other cities are obsessed with their quality of life—their sunshine, their libraries, their universities, their income levels. We're obsessed with our *way* of life."[94]

But how to convey that way of life to tourists? That was the challenge for the hackathon teams, which had forty-eight hours to design an app that Super Bowl visitors could use during the week of the game. First up was Team Crawfinder, five young men led by an Asian American who navigated the app, which was projected onto a screen behind him. When you Googled "free crawfish boil," the team leader told us, the first results listed were for parties in Dallas and Washington, D.C. The team thought this was ridiculous: what city throws more crawfish boils than New Orleans? Shouldn't there be an app to help Super Bowl visitors find the nearest free "mudbug" party? The app provided those hosts with the option of attaching a song to their post, so that, say, Jimi Hendrix fans could find a "Foxy Lady"–themed boil.

Matalin wondered what would happen if the boil got too full or sold out—would the app notify users? Throughout the afternoon, she focused on the technical nuts and bolts while her husband mused and plotted. Carville reclined in his chair, one fist pressed to his mouth. "It's interesting that Dallas has more crawfish boils," he observed. Someone in the audience called out, "They just publicize it. We have more!" "Good point," Carville admitted. He countered with questions: What was the publicity plan? Was the team considering partnerships with catering companies? It was fascinating to watch him work, the deft political strategist cum civic booster, coiled in a pinstriped shirt as ideas flew his way. A veteran of campaign war rooms from Washington to Kabul, Carville listened to the pitches and responded with angles. New Orleans was his newest candidate, the Super Bowl was the campaign and the apps were slogan ideas.

As they prepared their presentation to the NFL in 2009, the host committee wanted Carville and Matalin to deliver the pitch. According to committee member and Greater New Orleans Sports Foundation (GNOSF) CEO Jay Cicero, politics were frowned on in the Super Bowl selection process, so the couple's inclusion was delayed. Cicero joined Landrieu, Tom Benson and league officials at a September 2009 news conference to announce Carville and Matalin's selection as committee co-chairs. "They may be in a better role now than they would have in the pitch," Cicero told NOLA.com. "There is a really unique perspective that they bring to the table."[95] According to Benson's granddaughter, Saints VP Rita Benson LeBlanc, the couple gave the committee star power. "They understand the opportunity that we have here, and they've been proving what New Orleans means to them and what they could do to get the attention on all of our successes," she said.[96] According to Cicero, Carville and Matalin's new roles included "fundraising, managing staff, representing the organization at news conferences and Super Bowl meetings, and creating ways to present the city in a favorable light."[97]

"It's very exciting," Matalin said. "I love bragging about this city. I love sharing this city. I like watching people get enthusiastic about this city. I love the recovery."[98] In a city historically suspicious of (and vulnerable to) outside interlopers, the choice reflected the couple's popularity as messengers of the recovery. Carville's Louisiana roots and fiery persona coupled with Matalin's Republican credentials and ease among Uptown ladies to create an eloquent ambassadorial team for the new New Orleans. Like many of the recent transplants, their enthusiasm and ambitions shaped the image of the city as a hotbed of opportunity.

After Katrina, an influx of young, educated newcomers suggested a reversal of the city's decades-long "brain drain," the outflow of native talent to Atlanta, California or the Northeast in search of better career prospects. The catastrophe created jobs. The firing of all Orleans Parish public school teachers, the post-disaster need for urban planners and social workers and the numerous new nonprofits all factored into unprecedented demand for people willing to risk the hazards of the recovery. In 2008, the *Times Picayune* wondered, "Will newcomers stay?"[99]

"For young professionals and graduates across the country," wrote reporter Michelle Krupa, "New Orleans remains a magnet, blending a timeless allure with newfound dynamism." Interviews with transplants confirmed the wide-open nature of the employment landscape. "Instead of just working behind the scenes, I'm in the decision-making circles," said Krista Lois Colson, a thirty-year-old urban planner from Seattle who took a job with the Nagin administration. "I didn't expect to do that. It's good. You feel like you're actually part of it, and you can see the fruits of your labor." LSU surveyed members of the Young Urban Rebuilding Professionals (YURP) networking group and found that 95 percent of 263 surveyed members had college degrees, with 30 percent holding advanced degrees. Nearly one-quarter came from the Northeast. Though 80 percent were optimistic about the city, Krupa spoke to several transplants who were unsure how long they'd remain. "It feels very Wild Westy, still, because you always think it's going to get better, but it doesn't," said one twenty-seven-year-old. Another complained that the "most frustrating part about living here has been the ongoing corruption and the damage I think it's doing to our city's already fragile image."[100]

ONE HUNDRED DAYS IN AMERICA'S COOLEST HOT SPOT

The YURP organization eventually folded, but enthusiasm for the city as a professional destination continued to grow. The first wave of recovery-related transplants gave way to more traditional professionals, or at least aspiring professionals. By 2011, Forbes had ranked the New Orleans region at the top of its "Brain Magnets" list. There were new jobs in education and technology, with an emphasis on entrepreneurship and public service. But what separated New Orleans from other cities, according to Forbes and other media outlets, was the intangible "way of life" available to college-educated newcomers. With a booming music scene, unique neighborhoods and a reputation for funky exuberance, the city seemed to offer everything a young person might want in a midsized metropolis. Gentrification in the downtown Marigny and Bywater neighborhoods brought new restaurants and retail options. Business incubators like Idea Village and GNO Inc. touted the fertile environment for entrepreneurs, including state tax credits for digital media and a community of energetic start-ups. The rise of a tech sector seemed an indicator that, for the first time in decades, New Orleans was not only a fun place to spend a few days but also a place to start a career, even a family. The promise of economic vibrancy dovetailed with the tourism industry's messaging: everyone was welcome to fall in love with New Orleans. In the new New Orleans, the reasons for visiting translated into the reasons for staying—there might be a future in it.

"You can feel it," Carville told the *Times Picayune* in March 2008. "Everywhere you go, I sense people are really fired up about what's happening."[101] The duo's plans to relocate began soon after the storm, and by late 2007, Carville and Matalin were house hunting. Unlike the younger transplants in search of new careers and adventures, the couple had school-age daughters and long résumés. Yet they chose New Orleans, a sign to many that the city was viable and family friendly. Carville took a teaching position at Tulane and relocated his bipartisan think tank to the university but assured locals that New Orleans politics weren't his interest. "We're not coming down for politics," Carville said. "This is an exciting thing for our family." Whatever his intentions, the city soon drew him out.

A less energetic guest lecturer might have carved out a cozy niche in academia, content to accept the gravitas without breaking a sweat. Not Carville. He used his position at Tulane to insert himself into the New Orleans political arena with a survey published in late 2009. According to 1,008 potential voters polled by Carville's students, New Orleans was less divided on key issues than one might expect. Across color lines, New Orleanians were intent on "putting the conflicts of the past behind them" to deal with the urgent issues: crime, local schools, local corruption and long-term economic growth. In what many respondents called "the most important election in [their] lifetime," the majorities of blacks and whites were in search of a candidate with political experience who would reenergize the recovery.

"The much-talked-about racial divide in New Orleans is nowhere near as much as most people perceive it," said Carville. "If this election becomes about race, it will be because the politicians took it there, not because the people wanted it there."[102] His analysis seemed tailor-made for a candidate who hadn't yet declared, and some observers credited the poll with pulling Landrieu back into a contest he'd initially resisted. There were even whispers that Carville helped with Landrieu's strategy once the latter became a candidate. Regardless of intrigue, the numbers seemed to validate the argument that, despite the "shadow government" claims, New Orleans was ready to move on. A new city needed a new type of politics.

If local politics proved too juicy to resist, the *Deepwater Horizon* oil spill demanded a national spokesman for New Orleans. As the disaster dragged on, the federal government again became a target of the city's ire. While Jindal worked to position himself as Obama's equal and Landrieu adjusted to the shock of such an immediate blow to his new administration, Carville emerged as the voice of the people. His first cable news appearances with Matalin recalled Ray Nagin's demand during Katrina that the government "get off your asses and let's do something." The difference came in Carville's targets: an international corporation, part of an industry crucial to the state's economy, and a Democratic president. Carville took aim at both on behalf of New Orleans.

"I think [Obama's advisors] actually believe that BP has some kind of a good motivation here," he told CNN's Anderson Cooper. "They're naïve! BP is trying to save money, save everything they can…Somebody has got to shake [the administration] and say, 'These people don't wish you well! They're going to take you down!'"[103]

Carville's outrage as a New Orleanian was a stunning rebuke by a party loyalist. "No one doubts James's motivations here—he is a resident of a great city that is at terrible risk right now," said one White House official. "We just wish he would let us help him get his facts right."[104] Two weeks later, Carville appeared on Wolf Blitzer with a more humorous New Orleans story: "I called Ryan Berni and Mike Sherman, two of my close friends that work with me, that work in the mayor's office, and said, 'Meet me at Eleven 79,'" an Italian restaurant frequented mostly by locals.[105] Berni had worked for

ONE HUNDRED DAYS IN AMERICA'S COOLEST HOT SPOT

Carville's firm for five years before becoming Landrieu's press secretary, and Sherman was the city's director of intergovernmental affairs; Carville's ties to the new administration were deep. Upon entering the restaurant, Carville was directed to a table where the U.S. Coast Guard's Thad Allen sat with BP's CEO, Tony Hayward, then considered public enemy number one on the Gulf Coast. After amiable introductions, Hayward asked Carville to meet him for dinner in a year, when, the CEO predicted, BP would be vindicated as a responsible partner. "I'm skeptical," replied Carville, but he agreed to the date. "I'd love to be wrong."[106] Hayward stepped down two months later. Carville, though, had cemented his role as the region's defender.

When he wasn't busy blasting corporate misconduct, Carville made himself—and his home—available for business interests. When Goldman Sachs launched an initiative to support ten thousand small businesses in the city, Carville and Matalin hosted a party for participants. When *Inc.* magazine declared New Orleans "the coolest start-up city in America" in 2011, it cited as proof the reception held for New Orleans Entrepreneur Week at Carville and Matalin's "posh Uptown antebellum mansion." Winners of a pitch contest received a limousine ride to the party. Organized by a small business incubator, Idea Village, the week brought speakers and aspiring entrepreneurs together to discuss the city's business climate, connect with investors and generate new ideas. Described as "a festival of aspiring business owners," the week was a model for the Super Bowl hackathon, with Carville and Matalin serving as judges for similar competitions. Inspired by the city's resilience and civic pride, the couple leant their celebrity to the reinvention of the New Orleans economy.

While the national media celebrated the city's business environment, it remained unclear what overall impact the transplants had on the city. In some neighborhoods, the housing market boomed, while federal grants tied to the recovery continued to propel large-scale construction projects. The broader picture was positive: the unemployment rate in metro New Orleans for November 2012 stood at 4.7 percent, significantly lower than the nationwide rate of 8 percent. Other measurements suggested that long-term economic issues remained. According to census data analyzed by the Greater New Orleans Data Center, the poverty rate for Orleans Parish in 2012 exceeded that of 1999, 29 percent to 28 percent, with children in poverty remaining flat at 41 percent. The city had more adults with bachelor's degrees, at 34 percent in 2012 compared to 26 percent in 2000, but the median household income had dropped from $37,000 to $34,000 over the same period. Median rents grew from $688 in 2004 to $861 in 2012, in part reflecting higher taxes and insurance rates for landlords. New residents continued to arrive at a higher rate than before the storm, but the city was more expensive, in part due to those arrivals. The entrepreneurs feted by GNO Inc. and the Idea Village found the "way of life" vibrant, close-knit and conducive to business. But these anecdotal successes clouded the picture of a city still struggling through its short- and long-term economic challenges. Festivals were great, but could the tech sector generate the kind of tax revenue Landrieu needed for the consent decrees? For now, the start-ups and entrepreneurs were useful, if uncertain, indicators that New Orleans was on the rise.

In the Peter Mayer conference room, new ideas emerged from the minds of tired competitors. The "Heartbucket" app offered visitors the chance to rate their service experiences, which were "being curated by our service industry workers—the bartenders, bellmen and waiters," said the team's spokesman. By "capturing these moments," visitors were "hopefully helping out the person who helped you out." The difference between the Heartbucket app and sites like Yelp and TripAdvisor was that reviews were limited to two hundred words, and "we only have positive interactions." Next up was "Digital Tip Jar," which let visitors tip performers using their credit cards. "Live music is the heart and soul of our culture," said the team leader, himself a musician. Bands could post a QR code next to the stage, which app users would scan to send tips if they enjoyed the music. The transaction captured names and e-mail addresses for future marketing efforts.

Team Eat Now NOLA offered a frightening scenario: hordes of hungry and possibly intoxicated football fans roaming aimlessly in search of food. The solution: an app that provided wait times at local restaurants. Could those fans search for the closest restaurants, too? Matalin asked. That was the next step, the guys assured her. A late-arriving team member was introduced, a designer from Germany by way of Lafayette. "I hope you know how rich we are in German history in New Orleans," Carville told him. In a similar vein was Team Dome Waits, which consisted of two men, one considerably older than the other. Their app showed a map of the Superdome. By clicking on a bathroom icon, users saw the length of the line to use the facilities. If a user was hungry for chicken nuggets, the app identified locations and wait times in the Dome. Matalin wondered who would provide those times. Someone in the audience suggested "leveraging the cameras" inside the stadium.

As useful as these apps sounded, they relied in large part on the old economy of New Orleans. The hostesses, bellmen and guitar players still performed the basic activities, physically demanding and with inconsistent pay. The apps made things easier for the Super Bowl visitor, but how would these tools impact the economy? Service workers might curate moments, but they faced higher rents and irregular income. The tech entrepreneurs depended on the New Orleanians willing to boil crawfish, clean toilets and, maybe, report on wait lines for the men's room. As products dreamed up for tourism, the apps reflected the trickle-down nature of that industry. An easier city was more appealing, which meant more tourists, which meant more restaurant customers and more tips to pay more in rent. The promise of a new New Orleans traveled through more hands, but the rewards for New Orleanians remained unsure.

When I arrived that day, all but one of the teams were holed up in boardrooms, the hackers peering into laptops surrounded by empty drink containers. The next team to present sat on the floor of the lobby with paper and markers. Now they took the stage with only a poster board to convey their idea. It was, their leader made clear, a very big idea. "Whenever New Orleans tweets," he began, "individuals are connected." The proposed app would track, map and categorize all social media activity in New Orleans during the week of the Super Bowl. As the central tool for the host committee's "social media command center," the app would allow "journalists to detect what's hot right there, and potentially change course, because something unexpected occurred. Thank you." He pointed to a box in the center of the poster board. "Here we have a personal laptop interface for the press. And here in the middle we have the most important part of this." He pointed to a circle inside the laptop. "If you see something interesting on the dashboard, you press a button. That button gives you a bookmark on your timeline. We're storing every piece of data that comes through the system." The young man spoke in herky-jerky sentences, with a slightly grave tone. During the presentation, he said "shit" twice and apologized both times. The team hadn't completed the app in forty-eight hours, he explained, because of its ambitious scope. "This is the buffet, and we'd like to help New Orleans find the best place for their meal."

The audience applauded, and Travis stepped forward to reiterate the app's potential. "This is something that can scale for the World Cup, the Olympics, any big event that is in the city. This can be an entire company, and we've gotta give them credit for working so hard on such a big project." Carville asked if the app would be ready in three weeks for the start of media coverage.

"Absolutely," said the team leader. "It will happen."

"Somebody let Mary and I know," Carville said. "This thing gets up and running, we'll drive people to it. Hey, we'll come by and check out the command center, you know. OK? But be sure it's up and running and working." A few people giggled.

Matalin asked for an explanation of the app in a few words. Another team member said, "It's kind of like a Wikipedia for events as they happen." Someone in the audience noted that Wikipedia was, after all, a multimillion-dollar company.

"If it happened during that weekend in New Orleans," said the team leader, "there's almost no way in hell that system doesn't know about." It seemed like a big promise for a team armed with only a poster board.

The last team unveiled "NOLA Parks," another Google Maps–based app. The presenter was a tall guy holding a potent prop: an infant in pink pajamas who appeared surprisingly unfazed by the audience. There were approximately two hundred parks in the city, the young father explained. "Say you're tired of drinking and the Super Bowl and you say, 'I want to go for a run or play tennis.'" With NOLA Parks, the visitor could find the nearest park, but so could the local kid in search of a basketball court. Right now, both potential park goers would need to download an excel sheet from the New Orleans Recreational Department's website. The app provided a service to the entire city.

Carville had a shrewd sales hook. "Try this experiment," he said. "Ask someone how many parks are in this city. Just try that." Almost no one would know the answer, he said, providing a useful introduction when pitching the app to investors. For pitch after pitch, Carville found the old-fashioned messaging for the new media solutions. He didn't address a central question: would a neighborhood kid really need an app to find his local park?

With the presentations finished, Travis invited us to the after-party at the Little Gem Saloon on Poydras, where the winning apps would be revealed. "Hopefully," he said, "two years from now, people will look at this as a turning point." He thanked Peter Mayer, the Super Bowl host committee and the teams.

A few hours later, I stood on the Little Gem balcony with a member of Partners-N-Crime, a popular local hip-hop group. PNC was tonight's musical act; Travis was an old friend of the group. We sipped our drinks, marveled at the changes in the Central Business District and talked football. Inside, the upstairs lounge featured a small stage, red walls and a long bar where the bartenders made brisk work of the techie crowd, who preyed on free cans of the NOLA Brewery's Hopitoulas IPA microbrew. Soon Travis took the stage for the announcement of the three runners-up and the grand prize winner. First, he listed the impressive prizes awaiting the awardees, including trips to the Bonnaroo music festival, tickets to parties during Super Bowl week, one hundred pounds of crawfish and meetings with "angel" investors. For their community spirit, NOLA Parks received a special $1,000 grant from local developers Turbo Squid. Digital Tip Jar took third place, which meant a case of margaritas and a sit-down with famous New Orleans rapper Juvenile. Second place and the Bonnaroo tickets went to Gigs Guru. The grand prize was awarded to Eat Now NOLA, who would fly off to meetings with investors interested in the restaurant-based app.

After everyone posed for photos, PNC took the stage for a set of brass band–inflected songs, the background tracks cued up by Travis from his MacBook Pro. The crowd sucked down microbrews as a sudden rainstorm cleared all but the smokers from the balcony. Carville disappeared after the awards announcement, but Matalin remained to clap along to the music.

Perhaps tech made sense for New Orleans. It was a place with a long tradition of gambling; risk was ever present. Throughout its history, New Orleans has served as a base for plots hatched by tycoons and desperate transients. Booms and busts ran in cycles, but the intoxicating lure of get-rich-quick schemes never faded in a city where wealth was easy to spot. With Carville and Matalin as their guides, the hackers were part of a new bonanza where the spoils were some combination of hometown fame and national prominence. If the Super Bowl brought bright lights and business opportunities, the entrepreneur took advantage of it to promote his talents. Like the service worker, he scored when the big players were in town. He celebrated the city so the outsiders grew interested enough to pay for easier access to its mysteries.

The next day, Forbes.com, a frequent source of business news about New Orleans, praised Laurendine for creating "possibly the coolest Hackathon." Mary Matalin agreed: "Travis is really pioneering something here, and is on his way to turning New Orleans into tech central south. In 35 years of working with presidential campaigns, I have never seen anything like this." The hackathon, she said, reflected the city's lifestyle and creativity. "So organic. So entrepreneurial. So New Orleans."[107]

CHAPTER 8
JANUARY 16, 2013
(EIGHTEEN DAYS TO GO)

MUSIC BUSINESS

Three days after the hackathon, Mary Matalin continued to marvel at the ideas generated by the young entrepreneurs. "All of this extends beyond the Super Bowl," she said, "and we're going to be the tech center of the South." Her husband sat next to her, along with Mayor Landrieu and Mark Romig, who served as the interviewer for the host committee's media luncheon at the House of Blues in the French Quarter. The luncheon served as the committee's final press conference before the game, a last message to the local audience. "It's our time to shine," Landrieu told reporters. "It's our time to tell the story."[108]

Several speakers unveiled plans for the week. NFL vice-president of events Frank Supovitz described the opening night celebration on January 31, including fireworks and the arrival by barge of the Super Bowl XLVII roman numerals, large chrome figures that would sit on the river in front of Woldenberg Park. The park would become Verizon Super Bowl Boulevard, a free four-day music festival produced by New Orleans Jazz and Heritage Festival co-founder and director Quint Davis. Featuring more than thirty local acts, the production was, Davis said, "the Super Bowl done New Orleans style."[109]

The luncheon closed with a performance by one of the acts scheduled to play on Super Bowl Boulevard, the ToBeContinued (TBC) Brass Band. As the speakers left the stage, Landrieu greeted the musicians. Afterward, band members recalled the interaction. "When he was coming off the stage," said trombonist Devin Vance, "he was like, 'Hey you guys.' He knew who we

Darryl Parlow of ToBeContinued Brass Band. *Photo by Zack Smith Photography.*

were, he spoke to us and we was like, 'Hey, what's up with Bourbon Street?' He just went through the door."

For TBC, the brush-off was more of the same. They'd had a problematic relationship with the city for years, and though they'd been paid to perform, not talk, as part of the official function, they couldn't pass up the chance to address it with the mayor. "On different occasions, he mentioned our name in certain ways," said Vance. "That's why we wanted to talk to him. We see you face to face, just not over the phone, every band member right here. 'Oh, wait, what's up—I'm gone.'"

Vance sounded irritated, while other band members laughed or shook their heads. "I don't like how they could fix everything for the Super Bowl but they can't fix the streets in our neighborhood," said Vance. "They can spend so much money to make the city look pretty for something big like that, but you drive down my streets, [and] they got potholes every block. You can spend that much money to fix the French Quarter for somebody who's going to be here for a couple days for the Super Bowl?"[110]

TBC's experience of the Super Bowl reflected in part their own distinctive history as artists, but it also reflected the realities of musicians in the changing city. They were part of the official entertainment—they represented the "New Orleans style" marketed to visitors, yet their dialogue with people in power was riddled with frustration and perceived offenses. As African American men in their twenties, they belonged to a demographic accustomed to indifference, if not hostility, from authority figures. As New Orleans musicians, they were essential to the city—its economy, its global image, its culture. The Super Bowl generated numerous gigs for local bands, from private parties to Bourbon Street clubs to the sponsored festivities on the river. TBC traversed their particular engagements with the confidence of a battle-hardened platoon, curious but unfazed. We talked in several locations over the ensuing weeks, but the night after the host committee press conference, I met them on their turf.

Celebration Hall sat on St. Bernard Avenue in the Seventh Ward, just across Claiborne Avenue from a popular strip of nightclubs. Its brick first floor and corner door suggested a business, but nothing else about the exterior spoke to the energy the building contained on Wednesday nights, when TBC played their weekly gig. Inside the club, a wrought-iron railing marked off the white-tiled dance floor, where a woman in a brown jumpsuit warmed up to a 2Chainz song played by DJ Action Jackson. TBC was a relatively young band, but the customers tonight skewed a little older, with men still wearing their utility company uniforms or shirts stitched with the names of social clubs: "Undefeated Gents," "Men of Unity." I ordered a Heineken from a pretty bartender whose lip gloss pearled under the dance floor lights. TBC's Edward "Juicy" Jackson arrived, and we stepped outside through a rear door.

One of three trombonists in the band, Jackson served as its leader onstage and, in my conversations with TBC, its main spokesman. Juicy combined the wisdom of an octogenarian with an adolescent's sensitivity and pride, delivering boasts that sounded like pleas for reason, facts that cloaked threats to anyone who doubted his band. Though measured with outsiders, he cracked up the other musicians regularly. He was a large man who might've carried a tuba by default but instead played his horn like a nimble knife fighter.

Trumpeter Darryl Parlow joined us on a slab of poured concrete. The night was cold, and the native New Orleanians laughed that I, the guy from up north, was shivering. I asked how the media luncheon paid. "For the time of the Super Bowl, we don't push the gig scale up ourselves," Jackson said. "They come in with a price, but we already know what ballpark we're gonna go for. Between that and what's going on, we looking to make double, triple—at least double what's our normal price we play for."

"It's the Super Bowl," Parlow emphasized.

The gigs paid great during the week of the game, but the extra income didn't distract from TBC's issue with Landrieu. For almost ten years, the band claimed the corner of Bourbon and Canal Streets as its personal performance space. The members were in high school when they began to play on Bourbon in 2003, a time when ragtag brass bands were still common along the street. "Four, five [o'clock] after school, we did that for a little while," Jackson recalled. The band played on the 400 and, later, 300 blocks until "after we got into it heavy with the police, when they found out who we was, they pushed us to the 100 block, just like, we could play there. They moved us." Under that loose arrangement with the NOPD, TBC set up in the unofficial gateway to the French Quarter, a prime spot for being seen—and tipped—by tourists. With their backs against a Foot Locker store and their instruments pointed into the odd acoustics offered by the side of a hotel, they became a band. The inflow of Bourbon Street visitors brought them nightly audiences. "You never know who'll come out on Bourbon Street," said Parlow. Was the money good? I asked. "It's not really the money," Jackson said. "It's the interaction. That's where we started, that's where we feel most comfortable. That's where we feel like the band sounds the best."

Problems with traffic and safety increased, due in part to TBC's magnetism. As crowds crew, the band attempted to self-police the area (Jackson: "We had martial law out there"), but the challenges were bigger than live music. Despite the importance of Bourbon to the city's economy, crime issues persisted in the Quarter. On Halloween night 2011, sixteen people were shot and two killed in separate incidents just blocks from the band's post. Landrieu blamed a "culture of violence" among young black men armed with unregistered weapons. "This continues to be a battle for the future of our city," the mayor said. NOCVB president Stephen Perry lamented the impact on the city's image: "Tourists are critical, not only to the economic health of the city, but our employees and residents. The time has come for us to have zero tolerance."[111] Not long after, the police made clear that TBC could no longer play in front of the Foot Locker. "Around [January 2012], they started cracking down, and they got us up out of there," said Jackson. "They really enforced that we had to go. We played out on Bourbon one time in 2012."

How the other incidents influenced the treatment of TBC was unclear, but so, too, was the administration's attitude toward live music. When I spoke to Scott Hutcheson, head of the city's Office of Cultural Economy, he called the situation "a challenge of balance." "There is certainly no law that prevents somebody from playing on that 100 block of Bourbon," he said. "There have been different challenges with finding the balance there—sound, giving passage on the sidewalk and the street—and we've actually done some things that make it a little more friendly. Parking is no longer available on that street in the evening, and that really helped a lot." When asked about the mayor's interaction with the band at the media luncheon, Hutcheson had no comment.

"ToBeContinued has been a great ambassador for the city," he concluded.[112]

The story of TBC's time on Bourbon was symptomatic of the historical relationship between music and government in New Orleans. The band established itself on Bourbon through an informal negotiation with the police; flourished as the kind of authentic, interactive tourist attraction popular among visitors; and then lost its spot due to a change in policy that remained unexplained, if it was changed at all. It was often said that enforcement, not the law, was the issue in New Orleans. Whether the result of the city's libertine culture or the arbitrary habits of local law enforcement, authorities had failed to make rules that were both equitable and equally applied. In the new era of good government and a focused tourism industry, music became a conflict zone. Celebrated by marketers and Super Bowl organizers as New Orleans icons, Jackson and other musicians struggled to understand their place in a city that owed its popularity in large part to their work. The so-called war on live music was underway.

Tulane University musicologist Matt Sakakeeny observed that "noise complaints in New Orleans are as old as the city itself," citing a history of clashes between moralizing, often racist opponents of free expression and the local talents who invented jazz on the city's streets. "[M]usic shaped understandings of geographical, racial and conceptual boundaries at the precise moment when those lines were being redrawn," Sakakeeny wrote in a brief history of music "wars" since the late nineteenth century.[113] The more recent furor centered not on questions of the artistic value of New Orleans music but on the city's boundaries, which again were in the midst of a redraft as the new New Orleans emerged. The conflict became public in July 2012, when, in preparation for the Essence Music Festival, the city checked the permits and occupational licenses of one hundred businesses in the French Quarter, Marigny and Central Business District. Around forty businesses were cited; among them were two popular music venues, the Circle Bar and Siberia. Similar actions had temporarily halted live performances in several other bars. Music fans rushed to the clubs' defense. In the birthplace of jazz, enforced silence was seen as the real crime. "Why does Mayor Landrieu hate live music?" asked one blogger.[114] It was an overheated question but indicative of the ire directed at a politician who regularly championed the cultural economy and never missed an opportunity to join a parade, dance or even play rudimentary trumpet at the occasional public function. Press secretary Ryan Berni defended the permit checks. "Live music is important to us, and it's an important economic driver for this city," he said. "It just needs to match the zoning of the neighborhood."[115] Local music writer Alex Rawls saw valid points on both sides. The city's zoning ordinance was "an out-of-date document that doesn't suit where and how people live in New Orleans," Rawls wrote on his MySpiltMilk.com site. "It needs to be updated to better reflect the city's core values, one of those being creativity. Creativity is an essential part of who we are, and it's what tourists come here to connect to, to see if a little will rub off on them."[116]

Rawls's last point was important. The New Orleans way of life included a collective shrug at limitations on music. Play where you want to play: in the street, atop tables, on boats—wherever there was space and audience. That way of life was attractive to visitors who spent money in restaurants and clubs, creating one of the only growth industries in town. If you took the long view, there would be no Superdome, much less the 2013 Super Bowl, without the persistent musical genius that manifested over multiple generations in New Orleans. Along with Mardi Gras, live music kept New Orleans on the map as a tourist destination for at least a century and counting. But tourism couldn't grow in rickety venues that didn't abide by the law. Real industry required organization, accountability and guidelines, all of which sounded anathema to the very way of life that attracted visitors. Corporate sponsors needed assurances that New Orleans was a safe, regulated environment in which they could host meetings and parties. The administration was in a tough spot, but it didn't "hate live music" any more than it hated hotels and restaurants. The problem lay in the city's antiquated, rarely enforced ordinances that pertained to live music. Like TBC, the venues were used to relative freedom and the occasional, fleeting attention of the authorities.

Two months after the permit sweep, both Siberia and the Circle Bar resumed booking live acts. City officials worked with the owners to file the proper paperwork, and Landrieu officials accelerated plans for a streamlined permitting process. Hutcheson described the episode as another case of the administration's efforts at balance. "What you saw happen was not against musicians or the music," he said. "It was a business who was not in compliance with the licenses they had. The impact happened to be on musicians. This isn't about valuing or not valuing music. It's about a business owner satisfying his obligations as a business owner."[117]

Culture-as-business was a touchstone for Landrieu since his time in Baton Rouge. As mayor, he issued annual "Cultural Economy Snapshots," invariably positive reports on the impact of the "cultural sector" on the city's economy. According to the report for 2012, the sector provided 32,400 jobs, which was 13.8 percent of the total workforce and an increase over 2011.[118] Those workers earned over $1.1 billion in salaries at 1,722 "cultural businesses," which included everything from restaurants, festivals and film companies to museums, magazines and nightclubs. The data showed that music gigs were on the rise; an increasing number of festivals generated new opportunities for musicians. The film industry boomed, but culinary businesses outpaced all other segments combined, with $2.3 billion in gross sales and $49 million in sales taxes. Images of oyster shuckers and brass bands sat next to pie charts and line graphs. A Venn diagram broke jobs up into "cultural jobs," "cultural jobs that impact tourism" and "tourism jobs," with the middle group the largest, at 22,199 jobs. The report did not break out musicians into their own category of analysis but kept them within "entertainment," along with the film industry. Average salaries for "entertainment" were $34,798, close to the mean household income for the city, $34,361. The broad grouping and the use of averages left a large part of the cultural economy picture unclear. Was a major player like Quint Davis grouped with a brass band trombonist in the calculation of average salaries? What were musicians earning? Were they making enough to support families in a city with a rising cost of living? The annual snapshots never ventured to answer such questions. Instead, the 2012 report closed with a letter from the mayor, who believed the numbers "illustrate[d] that culture is inseparable from our way of life in New Orleans. We enjoy a diversity of cultural riches that most cities can only dream about."

Another report suggested some disconnect between those cultural riches and the bank statements of the musicians who made them possible. Sweet Home New Orleans, a nonprofit that helped "New Orleans musicians make a living, while living in New Orleans," issued its own annual reports on the economic status of the estimated four thousand musicians in the city.[119] "2012 was, by most measures, a good year for the New Orleans cultural economy," wrote the report's authors, "and an inconsistent one, at best, for New Orleans musicians." Sweet Home agreed with the Cultural Snapshot's finding that the entertainment sector was growing "but that growth is not trickling down to the artists who create the culture." The surveyed musicians earned, on average, $17,800 in 2012, approximately the same level since 2008. Positive signs included new festivals, increased work in music education and the opportunities provided by HBO's *Tremé*, which continued to serve as "a boon to local musicians." The organization called on the city to create a Music Business Office under the Department of Cultural Economy to "prioritize the development of Music Business as an indigenous industry."

If the administration and musicians' advocates agreed that music was a business, that didn't make the business any easier for musicians. "I wouldn't say we the bottom of the barrel," said TBC's Maize, "but we not too far from there. We make enough money to pay our bills—water bill, light bill…we not homeowners; we own our cars and pay out. We make enough to pay that." The band had established an LLC but was unsuccessful when it filed a lost income claim after *Deepwater Horizon*. "They're trying to say that, being street musicians, you need receipts," Vance said. "At that point [April 2010], we went from making $100 a night to making $8 a night. That's how we were surviving."

Musicians continued to survive in a cash-based industry that resisted the economic impact reports, never mind the requirements of federal disaster relief. Bands, particularly those playing traditional New Orleans music, benefited from the greater emphasis on tourism through more convention gigs, more second-line parades for French Quarter weddings. The tourism industry employed the images and mystique of brass bands and Mardi Gras Indians in its advertisements, websites and pitches, usually without compensating the culture bearers. But brass bands were particularly problematic as mascots. Take the trumpet or bass drum away from many of those musicians, and you had a young, black male, usually from a disadvantaged neighborhood, who was just an instrument away from the prevalent dangers of the city. In fact, for many bands, the distance was nonexistent. In 2010, TBC saxophonist Brandon Franklin was shot and killed in a domestic dispute. An assistant band director at a local high school, Franklin was visible on the cover of TBC's forthcoming album, his face watching over them from the clouds. When the image-makers of the new New Orleans borrowed the figures of parading brass bands as proof of the city's vibrant way of life, they paid homage in a way to the culture. New Orleans was not just Bourbon Street, streetcars and Super Bowls—indigenous music mattered. Yet those young men were impossible to simplify with slogans, just as their art was difficult to quantify with business terms. No matter how many official gigs they scored, the members of TBC belonged to an endangered population.

Violence was not the only threat. The economic picture for African American men in the mostly African American city was almost as frightening as the murder rate. According to a report from Loyola University's Lindy Boggs National Center for Community Literacy, by 2011, "more than half of all African American men in New Orleans were either unemployed or had given up looking for work entirely." Thirty years of industrial restructuring had impacted jobs in construction, manufacturing, utilities and other industries that historically employed African American men in New Orleans. The declines coincided with the rise of the tourism industry. The "accommodation and food service" sector was now the largest employer of African American men. "But with wages averaging about $26K annually, and 9 out of 10 jobs paying too little to support the basic expenses of one person living alone, the tourism industry is not attractive for men who want to provide for a family."[120] The city needed more workers with technical skills, including African American men who could fill jobs in the petrochemical and construction industries. Trombone players and oyster shuckers were important and certainly great for promoting New Orleans in magazines and Cultural Economy snapshots; they weren't models for saving a struggling demographic. The brothers and cousins of brass band members needed help.

At Celebration Hall, I'd paid five dollars at the door, four dollars for my first Heineken and another four dollars for my second. TBC assembled under a halo of white Christmas lights, their backdrop a disheveled curtain. People filled both sides of the dance floor. I leaned against the bar as the music began. Soon the harmonies slashed the air, dramatic minor keys coaxed by the slither and pop of the snare and the demanding bass drum. Throughout the room, the bodies reacted because, of course, this was dance music, but played with a life-and-death seriousness captured in Juicy's face and in the unique postures of each member. The dynamics of the group sounded initially like an aural brawl until the solos, which brought the featured instruments into relief before the group swallowed them up again. The crowd, too, moved in a collective fever, out of which the dancers' individualized styles broke free. Men jumped high to cheers from other men or offered their backs to women, who bounced off their shoulder blades. TBC seemed to carry the entire room on its backs in a rush toward a breaking point and then pivoted suddenly into Bell Biv Devoe's "Poison." The line "It's driving me out of my mind" never felt truer. The crowd sang along.

When Maize talked about the "bottom of the barrel," he described not just an economic condition but also a vantage point. The working brass band witnessed everything from corporate extravagance to street corner shootouts. For TBC, the changes brought on by the Super Bowl were transparent. For the band, Maize said, there was "more good than bad from the Super Bowl." He put himself in the shoes of a non-musician. "If I'm a youngster, I don't have an instrument, I'm out the projects, my momma on crack or whatever—money rule the world." The selective infrastructure improvements sent a message about power. "You see the streetcar passing on the streets…everything's done in a certain amount of time. What a coincidence! It makes you suspicious."

Still, TBC would take advantage of the Super Bowl to further its mission. The band planned to release a new album during the week of the game, its first recording since its popular mixtape, "Sorry 4 the Wait," also the name of a recent Lil Wayne compilation. Jackson claimed the rapper as the band's role model. Wayne, he said, was a pioneer who borrowed from others to make his own name. It showed, he said, an ability to relate to others.

"I was born with certain things that I have to deal with, and I have to take those things and build off them," he said. "I have to make them trophies instead of bruises. I have to make them a gold medal instead of a criminal record. You have to learn how to accept the bad and build off it and tell people about it and relate to them and not be afraid to relate. Don't be scared to be yourself."

As New Orleans approached its turn in the spotlight, Juicy's words could apply citywide. There were deep problems, created over centuries, and out of which America's greatest musical form emerged. The problems remained, but now music was seen as a solution, a salvation for some and a profit engine for others. How the New Orleans way of life translated into entertainment as well as a safe, sustainable place to live—that was the question. What facets of that lifestyle would be sacrificed for a better business environment? Could the city evolve without altering its essential relationship to music?

TBC had an original song, written back in 2003, when they started playing together on Bourbon Street. Its chorus served a mission statement:

We them folks that bring that noise
Got amplifiers in our horns
We them people
To be continued.

CHAPTER 9
JANUARY 19, 2013 (FIFTEEN DAYS TO GO)

"BE NICE OR LEAVE"

We realize that the Super Bowl is a game played on the world's largest stage, and every single one of you is critical to bringing that show to life."

From where I sat, the man bore some resemblance to Lance Armstrong. He was certainly fit and, it became clear, quite an effective leader.

"You're going to remember this moment," he told the audience gathered in the lower section of the end zone seats at the Superdome. "This is your moment." With his encouragement, we turned to congratulate our neighbors. On my right was a middle-aged white woman, who said she worked for SMG, the company that managed the stadium. To my left sat a young black woman with thick-rimmed glasses, who told me she was just here for the experience. The rest of the crowd sounded happy to be here, applauding loudly as the man introduced each member of the Disney Institute Super Bowl Fans First Team.

"From the University of Illinois," he bellowed like a PA announcer, "wide receiver Amy…"

The Super Bowl Teammate Rally brought together volunteers and temporary employees hired for the game for an appreciation event that included hospitality training from the Disney team. Also on hand were Saints cheerleaders, current and former Saints players, several musical acts, Carville and Matalin and Tom and Gayle Benson, each taking a turn on a stage set up in the end zone. With black-and-gold jerseys and hats prevalent in the crowd, the rally felt like a decidedly local affair. The Disney leader styled his presentation accordingly, donning foam Saints #1 hands to quiet the crowd with Saints quarterback Drew Brees's signature arm flapping. Mentions of the home team were one way of appealing to local pride, an important factor in the success of Super Bowl week. Thousands of visitors were about to descend on New Orleans, and today's audience would be there to meet them on downtown street corners and at official events to answer questions and give directions. The morning included a series of gentle nudges: be hospitable and make the city look good. Despite New Orleans' reputation for warm receptions, there was cause for concern.

When it came to hospitality, the Disney leader said, Indianapolis was the standard for New Orleans and any other host site. Originally scoffed at for its cold weather, the midwestern city won over most critics with its revitalized downtown, the ease of transportation to and from the game and the warmth of the residents. The success of Indianapolis didn't just set the bar for its reception; it also opened up the possibility of hosting the game to any NFL city, or at least any city willing to spend tax dollars to fund a new football stadium. New Orleans and Miami were tied for the most Super Bowls hosted, but the competition was wide open now, and weather was not the only factor.

"Satisfaction is dangerous," the Disney leader told us. Quality hospitality should elicit a reaction: "Wow." Not "Wow!" as in blown away by a welcome slightly overdone, but an impressed "wow" from an informed, grateful visitor. At his request, we stood and put our hands in the sky. "Stretch it out a little farther," the Disney leader said. "This isn't about going the extra mile. This is about going the extra inch, just enough but not overboard. When you add up all those inches, it makes a mile." In a city known for its robust celebrations, it was unusual to hear a request for measured response.

A giant Mercedes Benz logo hung from the peak of the Superdome ceiling. No matter how many times I'd been inside the stadium in recent years, I always thought of the torn roof left by Katrina and the hellacious conditions that unfolded on that same floor where the boys played. In place of that terrifying wound was the emblem of the car that Tom Benson sold in his San Antonio dealerships. As part of his 2010 deal with the state, Benson received ownership of naming rights for the Dome, with the first $1 million of any sale going to him and the balance split with the state. In October 2011, Benson sold the naming rights for ten years to the German manufacturer for a reported $50 to $60 million, and the building became the Mercedes Benz Superdome. Both sides claimed the idea came from Benson's wife, Gayle, who asked her husband one day, "What about Mercedes?" The agreement also offset the subsidies that Baton Rouge owed annually to the Saints.[121]

Efforts to sell the name to Pan-American Life Insurance, Bacardi and local power company Entergy had failed a decade earlier. Now Mercedes-Benz USA CEO Ernst Lieb flew in to announce the deal. "This is tremendous for us," Lieb said. "We are basically looking at, 'Where are our customers, where are we today selling our cars,' and we have cars starting at $31,000. And down the road you will see that we are going to go a lot more forceful into that segment, even below $30,000, which means many of the 73,000 people who are going to come in here for the games actually can afford a car like this." That month, a new $1.6 million state-of-the-art lighting system illuminated the stadium's curved walls with a spectrum of animated colors. Once an unmarketable relic and then a national tragedy, the Dome was now a world-class facility with an international sponsor.[122]

When the Disney team finished, Mayor Landrieu took the stage to the anthem "Unbelievable." In dark blue jeans and the same black Super Bowl Volunteer windbreaker given to the rest of us, the mayor popped a dance step before settling into a director's chair next to a new emcee, a black man with high cheekbones and a glistening bald head. "What's up, New Orleans?" the mayor drawled. The crowd roared, and several people stood up to applaud. "I'm trying to teach all these people coming to town how to talk 'New Orleans.' Don't scare people when you say, 'Where y'at, baby?' The Disney people wouldn't teach us to talk like that."

The emcee tried to take control. "We ballin' in New Orleans?" he asked the mayor, who continued to address the crowd. "Woo, y'all look good. Y'all ready for Mardi Gras?" Apparently everybody was. Tell us, the host asked, about all the cool things happening in town. "First of all," said Landrieu, "I can't tell y'all how much I love y'all. I appreciate y'all so much." When the NFL raved about Indianapolis hospitality, he told them, "Listen here: I don't know what they got up there, but their people are not nicer than our people. Y'all don't need to worry about that." The league, the mayor recalled, had questioned the city's preparations. "They said about us, 'Y'all slow, y'all say you're going to do things and you don't do things and all that stuff you want to do is not going to be finished.' And I said, 'Not now. Not in this New Orleans, where we are on time, on task and under budget. Things are gonna get done!'" The crowd seemed genuinely appreciative of Landrieu's emphatic defense of the city against the skeptical NFL.

Still, the mayor felt the need to warn us to mind our manners. His son asked him if a no-fly zone was possible in case the hated Atlanta Falcons made the game. "We're going to be the host of the Super Bowl," Landrieu had replied. "So we gotta be nice or leave." Everyone laughed knowingly, but the mayor grew serious. "[Y]'all remember a couple years ago, we were fifteen feet under water, with the only thing we had on our backs and our garbage bags with our stuff in 'em? Yes, indeed, everybody was in the boat. And we were under water. We were last on the list for everything that counted. Guess what? We're on the top of the world today. Right? And we're on top of all the lists that matter. People [are] talking good about us. When's the last time people talked good about New Orleans? A long time ago."

The mayor knew that New Orleans people were the city's greatest asset. "So what we have to do, if we want to leave people smiling—we've gotta go out of our way to welcome everybody that comes. Now, look at me: I'm talking about everybody. Y'all know who I'm talking about?" Scattered boos were audible amid the chuckling. "You gotta be on your best behavior. Now, I know. I know what you wanna say. I know what you wanna do. But it's like if you invite somebody over to your house—you gotta be nice to everybody. Because listen to me, we want another Super Bowl, don't we?" Yes, we cried. "Do what you do better than anybody in the world and be the best host because you've got the greatest city, and if you do that, baby, we gonna be fine. Everything's gonna be beautiful, and this is going to be the best Super Bowl that ever was."

He departed to loud applause. Almost three months had passed since the press conference held during the taxicab protest. The audience today required a folksier tone, but the message was unchanged. The new New Orleans awaited the world, ready to tell its story of rejuvenation. At the helm was a proud, efficient administration representing a united population.

As a visible symbol of the turnaround, the Saints were an essential part of that narrative. Since 2007, sports announcers, politicians and regular citizens cited the relationship between team and fan base as a crucial catalyst in the recovery, each gridiron success another step forward for New Orleans. "Who Dats" became the face of the city, an eccentric, vibrant representation broadcast every week to NFL audiences. The problem was, in January 2013, the "Who Dats" were angry with the NFL. The city's relationship with the league had reached its nadir.

I had good seats for the ascent. During the 2009–10 season, I worked as a DJ at Handsome Willy's Patio Bar during Saints home games. Located five blocks from the Superdome and surrounded by parking lots, the bar was a nexus for fans. The area around the stadium was bereft of pre- and post-game drinking options, but Willy's opened early and didn't close until the last "Who Dat" staggered out in the wee hours of Monday. Proprietor Justin Micaroni became one of my closest friends in the city that year, as did the bartenders and

ONE HUNDRED DAYS IN AMERICA'S COOLEST HOT SPOT

Handsome Willy's Patio Bar erupts in the moments following the Saints' 2010 Super Bowl victory. *Photo by Rachel Leifer.*

several regulars. In April 2005, Micaroni bought the place with Brian Greiner, a childhood friend from Long Island, and writer Jarret Lofstead. They took over a watering hole just one hundred yards away from Charity Hospital, a built-in market. Then the levees broke, the state closed Charity and the young owners fought to drag the bar back to functionality. Saints home games gave Willy's a shot in the arm each fall, but nothing before or since could compare to that championship season. Those Sundays unfolded in a dramatic arc of morning meet-ups between a growing crowd of mainstays, a flurry of downed shots and energetic dancing before kick-off and then a lull as we watched the Saints win their first thirteen games, including six in a row at home. The victory celebrations were mad and grew more emotional as the unthinkable appeared on the horizon. It seemed like half of New Orleans poured in and out of the bar over those five months up until February 7. When the final second ticked off the clock in Super Bowl XLIV, I hit play on Queen's "We Are the Champions," and the entire bar broke into tears and screams.

Plied by quotes from ecstatic locals, the nation embraced the story of football saving the city. "And the city Katrina once left for dead was very much alive," noted the *Washington Post*.[123] When the Saints visited the White House, President Obama praised the players for their leadership in the region: "Not only did the team come back—it took its city's hands and helped its city back on its feet. This team took the hopes and the dreams of a shattered city and placed them squarely on its shoulders." The Saints as saviors oversimplified more than four years of frustration and resilience in south Louisiana, but the sentiment was hard to dispute: New Orleans felt different after that game. The game seemed to rebuke doubts about New Orleans and New Orleanians, providing symbolic proof that the residents refused to give up. For once, there was something larger than Mardi Gras and, at least momentarily, larger than Katrina, and no matter who you were, if you lived in the city, you could claim you were a part of something. I'll never forget that feeling.

Everyone, it seemed, was a Saints fan. "I keep thinking of the word 'magical' when you think about the relationship between the Saints and the Gulf Coast and the city of New Orleans," said NFL commissioner Roger Goodell after the game. "It was more than just a football game and more than just a football team. The hopes, dreams and struggles of that community were all reflected in that football team."[124] Goodell's sentiments echoed the words of observers around the nation: the Saints were America's team. Bitter reality struck six weeks later, when the *Deepwater Horizon* rig exploded in the Gulf of Mexico. The oil spill was a blunt reminder that, whatever happened in the Superdome, the city remained in a precarious region threatened by nature and industry. Still, the afterglow of the Saints' victory persisted into the next football season, even if the sudden disaster tempered the stories of gridiron-inspired rebirth.

And then things got complicated.

> *Kill the head, and the body will die.*
>
> *We've got to do everything in the world to make sure we kill Frank Gore's head. Go get that motherfucker on the sidelines.*
>
> *The NFL's a production business—don't ever forget about it. Where are we at right now?*
>
> *Remember me, remember me. I got the first one. (Rubs fingers together, indicating cash payment) Go lay that motherfucker out.*
>
> *Every single one of you, before you get off the pile, affect the head.*

ONE HUNDRED DAYS IN AMERICA'S COOLEST HOT SPOT

We need to find out in the first two series of the game, the little wide receiver, number 10, about his concussion. We need to decide if Crabtree wants to be a fake-ass prima donna, or he wants to be a tough guy.

Early, affect the head. Continue, touch and hit the head.[125]

These quotes come from a transcription of a video taken in the Saints locker room prior to the January 2012 playoff game against the San Francisco 49ers. Defensive coordinator Gregg Williams addressed his players in terms likely familiar to anyone experienced in the motivational tactics of football coaches, even in an era of increased concern over concussions. The problem came when Williams rubbed his fingers together. The gesture referenced a cash reward for players who knocked opponents out of the game, part of an illegal system of bounties allegedly embraced by players and coaches and endorsed by head coach Sean Payton. Two years after the country toasted the leadership and importance of the Saints, the juggernaut ran aground. In March 2012, the league suspended Payton and several of his staff for offering bounties to defensive players who injured or sidelined members of the opposing team. Payton was lost for a year. Williams was banished from coaching indefinitely, while GM Mickey Loomis, assistant head coach Joe Vitt and several Saints players received multiple-game suspensions. In a city still crazy about its football team, the punishment felt like a stomach punch. The tape of Williams came out a month after the NFL's initial announcement, its source a documentary filmmaker who followed former Saint Steve Gleason into the locker room. Ironically, it was Gleason who made the signature play of the team's rebirth, the 2006 blocked kick against the Falcons in the Saints first home game after Katrina. Now suffering from the MLS disease, Gleason was a civic hero whose perseverance was the focus of benefit concerts, fund drives and bumper stickers. His inadvertent involvement in the scandal only added to the ugliness. T-Shirts reading "Free Payton" and threatening NFL commissioner Roger Goodell popped up instantly in the French Quarter and along Magazine Street. Bars and restaurants posted Goodell's photo next to warnings that the man pictured would not be served. New Orleanians all too accustomed to defeat were indignant, but no one could hide from the facts. The team was warned in 2010 and again in 2011. Benson personally instructed the coaching staff to stop the bounties, and they ignored his orders. The NFL was already mired in a controversy over head injuries, and the league took the opportunity to punish one of its best stories. New Orleanians found themselves in the center of a furor debated on cable channels and in sports bars across the nation. The regulars at Handsome Willy's were exhausted and irate. For many New Orleanians, Goodell occupied the top villain post formerly held by FEMA during the post-Katrina recovery. Now the commissioner and his league prepared to enter the city for their annual corporate convention. Landrieu had good reason to remind everyone to "be nice or leave."

A few hours after the volunteer pep rally, the rescheduled Mardi Gras began in earnest in the French Quarter. Krewe du Vieux, a walking parade that began in the Marigny neighborhood before snaking through the Vieux Carré, was infamous for its bawdy floats and libertine membership. The floats combined political parody with sexually explicit imagery in the season's biggest send-up of the powerful, with costumed crowds packing the narrow streets to catch throws that referenced marijuana, corruption and other Carnival favorites. The parade was an annual roll call of the city's favorite targets, and this year's roster included heavy doses of scorn for the NFL.

The evening was cold when my wife and I arrived on Decatur Street near the Old U.S. Mint, just as the first marchers passed, led by one of twelve brass bands hired for the night, among them Juicy Jackson and TBC. After an

A float in the 2013 Krewe du Vieux parade. *Photo by Bart Everson.*

ONE HUNDRED DAYS IN AMERICA'S COOLEST HOT SPOT

Energizer Bunny with an engorged penis kicked off the lewdness, the first of multiple strikes at the *Times Picayune* appeared. "Make TP out of TP," read the back of a giant toilet bowl. A rolling shrine proclaiming, "All white and dead all over" preceded the float that appeared in several recaps the next day. "Super Hole XLVAG" consisted of a giant vagina, out of which poked Roger Goodell's papier-mâché head and arms, a Lombardi trophy in one hand. Subsequent floats included the commissioner in bondage, the commissioner atop an eight-foot-long phallus and, in a synergy of ire, the commissioner mounting a white cow emblazoned with the NFL logo, backed by a "Sometimes Picayune" front page. The paper's headline: "Top 10 Reasons Goodell Hates N.O.!" National sports websites ran images from the parade, and several writers caught up to the creators of "Super Hole XLVAG," Greg Guidry and Mike Alltmont. "If you ask just about anyone on the streets of New Orleans, 'Would you like to watch the demise of Roger Goodell by a giant man-eating vagina?' Their answers would be 'yes,'" Guidry told The Classical.[126]

Along with the *Times Picayune*, Goodell had taken the place of Ray Nagin as public enemy number one. In fact, the parade's sculpted jokes about Nagin were noticeably minimal for the first time in years. Even after he left office, the former mayor continued to serve as a Krewe du Vieux piñata, sometimes literally; by last year, I thought the jokes were tired. But the past refused to rest peacefully in New Orleans. The floats were already built when, the night before the parade, the former mayor burst back into the headlines. Just as the Super Bowl drew close, and with it the chance to showcase the new New Orleans, the contentious ghosts of the recovery emerged to complicate things.

On January 18, a grand jury indicted Nagin on twenty-one federal corruption counts. The charges included conspiracy, bribery and conspiracy to commit money laundering, with the mayor accused of taking payoffs totaling $235,000. Nagin's transgressions ranged from the acceptance of a trip to Jamaica covered by city vendors to trading his support for a new Home Depot outlet in exchange for the retailer granting contracts to the granite company he owned with his sons. Inside city hall, Nagin's technology office became a channel for kickbacks. "During what can only be described as a zany trip to Chicago and Las Vegas," wrote WWL-TV reporter David Hammer, the mayor, his wife and friends joined one vendor for the NFC Championship game, where the Saints lost to the Bears and members of the traveling party joked about the blatant conflicts of interests.[127]

The timing of the indictment worried observers. On the day of the announcement, WWL posed the question, "Will Nagin's indictment hurt New Orleans' reputation ahead of Super Bowl?"

"Now, just weeks before the Crescent City hosts Super Bowl XLVII, the city's former leader has been slapped with a sweeping federal indictment," said reporter Monica Hernandez. "As New Orleans prepares to take center stage in a worldwide event that will bring in hundreds of journalists, the ancillary focus will likely fall on the city's post-Katrina recovery and the leader who allegedly hindered it." NOMTC's Mark Romig was unmoved. "The news from today does not affect the planning or implementation of our tenth Super Bowl in any way whatsoever. We are focused on sharing three key messages: New Orleans is a great place to live and work, a great place to visit and a great place to host a Super Bowl. Period." Eyebrows were raised when, just five days after the indictment announcement, U.S. District Court judge Helen Berrigan rescheduled Nagin's arraignment date from January 31 to February 20. Berrigan gave no reason for the delay. While some wondered if the sides were negotiating a deal, others noted the convenience of avoiding the image of a former mayor entering a federal courtroom during Super Bowl week.[128]

On the afternoon following the indictment announcement, I turned on the black radio station WBOK as I drove across town. Hosts Paul Beaulieu and John Slade pored over the paperwork from the Nagin case. Beaulieu found two ironies in the whole situation. First, Nagin campaigned in 2002 as a pro-business, anti-corruption candidate with no political baggage. Once inaugurated, he immediately cracked down on alleged illegal activities in the city's inspection and taxicab bureaus, launched an investigation into fraud in federal housing contracts and dismantled the city's Utilities Bureau. "I've talked consistently about making sure we have city government that is open, honest, fair and fairly transparent in its dealings with the public," Nagin said. "We're trying to set a tone that says it's safe for outside investors to invest, because it's an environment where they can get a decent return." After six months in office, Nagin's approval ratings stood at 80 percent. A new, cleaner New Orleans seemed possible.[129] Now the crusader was the crucified.

Beaulieu relished a second irony. "You gave us Ray Nagin, white folk," he said. Most New Orleanians claimed crime was their number-one issue in the 2002 election to succeed Marc Morial. Faced with the choice between a successful crime fighter, NOPD chief Richard Pennington, and a political novice, "white folk" backed the latter. "If there's one thing white folk fear more than diphtheria, the plague and the continental flu," Beaulieu said, "it's the Morial name." Marc Morial's father, Ernest (aka "Dutch"), was the city's first black mayor, a confrontational, dynamic pioneer who won two terms. Sweeping generalizations aside, there was a core truth in the talk show host's observations. Promises of a new New Orleans marked Ray Nagin's ascent, backed by business interests in search of an alternative to what they saw as machine politics. Nagin was a white-collar executive, unafraid of the black political establishment. His demise, according to Beaulieu, came in the fevered months after Katrina, specifically after the mayor's infamous "Chocolate City" speech. "He then became the Django," Beaulieu said, referring to the 2013 Quentin Tarantino film. "The uppity black who can look in the eyes of the white folk and say, 'No, this will be Chocolate City. You ain't messing over my people.' Well, maybe he paid the price for that."[130]

Nagin's second term featured disappointment after disappointment for both black and white residents as recovery efforts stalled and the mayor grew more erratic. By the time he left office, Nagin had few friends left in political circles and few admirers among his fellow citizens. The willingness of Beaulieu to essentially blame the white elite for both Nagin's rise and his eventual fall belied his station's role as Nagin's last media mouthpiece, but it did reflect the general lack of empathy for the man who steered the city in the years after its near death. Nagin's failures returned to the limelight as disfigured relics of the old New Orleans, a cause of discomfort as the city put on its best face.

Local anger at Roger Goodell over Bountygate could be laughed off in ribald parades, but the indictment of a former mayor presented a more serious challenge to the image of the new New Orleans. On one hand, the charges showed that the city was serious about cleaning up its act; the current mayor benefited from comparisons to his disgraced predecessor. On the other hand, Nagin's reappearance was a reminder that Katrina was not vanquished through football games alone and that the city was barely removed from that divisive period. It was one thing to tell football fans to be nice. It was quite another to watch skeletons being pulled from the closet as honored guests knocked on your door.

CHAPTER 10
JANUARY 24, 2013 (TEN DAYS TO GO)

BIRDS

The service road from I-10 to Louis Armstrong Airport was well suited for first impressions or final reflections. If the airport was your destination, a lone sign thanked you for visiting New Orleans and the region. The occasional parked patrol car warned against last-minute speeders; sometimes the car was empty. A flat expanse of grass stretched to your right, where planes previewed your pending departure or perhaps carried your loved one or guest. Like most airport approaches, the view conjured feelings of anxiety and finality.

Headed toward I-10 and the city, billboards greeted you with promises of food, music and mischief. First came Chef Paul Prudhomme, proprietor of K-Paul and one of the first celebrity chefs to emerge from the city. The next sign advertised three affiliated Bourbon Street bars, followed by billboards for Acme Oyster House; Lafourche Parish, with its slogans "Dig In!" and "Really Cajun, Real Close"; the Davenport Lounge in the Ritz Carlton; the Louisiana Lottery; an assurance from the Convention and Visitors Bureau's: "We're Jazzed You're Here"; more Bourbon Street bars; and Tito's Traditional Vodka. Throughout the year, different ads appeared along this prime real estate, but a Bourbon Street gentlemen's club, Rick's Cabaret, controlled the final spot on the service road. On this day, a blonde in shoulder pads and helmet glared out from a black background next to an orange-lettered "BOUNTIFUL," a clever pun on the Saints' recent saga. French Quarter–style streetlamps ran down the road's narrow median.

If the tourism industry was intent on enhancing each step of the visitor's experience, the three-mile-long Airport Road provided a succession of familiar images. Here, the city remained Bourbon Street and excess. For all the changes awaiting a new arrival, Airport Road offered certainty.

There was renewed uncertainty, however, about the taxicabs that carried those tourists. Recent days brought increased complaints by drivers based in Kenner who, while outside the jurisdiction of the reforms enacted in New Orleans, were required to comply at the airport, which was owned by the City of New Orleans. Drivers claimed that New Orleans–based cabs received preferential treatment for installation of new equipment. In early December, two Kenner City Council members responded with a threat to the Super Bowl: if the December 31 deadline for cab compliance wasn't pushed back for airport cabbies, the council would delay approval of ongoing construction projects at Armstrong International. Airport officials agreed to suspend the deadline.[131]

This week, the ceasefire ended. The airport had announced the day before that Kenner-registered cabs working during Super Bowl week would be required to show paperwork that proved they'd ordered new equipment and were only awaiting installation. Angered taxi drivers floated the possibility of a protest at the airport during the week of the game; hostility to the reforms in New Orleans remained high. "You're taking people's livelihoods. You're putting people in debt who can't afford to go into debt," driver Addie Washington-Ranson told the *Baton Rouge Advocate*. Airport officials tried to remain calm. "We are looking forward to hosting the Super Bowl, and we are confident we will provide our passengers with a world-class experience," said COO Walter Krygowski.[132]

The airport was the gateway for the new New Orleans, and the Super Bowl served as the facility's deadline for $300 million in capital improvements, funded by bond issues and set into motion in 2009. Renovations to restrooms and one concourse, a new rental car facility, the opening of several locally themed restaurants, a fire station and various landscaping projects were aimed at making Armstrong International a world-class airport. On January 15, Landrieu and regional officials celebrated in the main terminal. "These are necessary improvements that will help sustain the airport for several years," the mayor said. "And with the Super Bowl putting New Orleans on the world stage, the timing couldn't be better."[133] Once labeled a "pit of corruption," the airport seemed poised to enter a new era. A recent arrival led the turnaround.

Iftikhar Ahmad was hired as aviation director in February 2010, not long after the Saints' Super Bowl win and Landrieu's election. Previously the director of the Dayton airport, Ahmad had a track record of successful capital projects and cost-cutting measures. Signed to a five-year contract, Ahmad became the second-highest-paid public official in the city after longtime Sewage and Water board director Marcia St. Martin, his $195,642 initial salary topping the $180,000 paid to NOPD superintendent Ronal Serpas. Ahmad cited the progress of the new New Orleans as a factor in his decision to relocate. "You want to put yourself in a place where you someday can look behind and you can smile to yourself and say, 'I gave it my all and made a difference.' That's possible here with New Orleans,"

Iftikhar Ahmad. *Photo courtesy of Louis Armstrong International Airport.*

Ahmad said. "There's this tremendous optimism in the air—you guys won the Super Bowl, you have a new mayor and I heard Mardi Gras was one of the largest you've seen. Surely, one would want to be a part of that."[134]

At the time of Ahmad's arrival, the airport was rarely mentioned as a symbol of civic optimism. Passenger numbers were down compared to previous years, and customer satisfaction had plummeted. JD Power lowered the airport from number four in its rankings of small airports in 2008 to twenty-three out of twenty-four in 2010. With its dated architecture and the dingy baggage claim level, Armstrong International often felt like a very nice airport in Central America, not the doorstep of a major tourism destination. The BCG report had good reason to list the airport as a priority for the tourism master plan.

Prospective reforms were complicated by administrative turmoil. Ahmad's predecessor resigned amid controversy and later pleaded guilty to Katrina-related fraud charges. He eventually served a year in prison, but not before collecting a six-figure severance package. Dan Packer, the board chair who hired Ahmad, stepped down in 2011 after an investigation revealed more than $76,000 in questionable charges on his airport credit card. Whatever fresh forms of excitement awaited them in the new New Orleans, visitors first passed through a den of cronyism.

"Let me just say…that in the past this organization had a bad reputation, and that reputation has been a pit of corruption," Inspector General Ed Quatrevaux told the aviation board during a March 2012 meeting. "In the past, this board took the low road to high life…In the past, this organization was consistent with the old New Orleans, steering jobs [and] business to favorites." After issuing his report on the credit card abuses, Quatrevaux set up a satellite office in the airport. Ahmad offered his support. "I would say that where he's at and where we're at is exactly the same point," he told Fox 8's Lee Zurik.[135] Instead of a civic embarrassment, Armstrong International would serve as a frontier in the fight against corruption.

When Ahmad and I spoke via phone in December, he addressed the airport's tarnished reputation. "Any charges that I make to my corporate card, I post them on our website," he said. "I can tell you exactly who I've met with, what we spent money on, what we discussed, exactly where we met—we make all of that public on our website. It's a message to people out there that this is a new airport." Transparency had tangible results. By putting old contracts out to bid, Ahmad predicted, the airport would save $25 million over the next five years. Cutting costs meant increasing profits, which attracted more airlines, thus delivering more visitors to the region. "New Orleans is a tourism-based economy for the most part. That makes the airport an integral part of the supply chain. For a quality-of-life point of view, this airport is integral to the strategic positioning of this area and the surrounding region," Ahmad said. His description of the city's "supply chain" was instructive. New routes and services would "put pressure on our hotels, put pressure on our restaurants, put pressure on our gas stations, and all our other parishes," he said. More arriving passengers triggered a chain reaction. "When you hire more people, more money is changing hands. So when you were talking about impact on people, your property value goes up, and it is a rising tide that will lift my neighbors, my people, my city, my parish, my state."

It seemed like a tidy equation, but so far Ahmad had proof of his effectiveness. Within six months of taking office, he reversed the trend that mattered most: monthly passenger traffic. Now almost two years into his tenure, he saw the Super Bowl as a milestone in a larger journey. "I knew about the deadline and that the game was coming and that we had to get the airport ready," he said. "But really, it has been one of the many, many things we have been focused on." The bigger goal was a new terminal, part of a seven-year plan to "put New Orleans on a different level than other cities" in time for the 2018 tricentennial. Along with better services and finances, the airport needed to symbolize something greater for area residents.

ONE HUNDRED DAYS IN AMERICA'S COOLEST HOT SPOT

The dispute with Kenner taxi drivers was unfortunate, Ahmad said, but the improved cabs were another link in the supply chain that connected runways to tourism to community revitalization. "It goes back into the whole airport-as-a-front-door to the state of Louisiana, the city of New Orleans." A better airport created a better image, which fostered a business-friendly environment that attracted corporations "to bring their families here and raise them like I did, like my colleagues here at the airport did…and to invest in our business to create opportunities for those investments for our neighborhood. Everybody will have to make some sacrifices for the good of all…and I believe that, at the end of the day, we will all get ahead."[136]

How those sacrifices impacted the families of the taxi industry remained uncertain, but Ahmad's emphasis on transparency and his methodical approach to expanding the airport made sense. Among the officials hired to reform city agencies, he stood out as a shrewd professional who understood the terrain. The airport renovations provided an opportunity for the Landrieu administration to demonstrate the use of big events as deadlines for highly visible capital projects.

On this day, I sat down on a freshly installed, S-shaped couch in front of a new retail outlet, Creole Kitchen. Locals had long complained that the shops and restaurants at the airport failed to convey the "real" New Orleans. The renovations included new eateries with local ties like Zatarain's Kitchen, Copeland's Cheesecake Bistro and a Dooky Chase restaurant, while a Saints apparel store and Perlis Cajun Clothing offered visitors homegrown fashions. Creole Kitchen brimmed with locally made Zapp's potato chips, pralines and boxes of king cake. Clusters of plastic red peppers and garlic adorned walls printed with words like "voodoo," "file gumbo" and "fleur de lis." The merchandise was overpriced airport fare, but the New Orleans iconography was more immediately available for purchase than ever before.

Inside the Saints store, numerous screens replayed the 2010 Super Bowl. The shelves bulged with the finest selection of Saints apparel I'd ever encountered, including ten types of team caps, plus scarves, bedding sets, commemorative coins, steering wheel covers and piggy banks. For the upcoming Super Bowl XLVII, a display offered shot glasses, #47 jerseys, golf shirts, bomber jackets and clocks bearing the game's logo. At the register, I spoke to the cashier, a short woman in a blue Super Bowl pullover. Amid the team cheer, she was a droll ambassador for a mostly empty store. She told me the Sugar Bowl sucked for sales but that the Super Bowl and Mardi Gras would be much better, not that she was all that excited about it. Behind her on a wall of monitors, author Anne Rice appeared amid images of the flooded city post-Katrina. Well stocked and narrowly focused, the store banked on the alignment of team and city as a recipe for souvenir sales.

In the main terminal, the cosmetic upgrades were obvious. Wood paneling spruced up the walls, wave-shaped orange mobiles hung about the ticketing area and the restroom entrances were newly tiled. Between the monitors showing departures and arrivals, a screen displayed a message: "Welcome to Louis Armstrong New Orleans International Airport for Super Bowl XLVII. Arrive a Fan, Leave as Family."

I walked to the Gate A ramp to wait for my wife, who'd been visiting her sister in Baltimore. A black man with a silver beard milled about, looking toward security and checking his phone. I recognized his fedora, and when we caught each other's eyes, we asked simultaneously, "Don't I know you?" Yes, we did. Curtis Moore of the Praline Connection had catered several events at my workplace. With two outlets in the terminal, Moore was relieved that the renovations were finished so that business could get back to normal. The Super Bowl was great, but so, too, was the upheaval.

Moore and his business partner, Cecil Kaigler, opened the Praline Connection on Frenchmen Street in 1990. He recalled the street in those days: "Dead. People thought I was crazy when I came down here to open a restaurant. Place was a mess. It was just a dead area." The partners caught a break when a local food critic gave their new business a stellar review. Within three months, "we became famous." Moore had toured Africa, Europe and the Middle East cooking New Orleans food. Today's Frenchmen Street was an internationally known strip of music venues and eateries; Moore had chosen wisely. "I think we have the next Bourbon Street. Only difference is it's a little cleaner!" Moore said.

The airport location opened a few years later. "They were looking for minorities running businesses and people who were known for what they were doing," Moore recalled. "At the time, we were riding high, pretty successful. It wasn't a bad shot for them, and we've been doing good ever since." The hospitality management company Delaware North oversaw concessions at Armstrong International, with Praline Connection classified as a subcontractor. Moore paid a base rent of $59 per square foot to the aviation board, plus a percentage of sales. The renovations were costly for an independent businessman. To meet the requirements of the facelift, Moore took out a $190,000 line of credit. More than twenty years into a successful operation, he wasn't worried about the debt, but the construction had forced him to close both restaurants for five weeks during the busy holiday travel season. "They wanted to make that big impression with the Super Bowl," he said. "It was a matter of when they were going to close it down. I guess they could've done it earlier, but you know they procrastinate, and then they had a limited time to do it. That was the worst time. For the workers, these people live off paychecks. To miss all Christmas, I couldn't imagine. I gave 'em a party and a bonus, and they were appreciative of that." He shrugged. The locations employed fifteen people.

Moore took the changes at the airport in stride. "It looks so much nicer now. My people lost—and I lost a lot too—but that's the only way it could happen. Somebody had to lose." Recently, Delaware North directed all vendors to purchase new computers so that the company could track sales, apparently a part of Ahmad's fight against waste and fraud. Moore assented. "I guess they don't trust us!" He laughed. "Which is OK with me because ever since I opened my business, I always did what I was supposed to do. I am not going to jail!" He'd survived the mishaps of earlier regimes. "If they want a computer I can afford, I get one. They want access to do it, [they can] do what they want with it."[137]

Moore was good humored, but airport concessions had a rocky history. In October 2011, Delaware North cut ties with a company owned by imprisoned businessman Stan "Pampy" Barre, a former NOPD officer and close associate of mayors Dutch and Marc Morial. Under a contract awarded by Marc Morial's administration, Delaware North had partnered with Pampy's Inc. to manage all concessions, thus helping the larger company meet disadvantaged business enterprise goals set by the Federal Aviation Administration. Critics cited the contract as the source of the airport's shoddy eating options and poor service. In 2007, Barre was convicted on corruption charges related to another city contract. In exchange for a five-year sentence, he cooperated with U.S. attorney Jim Letten's office to ensnare a city councilman and a school board member in separate schemes, later bragging that his work as an informant opened the floodgate for multiple convictions. "I connected so many dots for them, it's incredible," he told the *Times Picayune*. "The next time they look at a situation, they're going to be in so much better shape because of the things we talked about. They didn't have any idea of who belonged where, especially in black politics and business."

After his conviction, Barre agreed to disinvest himself from Pampy's Inc. to salvage the contract with Delaware North and the corporation's DBE compliance. In reality, Barre continued to direct operations from a Florida jail cell until last year, when Delaware North ended the contract via an "amicable settlement."[138]

Improving the airport meant more than adding quality jambalaya in the concourse. From Ahmad's online credit card statements to Moore's new computer, the changes at Armstrong International reflected the facility's slow emergence from decades of corruption. Reform meant skirmishes with taxi drivers and lost wages for food servers, but as Moore said, "somebody has to lose." The real proof of reform would come when the capital projects ended without resignations and jail sentences. For now, the new façades and Ahmad's promises to the community seemed to rebuke the lecherous past. After years of embarrassments and shady deals, the airport's new leadership provided a fitting front door as the city awaited the Super Bowl.

A few hours after my conversation with Curtis Moore, I passed through security checkpoints into the most heavily guarded zone of the city: Dave Dixon Drive. The stretch of Girod Street between Loyola and Claiborne Avenues was renamed in December for the late "father of the Superdome," and now the thoroughfare between the New Orleans Arena and the Dome buzzed with Super Bowl preparations; Dixon would've loved it. The NFL logo hung on the front of a glass pavilion erected for league-sponsored parties. Eighteen-wheelers surrounded the stadium's loading docks, technicians unspooled cable and police officers checked badges at the entrance to Champions Square. After several displays of my press pass, I weaved through the golf carts and uniforms to the rear entrance of the arena. Super Bowl preparations could wait: Tom Benson had an announcement to make.

The New Orleans Arena opened in 1999. A minor-league hockey team, the New Orleans Brass, was its first tenant, brought to town by an ownership group including Ray Nagin. Hockey was on odd fit for the city, and the team folded after three years, just as the arena welcomed a better prospect. On May 9, 2002, a second-line parade led Charlotte Hornets owners George Shinn and Ray Woolridge to a press conference, where the duo announced the NBA's approval of their move from North Carolina to Louisiana. The team left the Queen City in disgrace after a series of scandals, poor personnel decisions and a failed attempt at a new arena. "It's hard to uproot, but we had no choice," said Shinn at the press conference.[139]

Over the next ten seasons in New Orleans, the Hornets were a middling product on the court but a struggling one at the gate. Attendance peaked at nineteenth out of thirty teams in 2008–09. After Katrina, Shinn flirted with Oklahoma City, where the displaced team played to sold-out crowds. The Hornets' eventual return to New Orleans was the Saints' story in miniature as point guard Chris Paul led them to the second round of the 2008 playoffs and civic embrace. That year, the city hosted the NBA All-Star Game, where the ongoing recovery provided readymade opportunities for the league's charity efforts as players wielded paintbrushes, lifted drywall and dedicated new courts. Several media reports mentioned the escalating murder rate, but most reporters were more impressed with the local hospitality and the short walk from hotels to the arena. The weekend proved New Orleans was again open for the business of major sporting events.

The Hornets remained fragile. In 2009, Shinn tried to sell the team to minority owner Gary Chouest, a Louisianan billionaire who'd earned his fortune servicing the offshore oil industry. When the *Deepwater Horizon* catastrophe shut down business in the Gulf in April 2010, Chouest pulled his offer. A few months later, Shinn announced he was on the verge of bankruptcy. Once again, the city faced the prospect of losing its team.

Commissioner David Stern rode to the rescue. The NBA took the unprecedented step of purchasing the team from Shinn, reportedly for $318 million. When the season ended, Stern began negotiations that led to the second labor stoppage of his reign. Once again, the city served as a convenient symbol for powerful forces: the Hornets were an example of a valiant small-market team handicapped by the players' greed. The league missed two months of the regular season, and when it resumed, Stern made a mess of the Hornets, calling off a trade of Paul to the Lakers. ESPN's Bill Simmons called it Stern's "Watergate" and said it was a sign that the commissioner was "losing control of his league."[140] After shipping Paul to the Clippers, Stern watched the Hornets crawl toward the second-worst record in the league. Instead of being proof that the new collective bargaining agreement benefited weaker teams, the team was an albatross.

Then Tom Benson called.

"The city is one of the country's treasures, and we really have found the perfect owner," Stern said at an April 13, 2012 press conference, echoing Edwin Edwards's description of Benson as "a miracle" twenty-five years earlier.[141] Along with the reported $338 million sale, Stern and Benson worked out a new lease with the state that included a $50 million facelift for the arena. Forbes reported that the league broke even on the deal. A week after the announcement, Stern and Benson joined again to announce that New Orleans would host the 2014 All-Star Game. The commissioner denied that the game was awarded as part of the sale but continued to praise Benson as the perfect fit: "We would have to invent him if he didn't exist."[142] In the final stroke of fortune, the Hornets beat the odds and secured the top pick in the 2012 draft lottery. "This is just another step towards us winning it all," Benson said.[143]

This day was heralded as one more step. Inherited from Charlotte, the Hornets name would be replaced by something more appropriate for a team that seemed certain to remain in New Orleans. I emerged onto the court to join a gathering of media, politicians and team players and officials awaiting the announcement and the debut of new uniforms. The arena was dim, save for a spotlight above a stage with two large screens. The new name was hardly a secret, but a giddy feeling permeated the near darkness. Outside, the trucks unloaded the Super Bowl infrastructure, while inside we waited for a historic moment in New Orleans sports. Three months remained in the NBA season, but team officials wisely timed this announcement to take advantage of the NFL's arrival.

Finally, team play-by-play announcer Joel Meyers welcomed everyone and quickly cut to the chase. "At the conclusion of the current campaign, the franchise is going to be changing our name to the New Orleans Pelicans." A brief video explained the logic and history behind the decision. When Louisiana first welcomed explorers, the newcomers "saw how charitable the pelican was towards their young." Later, the state flag reflected this impression, its central image a mother pelican feeding its young. "It is a hunter, protector, has speed, precision, and is as unique as the Gulf South region." A photo of oiled pelicans represented those lost in *Deepwater Horizon*. The health of the bird and the coastal wetlands would be an integral part of the franchise's community efforts. The Pelicans would fight for the pelicans.

When the video ended, two bursts of fireworks popped off in the rafters. Ron Forman, chair of the Louisiana Sports and Exposition District and president of the Audubon Nature Institute, remembered Benson's leadership after Katrina, or at least after the incident at Tiger Stadium: "Tom stood up and said, 'I have a vision: the Saints are going to lead, not just in winning football games, but lead the rebuilding of the city.'" That prediction had come to pass, Forman said. "The public relations we got out of becoming America's team overcame the negative. We became the city alive again, and it became much more than a football team." The Pelicans, he said, could have a similar impact on Louisiana's wetlands. "[The Pelicans] are going to be the leaders to rebuilding our coast." Sports would rescue New Orleans again.

Mayor Landrieu followed Forman. He compared the name change to the event about to unfold next door. "The magic to this is that a Super Bowl is not an end in and of itself. Having a franchise on the football or the basketball side is not just an end of itself. It's how you use it. The magic about the Bensons is they have used this as a means to make New Orleans and Louisiana a great place for all of us to live." He introduced "the Papa Pelican, the Big Daddy of 'em all, Mr. Tom Benson."

Benson moved slowly in a navy blue suit and tie, topped by a new Pelicans hat. His Seventh Ward accent remained strong. "The New Orleans Saints means a great deal to this community, known throughout the world. Now, with the New Orleans Pelicans, we're gonna get it known throughout the world, too, huh?" He made a rare mention of Bountygate. "I think we're proud of our football team. We didn't have the year we wanted this past year. But now we got back everybody on the job. In fact, Payton was back in the office today. I didn't think he and Gayle would ever quit hugging, but it was all right. This is an exciting time." He thanked the city and the state for their cooperation. The most powerful man in New Orleans could no longer perform the Benson Boogie, but his satisfaction was clear.

The ceremony ended, and the media followed the VIPs into the well-lit tunnel. Rodney Richardson, the designer behind the team's new logo—a fierce, red-eyed pelican—explained the rebranding process. "Brands are built around stories," he said. "Those stories of who we are and where we come from, those are the most impacting stories of all." They'd discussed countless possibilities in favor of local relevance. "You can't ignore those things. A lot of folks want you to follow trends. They want things they expect, what they think all sports [logos] are supposed to be. This club said, 'We don't want to be what everybody wants us to be. We want to be uniquely New Orleans.'"

Back on Dave Dixon Drive, I thought about the long road traveled by professional sports in New Orleans. Dixon proposed the Superdome and the Saints as a means of legitimatization, a way to leapfrog past Houston and Atlanta into modernity; joining the big leagues might even cure the city's racist reputation. Until Katrina, those predictions had mixed results, just like the local teams. After the storm, however, the embrace of New Orleans became central to the teams' brands. There was a story to build around. Loyalty to the endangered city made business sense at home and across the nation, where the Pelicans were now part of a winning brand. Fans didn't just buy jerseys—they bought a symbol of resilience and care. The transplanted basketball team was now locally owned and locally themed. That alone sparked hope and sales, if not the immediate restoration of the wetlands.

I'd parked in a garage near the entrance to Champion Square. As I reached the second floor, I recognized a sandy-haired man in a Hawaiian shirt: Quint Davis, director of the New Orleans Jazz & Heritage Festival. I caught up to him and introduced myself.

Davis, of course, needed no introduction to any local interested in music and the music business. One could argue that Jazz Fest was the most important development in New Orleans music since the birth of Louis Armstrong.[144] When renowned promoter George Wein launched the festival in 1970, he hired Davis and fellow Tulane undergrad Allison Miner to book musicians to play for a few hundred people in Congo Square and Municipal Auditorium. Tickets were $3, and total sales were less than $50,000. An avid music fan and aspiring producer, Davis was the son of architect Arthur Davis, a partner in the influential New Orleans firm that designed the Superdome and later the arena. The younger Davis built Jazz Fest into a global brand that rivaled Mardi Gras as the city's largest annual tourist attraction, with a reported 450,000 attendees over two weekends in 2012. If anyone understood the transformation of local culture into a marketable brand, it was Davis. He was also, I knew, a huge basketball fan.

I complimented the pelicans in the print of his shirt. "I mean, if they'd have done frogs or something, I'd have looked really stupid," he admitted, "but I was hoping it was pelicans." Davis had a familiar, frank manner, somewhere between a film director and a burgomaster. He lamented the loss of the New Orleans Jazz name, "one of the greatest brands ever" but unfortunately exiled to Utah in 1979. "I really will never get over that." We agreed that the Pelicans logos were much stronger than imagined, the red eyes expressing the necessary ferocity. Davis thought the name change reflected the team's improved standing. "I just think it's all part of Mr. Benson anchoring New Orleans as a major-league city and ensuring that we have NFL and NBA franchises," he said. "That's a huge thing for this city that takes billions of dollars to do. Now he's branded it to the city." The Saints operation would transform the Pelicans. "You've got the marketing team, you got the ticket-selling team, you have all your corporate relationships." Davis knew the importance of those relationships: after Katrina, he secured a long-term partnership with Shell Oil that righted the festival's teetering ship. I asked about his involvement with the Super Bowl.

"These are some of the smartest, most dynamic people, but they have grown, just like Jazz Fest. We were in Congo Square—now look at us. Super Bowl is the same thing." As a producer, Davis appreciated the persistence and vision involved in expanding the game's footprint. "They have grown this thing exponentially year to year to year," he said. "It's not what it was five years ago. It is the closest thing to an annual Olympics, and I think the incredibly brilliant thing—you know, they said in there that Landrieu was just voted one of the top five mayors. He should've been number one."

ONE HUNDRED DAYS IN AMERICA'S COOLEST HOT SPOT

Landrieu's ingenious strategy was to approach the Super Bowl the way other cities approached the Olympics. "When an Olympics goes to a city, they undo, redo and overdo everything," said Davis. "They build new venues; it changes the city. And then when the thing is over, it's got permanent improvements forever. And to me, Mitch seized on the opportunity of the American Olympics, if you will, coming here and used it like you would an Olympics. To redo the streets, to redo the lights, to finish the streetcar—all kinds of stuff that are permanent improvements to the city and that will be here until after the Super Bowl is gone."

Standing a few hundred feet from two stadiums designed by his father's firm, Davis spoke with authority. Again, he expressed admiration for the NFL: "It's when imagination meets resources. When you've got the resources, you can make your imagination happen. What's the dollars of it, what's the impact? What, are you fucking kidding me? Thirty-second [advertisement] slots are $5 million. We're on the television for a week. It's New Orleans every time out of their mouth. You can't get that. When you are the center of the world—we have five thousand media people here. That's the volume. I don't care if there's one penny spent." The brand needed all the help it could get, and now the greatest show on earth had arrived to change the narrative.

"We've had Katrina, we've had the oil spill. We're trying to let the world know that there's not still water in the streets, that our fish aren't still poisoned—it's hard to get beyond those. Reality is easy to fix; perception is hard."[145]

We shook hands and walked to our cars, his German, mine Korean. After he pulled out, I considered the different efforts required of reality and perception. Oily birds were reality; basketball jerseys were perception. Still entangled in troubled realities, the city continued to excel at spectacles like Jazz Fest and the Super Bowl that banked on positive perceptions to attract visitors and dollars. The promise of the new New Orleans was that perception—the brand—could pay to fix reality. Used to attract visitors and sporting events, the story of the recovery was crucial to the economy of the recovery. Davis's Olympic analogy summed up perfectly the approach of city officials. By emphasizing the urgency and grand promise of the Super Bowl, Landrieu and others forced reality to get in line. Spectacle begot bricks and mortar to encourage more spectacles. And now the biggest spectacle in contemporary America had arrived in New Orleans. Perception and reality would meet.

CHAPTER 11
JANUARY 26, 2013
(EIGHT DAYS TO GO)

THE CLEAN ZONE OF TOMBSTONE

The mule greeted his driver every morning at 8:30 a.m. inside a barn in the Marigny. Now ten years old, the mule waited as the driver wiped down the animal's black coat, strapped on the harness and hooked the mule to the buggy. The driver was the only one the mule, Shine, had ever known, his sole trainer when the mule was five and ready to start working. They got along well. Each day, a stable hand fed Shine four scoops of feed and eight sticks of hay. And once a week, a man came to check his shoes, though the driver could handle that in a pinch. The mule had recently returned from a two-month vacation on the Northshore, where the company sent animals for a break from the stress of French Quarter traffic. Even with an experienced driver and willing mule, accidents were not uncommon. At 9:00 a.m., the mule pulled the buggy out of the stable and headed toward Jackson Square.

At the square, they parked along the designated stretch of curb on Decatur Street, known as the hack stand, where the driver, John Cosentino, checked in with co-workers and waited for the day's first passengers. They were glad to be back at the hack stand because for most of the previous ten days, the area had been unavailable to the buggies. The centuries-old plaza was in the middle of a transformation to a media nerve center for CBS, the network carrying this year's Super Bowl. Several stages were set up along the path that circled the park opposite St. Louis Cathedral. The morning shows, the NFL pre-game shows and the network news all had locations prepared where on-air talent would chatter in front of the square's iconic backdrop. As I climbed into the buggy this morning, a live band ran through its sound check.

The Super Bowl might serve as the debut for a new New Orleans, but the cameras still loved the French Quarter. Almost three hundred years old, newly repaved, persistently dangerous, dependably untamed, prowled by thieves and scam artists, plump with visiting drunks, relatively cheap and open all night, the neighborhood was unlike any other national landmark or nationally televised backdrop. For the next eight days, the French Quarter would bear the burden of the city's image, broadcasting to the world that New Orleans was back and ready to party. American viewers recognized the wrought-iron balconies and oversized drinks, the buggies and street musicians. If the city really was rebuilt and better than ever, the Quarter remained the preferred location for the networks. As the media set up camp, the men and women who worked in the neighborhood had the most interesting viewpoints on the neighborhood, the visitors and progress.

Born and raised downtown, John had a wry, matter-of-fact posture well suited for narrating tours. He looked like a hip German farmer, tan with light whiskers that dusted his round face, dark-rimmed glasses and a wide-brimmed hat. His father had retired from the local passport office, and his mother was a librarian in the St. Bernard Parish schools. Now in his mid-thirties, John estimated he was the most senior driver on the street this morning.

"I started driving buggies for the Bayou Classic in '99," he said. The Bayou Classic was the annual Thanksgiving football game between Grambling and Southern, two historically black universities that brought fans and alumni to the Superdome. "I wasn't making any money teaching, and a buddy of mine was driving the buggies, so I'd teach during the day and drive at night. After awhile, I gave up teaching." When he started, most of the drivers were older black men. "Now almost all those guys are gone. I don't know why younger black guys don't want to do this job—it's not the worst job in the world. You just gotta be able to pee in a cup and pass a criminal background check. I make about $50,000 a year sitting on this buggy." He'd worked the night shift before Katrina, but the business never fully bounced back for those hours and he had a young son, so now he stuck to days. The mule was allowed five hours of active work carrying passengers, which usually meant they'd finish by 4:00 p.m. On a good day, John made $400; on slow days like today, when he'd likely give three tours and then go home, he made between $100 and $120. A minimum half-hour tour for four people was $90. Drivers took in 35 percent of fares, plus tips. I agreed with John: this was a good gig.

Like any job, there were hassles and downsides. The buggies were regulated by the Taxicab Bureau, which required two permits totaling sixty dollars, renewable biannually, as well as a background check, fingerprinting and drug testing. "It's a rigmarole," John said. Navigating the Quarter was old hat, but shit happened. "Wheels fall off, cars hit mules, you smash up cars," especially when he trained one of the company's new animals. If a mule refused to stop, the only choice was to run the entire rig into a wall or car; usually the mule pulled up before collision. Misinformation hurt business, particularly the night shifts. "They have people in the hotels telling the guests it's dangerous to go out at night. It's nonsense. As long you stay on a major street and don't bet a man at his own game, you're not going to have problems in the Quarter." The Paths to Progress streetscape upgrades impacted the buggies. "We got shut down for a week or so when they were repaving Decatur Street. I guess that's another lasting impression of this stuff, but they were improvements they were going to do anyway." The construction didn't affect the tour routes, though. "I been doing this so long, I can get around all this stuff. We're not selling distance; we're selling time. You can talk about whatever you feel like, whatever street you're on."

Secure in a timeworn trade, John was nonplussed about most things. The Super Bowl was more disruption than bonus, but he saw both sides: "It's going to be a wash for me. I've lost the hack stand so many days. I've had a bad month; I can't make it all up in three days. For me, it's not the greatest of things. The plus of it is the good advertising. Media all over the world, people see New Orleans is up and running, it's a fun place, come down." CBS, at least, had tried to work with the drivers, providing a schedule for load in and the various televised events. John had endured the chaos in 2010 when the NFL staged a season kickoff concert in Jackson Square that drew the ire of locals who lived and worked in the neighborhood. With little notification, the league took over the entire square for two days, pushing out buggy drivers and the permitted artists who sold work around the park. Taylor Swift and the Dave Matthews Band performed on a massive stage mounted on Washington Artillery Park across Decatur from the hack stand. "Nobody came to us with any information whatsoever," said one shop owner, part of a group that forced meetings with city officials when word spread of the coming takeover. "We had to solicit it. We weren't consulted in any way. Basically, the NFL was given free rein and had no restrictions whatsoever."[146]

The concert revealed the overlapping jurisdictions inside city hall, with the Department of Parks and Parkways charged with maintenance inside the park's gates and the Department of Sanitation overseeing the pedestrian malls. City Councilwoman Kristen Gisleson Palmer formed a task force of residents and business owners that issued a list of recommendations, including a single entity for maintenance in the square, background checks for tarot card readers and penalties for buggy drivers who failed to clean up manure. Jackson Square was "not a frozen piece of history," the task force reported. "Instead, it's a vibrant residential, commercial and tourist hub that is under increasing pressure because of its popularity."[147] That position was inarguable, but further solutions proposed by the task force uncovered the divergent takes on the proper management of the space.

No matter the politics, John was at peace with the Super Bowl headache. Word from headquarters indicated the buggies would be out of service on game day. John shrugged. "We make more money if nothing special's in town, if it's just a normal weekend and the sun's shining. It doesn't get clogged up. Less people are going to be in town because people are going to be scared away from this kind of stuff."

The city had improved since Katrina, though nothing was guaranteed. "I went to Krewe du Vieux. The big complaints of the Krewe du Vieux were the crummy paper's publishing less and the coach got suspended for a year. If those are our big problems, hey, New Orleans is doing pretty well." John was from here, worked in the heart of the tourism industry and had no plans to leave, "as long as the levees hold and we miss out on the hurricanes the next forty years. I don't know if this place is going to be around long enough for my son, but you never know." Like they did most mornings, he and Shine waited for passengers.

Marlo Barrea started driving a pedicab in October after she got back from Alaska. She had a degree from Oberlin and a second job in a kitchen. She lived where she was raised, across the river in Algiers Point, and despite the Mohawk and jaded façade, still exuded a girlish sensitivity. Marlo wrote poetry and designed small books and worried about her little sister. We knew each other from Handsome Willy's, where she'd tended bar during Saints games.

We sat in the cab outside Café Envie on Decatur Street. Her company-issued radio crackled: "You know it's going to be a good day when there's a guy getting arrested at 10:45 on Bourbon Street." Marlo explained that the taxicab bureau regulated the pedicabs, and just like the cabbies and buggy drivers, she was aghast at the inefficiencies of that office. "Hell in and of itself." She spent forty dollars on her permit, fifty dollars on a federal background check and twenty dollars on a drug test to secure a license, which the bureau immediately informed her would expire in two weeks. Though the company begged successfully for a reprieve, it was clear that the rules and practices of the new industry were highly irregular. Drivers charged passengers one dollar per block, but they cut

ONE HUNDRED DAYS IN AMERICA'S COOLEST HOT SPOT

Decatur Street in front of Jackson Square, January 28, 2013. *Photo by author.*

deals during special events. Seventy drivers competed for the company's fifteen licensed bikes so that by 10:00 a.m., she was lucky to grab one of three remaining bikes. Today would likely be a slow day. The company charged drivers rent based on its expectations.

"A Wednesday might be $30, a Saints game $150. The Super Bowl, I think, is $250. And, of course, there's two shifts, a day shift and a night shift. Today is $75, and tonight is $150. Sundays are the worst—last Sunday, they lowered the rent to $5." Just a year out of college, Marlo was young enough to enjoy some parts of the job. "I get to be outside and get some exercise. It's these very brief interactions that you get to meet people. I've had so many people willing to tell you anything cause they're never going to see you again." Still, she knew the city, and like John, she refused to work the night shift. "Our shirts say, 'Need a Ride?' Think of all the lewd comments you get during the day. It just looks so incredibly lonely, and you're dealing with drunk people all night."

Last Sunday, she was working in the kitchen when her co-worker got a phone call. The co-worker's fourteen-year-old son had been shot. "He got shot in his thigh, on his calf, in his shoulder, and his arm. He's trying to run, so the bullet traveled from his shoulder, punctured his lungs twice and almost hit his colon, which would've meant he had to wear a bag for the rest of his life. Fourteen-year-old kid."

The boy was one of five people shot outside a grocery store on Martin Luther King Boulevard in Central City just thirty minutes after the annual MLK Day parade passed the corner. The gunmen fired from a moving sedan into a group of teens. Though the shooting appeared unrelated to the parade, the timing and location seemed poignant, and the incident made national news just two weeks prior to the Super Bowl. "It's the state of affairs in our nation that young men do not heed the words of Martin Luther King Jr.," Superintendent Serpas said.[148]

"I grew up thinking that that shit happened everywhere else, that it was normal," Marlo said. "It's not." She liked Alaska because she could hitchhike to work everyday and not feel fear. Her plan was to return there in April. "It's time to go. I think I'll come back and get my car. I don't know where I'm going to go, [but I'll] find somewhere else." Driving a pedicab was nice work, though, so maybe she'd pick it up in another city. In the meantime, she hoped to work once during Super Bowl weekend if she was lucky enough to score a shift.

Like generations of young people, both natives and transplants, Marlo made her way through the uneven territory that was service industry work in the French Quarter. Some people took to it and stayed, attracted by the cash economy, the multitude of job opportunities and the camaraderie of odd hours in a ribald environment. Others recoiled or got burned out. Money flowed during events like the Super Bowl, but the jobs remained mercurial, and the Quarter wasn't for the thin-skinned or the unsure. Endurance was the most important qualification.

"If it wants you, it'll keep you. If it doesn't want you, you can't stay," said the tarot card reader, referring to New Orleans. "It'll either destroy you here or it'll make you leave." We laughed. The CBS preparations continued, but foot traffic was relatively light on Jackson Square as we talked at his table near the downtown corner of Chartres Street. A deck of cards sat unmoved on the tablecloth.

His name was Mike, and he said he'd worked in the Quarter for fourteen years. "Well, I pulled into the city, was going to a horse farm in Ocala, had a job lined up for me. Took a wrong turn—it was my birthday. Pulled into town in my pickup truck, jumped out of my truck to take a piss on my tire. I'd been driving all night, got arrested. When I was arrested, they towed my truck. Every time I tried to get my truck back—my illusion of freedom—something else bad would happen. So I finally look at the sky and say, 'You know, you may have to hit me in the brick a few times, but I get it.' That's the synopsis." He was small with a squeaky voice, a stoner's giggle and lively eyes that spent every day reading the future of strangers. Wisps of gray hair curled over his ears from beneath a leather cowboy hat. "I'm a Quarter rat," he said with evident pride.

A boy hopped past and was introduced as Adrian, Mike's seven-year-old son. At the next table sat Adrian's mother. "We get along fine," he said of his ex-wife. "You get into these things as adults you don't really have to be a child to get back out of them." Mike possessed a professional's stash of one-liners—some cliché, some quite good. He also had a distinct vantage point on the conflicting forces that swirled around what he called "our village," adding that the French Quarter was "like an old friend who's always broke. You can have a lot of fun with him but you're going to be paying." In contrast to the hopeful motivations of young entrepreneurs and teachers who had arrived in recent years, his story was similar to earlier generations of transplants, the outcasts seeking refuge from the rest of America who found the dysfunction and danger fair tradeoffs for the freedom and cheap living. "This is a wild city on both sides of the coin," he said. "Wild joy and wild violence. We say it's on a knife's edge—whenever one suffers, the other runs up to take its place."

Football fans weren't really his market. "That's great for the bars, for the hotels, but not for our business. They're not in a spiritual frame of mind. They've already had their group prayer." Mike wasn't particularly worried about the impact of the Super Bowl; he'd weathered earlier attempts to clean up the Quarter. The tarot card readers were protected, he said, by the First Amendment. "There's no permit. Freedom of speech. You shouldn't have to pay for your rights. I'm not selling anything." Because the law didn't recognize his readings as an actual service or saleable good, he wasn't required to pay taxes.

Nevertheless, tarot card readers were vulnerable to other attempts to regulate the neighborhood. In November, at the request of the Landrieu administration, Councilwoman Gisleson Palmer proposed a ban on stopping, standing or loitering in Jackson Square from 1:00 a.m. to 5:00 a.m. Pedestrians could still walk through, but selling fortunes or sleeping on benches would be illegal. "They were going to really cream us over, block us all out," Mike said. Some businesses supported the legislation. "Jackson Square is used twenty-four hours a day, and it gets abused and it gets trashed and it needs to be cleaned," said gallery owner and photographer Louis Sahuc. "Its not about anybody really. It's about keeping the city clean, and that's the end of the story."¹⁴⁹ The dispute reflected the complex economy of the square. Brass bands, artists and tarot readers worked under various permitting arrangements, while storeowners paid rent and expected city services. Tourists, musicians and vagrants used the same benches in a civic space that dated back to the origins of the city. Fortunately for the tarot readers, the ACLU of Louisiana stepped into the fray. "Shutting off public streets to public activity, the law just doesn't permit that," said the ACLU's Marjorie Esman, who bemoaned the city's attempts to make the Quarter a "Constitution Free Zone." Gisleson Palmer withdrew the ordinance, but weeks later, the council passed separate legislation as part of the Super Bowl preparations. Famous for its pungency, funky bars and colorful characters, the French Quarter would become a "Clean Zone."¹⁵⁰

According to the Super Bowl XLVII Permit and Code Enforcement Guide published by the mayor's office, the "Clean Zone" was a set of temporary regulations meant "to protect the quality of life of residents and assist businesses in thriving" during the week of the game and to "facilitate a tremendous positive economic impact on the City of New Orleans and the State of Louisiana through regulation and control" of the designated area. The boundaries stretched far outside the French Quarter and the entertainment district around the Superdome, extending into the MidCity, Bywater and Seventh Ward neighborhoods and across the river to Algiers, an even larger section of the city than the borders of the failed Hospitality Zone. Within that diverse landscape, the rules were specific. Street vending was prohibited, including the activities covered by the Mardi Gras permit rules. Tents, stages and any "wireless communication facilities" not approved by the NFL were banned. Only the league could authorize giveaways, coupons or free products. In the ultimate measure of control, the Clean Zone disallowed multiple forms of advertisement, including "[i]nflatables, cold air balloons, banners, pennants, flags, building wraps, A-frame signs, projected image signs, electronic variable message signs, and light emitting diode signs." Mobile advertising, including "signs on or attached to a vehicle, portable device or person," were forbidden unless the signs consisted of "at least 60% Super Bowl/NFL branding, look and feel, and no more than 40% third-party commercial identification." In effect, the NFL had the final say on any commercial image within four miles of the Superdome, an area that included the city's main business district and the heart of its tourism industry.

As *Gambit*'s Charles Maldanado noted, the Landrieu administration didn't draft the language of the Clean Zone.¹⁵¹ Indianapolis had enacted the same regulations for the previous year's game, and other host cities had used some form of temporary legislation. The New Orleans rules were striking for the size of their jurisdiction and the apparent willingness of the city to agree to everything the NFL requested. In its eagerness to please its guest, the administration made an impossible set of promises. The lack of consideration for the signage and profits of local businesses echoed the failures of the Hospitality Zone. Enforcement was hard to imagine, and in the middle of Mardi Gras, the regulations could be read as banning costumes. In another city, the relative lockdown of a few blocks near the stadium was conceivable. In New Orleans, the administration and the NFL faced social, economic and political challenges to the weeklong brand exercise.

For the time being, I sat in the Clean Zone, across from Mike the tarot reader, who giggled at the whole thing. The fools could try all they want—the Quarter wouldn't change. He'd seen legislation come and go like so many service workers and bohemians. "This is Tombstone," he said, "people running away from someplace else where they couldn't be who they are." Despite the renewed spotlight, New Orleans would always be a magnet for the abnormal. "You don't see a place that's so welcoming of oddballs. Any other place in the country, if you've got facial tattoos, you aren't getting a job. Here, I can't even count the number of bartenders and service people with facial tattoos."

The Clean Zone's authors, I later reflected, likely hadn't considered the "branding, look and feel" of facial tattoos.

The machinery of Bourbon Street chugged to life at 4:00 p.m. Delivery trucks hugged the curbs outside restaurants, where waiters and dishwashers exchanged greetings as their shifts changed. In the daiquiri shops, the music was already too loud, but bartenders still had time to wash dishes and check their phones. Barkers prepared for happy hour; a guitar player passed with a case strapped to his back. End-of-work cigarettes were lit from the tip of final off-duty cigarettes. Late afternoon was the last respite before the storm of nighttime revelries.

In the doorways of strip clubs, women lounged in shiny bathing suits, chatting and waving to men who paused to consider the bare skin in broad daylight. It was an exchange nearly as old as New Orleans, a remnant of the brothels and "cribs" that had fueled the city's earliest tourism. However clean the zone, the most prominent commercial image on Bourbon Street was a half-naked woman. Television networks could find ideal backdrops throughout the Quarter, but much of this famous street was decidedly unsuitable for national broadcast.

The window of one club, Rick's Saloon, featured a swinging mannequin whose legs kicked in and out of the first-floor window. Rick's doubled as a

John Amos at his apartment on Bourbon Street. *Photo by Zack Smith Photography.*

sports bar, so the mannequin wore a referee's shirt. Entering the chalky air of the front room, I said hello to the bartender and then passed through a set of saloon doors to the club's main space. Then I climbed on stage.

I remained clothed. The DJ had waved for me to join him, as he usually did when I stopped by. We'd known each other about six months, during which time I'd written a magazine profile about him that earned my welcome in his tiny booth. Cramped with CD players and a sound system, the carpeted cloister offered a unique view of the strip club. Today, it's tables were mostly empty. On Saturdays, DJ John Amos came on at 3:00 p.m. and stayed until closing. As usual, he was optimistic about the evening and foresaw big crowds for the week of the Super Bowl. Plus, he was a 49ers fan.

Amos grew up in Bakersfield, California, where he sang in metal bands with friends who later played with Korn and Limp Bizkit. His life took a turn after a conversation at Denny's: "A friend of mine who was a doorman at clubs, he told me, 'I know you do your band thing, but what needs to happen…I'm going to give you a job, set you up so you can make your money and do your band thing.' Sounds cool." The work was mostly errands and menial tasks until the club's manager fired the DJ and asked Amos if he was interested. "He's like, 'You ever DJ before? I'm like, 'No.' He's like, 'They make a lot of money,' and I'm like, 'OK, let's go.'" Fifteen years later, he had stories of European tours ("we didn't want to fill the club with all Parisian girls because the Parisian girls tend to be prostitutes") and industry casualties ("this manager's watching gay porn, and I'm like, this chick's having a fucking brain hemorrhage"). After stints in Las Vegas and Los Angles, he hit New Orleans in July 2006, less than a year after Katrina. The city was in tatters, but his industry was bulletproof. "You're always going to have people who're going to need food," he said. "They're always going to wipe their ass, they're always going to need a casket to die in and they're always going to need some titties to look at. That's the thing you can always bank on: the vices of people."

Substantial muttonchops framed his hawkish face as he leaned into the microphone: "She's straight out of Miami and wants to show you her sunshine. Let's give it up, fellas, for Stacy!" In a lime string bikini, the dancer began her routine by spinning her raven hair wildly, her breasts shuddering lose as she untied her top. More dancers would arrive in a few hours. Throughout the night, Amos would repeatedly descend the stage and walk to a waitress station to consult the "rotation," a list showing available dancers and those working the VIP rooms. He'd announce the available names, play their songs and then move them to the second stage and call another name. "You really want to create a wave with the look of your girls," he said. "If you've got ten girls and you've got five blondes, four with black hair and a redhead, you want to go blonde, dark, blonde, dark—you don't want to just line them all up. You control that." Each girl got three songs until the rotation grew to seven, when he'd cut two songs. When the rotation reached twenty, a dancer performed for one song on each stage.

Television screens switched to ESPN filled the wall to our right, part of the sports bar theme that included mounted deer heads, pennants and waitresses in football jerseys. Amos wore a dark suit and a tight ponytail. Since we met, I'd grown to appreciate the intensity of his self-control. His last drink was six years ago. Other than weed and vitamins, he relied on a competitive streak to pull fourteen-hour shifts.

"It's the mindset of, I'm going to outwork you right now," he said. "And you're going to watch it, and it's going to suck because I'm going to watch it fuck with your head right now." His time on the road gave him a battle-tested veteran's confidence, and there was little romance in his view of the Quarter. "It's a shark tank filled with minnows, and when you bring in sharks from other regions, we eat everybody alive. And I hate to say that, because I think the people of Louisiana really work hard, and they're smart people. But they're not me. I've been through some shit, and I've been homeless before. Not because of a hurricane but because of hurricane me."

This was how you survived in the French Quarter.

CHAPTER 12
JANUARY 28, 2013
(SIX DAYS TO GO)

"WHAT IT LOOKS LIKE TO WIN"

The tent erected next to Union Passenger Terminal had a translucent roof that allowed the sunshine to fall more gently on the heads of the audience. Potted palms and cords of yellow, green and purple balloons trimmed the interior space, where few seats remained. Guests continued to arrive, most of them men and women in business suits. Dressed in gray uniforms, a group of Regional Transit Authority employees occupied a section of the seats closest to the stage. Assorted cameramen stood in the tent's rear, their backs to the new streetcar stop, where members of the St. Augustine Marching Band warmed up. It was a vivid Monday morning, the first day of the Super Bowl week and the official opening of the Loyola Avenue streetcar.

As a choir took the stage, I ran into Warren Bell, the city's first African American news anchor and a longtime public relations consultant, here today to record the ceremony for the RTA. Now in his sixties, Bell was a charmer who, over lunch, could offer some of the better political analysis in town, with reminiscences that doubled as critiques of both black and white political establishments. Today, though, he was on the job and upbeat about the city.

"The timing is so perfect, being the day after the two football teams arrived for the Super Bowl," he said. "Y'know, they thought this would be ready actually a few months sooner. But how better to kick it off when you have network crews coming? Because they're going to be sharing

Mayor Mitch Landrieu joins the parade on Loyola Avenue. *Photo courtesy of New Orleans Regional Transit Authority.*

this information with their audiences, and I just think it's a win-win for everybody." He worked for the RTA during the infamously delayed Canal Street line project, and the Loyola project was exemplary. "They had some glitches when they discovered underground channels of water that the Sewage and Water Board had built over a hundred years ago, but it's all good now."[152] Construction crews encountered another submerged obstacle: a giant cypress tree that required special equipment to remove. As hang-ups to progress in New Orleans, an old drainage technique and the petrified roots seemed poetic. Begun in June 2012, the Loyola line opened on this day, almost seven months past its planned completion date, a fact that went unmentioned in the morning's remarks. We were in the tent to celebrate the streetcar, the Super Bowl and, it soon became clear, the new New Orleans.

After the choir's performance, RTA director Justin Augustine opened the ceremony with promises of ceremonies to come. "This is the beginning of a brand-new era of streetcar expansion that will continue the revitalization of a once-dormant corridor," said Augustine, pointing to plans to continue the line down North Rampart Street and St. Claude Avenue. The federal government had already denied another Tiger Grant for that project, which instead would be funded through a $79 million bond sale. During a brief moment of candor in 2011, Augustine expressed fears that the St. Claude line would spark gentrification in adjacent neighborhoods.[153] Now he introduced the mayor.

Landrieu began his remarks about the streetcar with a nod to the Super Bowl. "First I want to recognize what I'm gonna start calling the first couple of New Orleans, James Carville and Mary Matalin. James is somewhere—there he is." Earlier, I had spotted Carville on his way into the bus station. Now he stood on the sidewalk holding his bottle of juice aloft. "Hey Mr. Mayor," Landrieu joked. He thanked the couple for their host committee efforts. "The entire world is going to be watching us this week, and they really quarterbacked that effort." It was a telling choice for Landrieu's first recognition: Carville and Matalin had little to do with this occasion, but the habits of one hundred days had fused the Super Bowl with the federal project. Next in line for thanks were Landrieu's deputy mayors, council members, state legislators and U.S. Department of Transportation secretary Ray LaHood, who sat to the mayor's right. Landrieu directed his comments to the secretary, but as he spoke, I couldn't help but wonder about his targeted audience.

"Mr. Secretary," he said, "this week the city of New Orleans is on top of the world and is beginning to lead on every list that really makes a difference on moving the needle for the young men and women that were sitting on this stage, whether it's healthcare reform, transportation, infrastructure, education reform, government reform. This city and the people of this city are, in my opinion, manifesting to the people of America what resilience and hard work and partnership, breaking down partisan lines, geographical lines—the people of New Orleans are showing America what it looks like to win."

Rumors floated in some circles that Landrieu harbored gubernatorial aspirations, hardly farfetched given his experience in statewide office and the growing sense that New Orleans was finally on track. Today's emphasis on citywide progress along with his defense of the federal stimulus plan gave the streetcar opening a more valedictory tone. If, as Warren Bell claimed, the national cameras were on the ground, the mayor met them with a bold plug for the new New Orleans.

The project was a partnership between the federal, state and city agencies that provided "a good example of what America is going to need to win the future. If we want to out-build, out-educate and out-innovate the rest of the world, then somebody has gotta find a way, shine the light and create the model. And Mr. Secretary, with your help, I believe that we have done this. This streetcar line is not just a red box on a rail going to nowhere. This streetcar line is a pathway to prosperity for the rest of America that, when taken together, not only produced jobs in terms of construction projects but also laid a foundation of government investment that attracted $2 billion of the private sector that helped rebuild a place called New Orleans, which is now going to be the focus of five thousand media folks from around the world."

Introduced by the mayor, Secretary LaHood embraced the coincidence of big game and big project. "So this is a win-win," he said. "This is a Super Bowl Sunday on Monday. That's what this is—that's what we're celebrating. This is the Super Bowl Sunday on Monday on Super Bowl week for the people of New Orleans." Bulky, with heavy eyebrows and silver hair around his temples, LaHood looked like a party boss. Along with his own defense of the stimulus, the former congressman from Peoria offered praise for Landrieu: "He gets up every day and tries to figure out what to do for New Orleans, how to make things happen. When we decided to invest $45 million in this project, it was because we had great trust in the mayor and his leadership and his vision." It was an odd admission. After all, the Tiger Grant application was submitted during the Nagin administration. The selection announcement came just nine days after Landrieu's victory in 2010; his inauguration came almost three months later.

On a day of congratulations, such details went unnoticed. Other officials made remarks, including U.S. representative Cedric Richmond, who mused that LaHood was here often enough: "I think he deserves an apartment in the Pontabla." The city owned several apartments in the historic building on Jackson Square; official use was a longtime point of speculation, thus Richmond's jest. "Since the press is here, that's probably not a suggestion we'll follow up on." City council president Jackie Clarkson, a steadfast Landrieu supporter, said she "thought it was very significant that I was given James Carville's seat—I thought that was important. I'm thrilled to sit by Mary Matalin and say to both of them, 'Thank you for what you're doing for our city.'"

RTA board chairwoman Barbara Major was one of the last to speak. A nonprofit veteran, Major had been appointed to the board by Nagin and elevated to chair in 2010 by Landrieu. She greeted the audience with exuberance: "To all my naysayers: kiss my…ring! Scared you, didn't I?" A few people laughed. In 2011, Major came under criticism after a review by the Louisiana Office of Community Development showed that she and her son had received $250,000 in low-interest loans from a nonprofit finance agency that employed Major.[154] The findings didn't halt her ascent to RTA chair. Now, she praised the progressive policies of the agency, thanked her workers and joked about another $40 million to cover the next stage of streetcar expansion. "I put on my good suit," she said. "People know I'm a jeans type of girl, but I heard Secretary LaHood was coming to town. And any brother that has $48 million, I want to say, the congressman was very, very professional. I'm just going to ask you outright: you got $48 million more? Cause we will show you what to do with it!" After the chairwoman concluded with a promise to meet LaHood later, Landrieu took the podium to chuckle, "Barbara, you bad."

As ribbon cuttings go, this morning was interesting—part grand boasts for the national audience, part local corruption humor. Carville sipped a cold drink outside Chep Morrison's rail terminal as Landrieu declared the city an exemplar of innovation and reform. On the first day of Super Bowl week, the new New Orleans was on full display under a dazzling blue sky.

The mayor asked that we cut the ceremony short: Secretary LaHood had been called back to Washington but wanted to see the streetcar's first ride. "Please tell President Obama when you see him at 4:30 how much we love him and how much we thank him for investing in a great city," Landrieu said. "New Orleans, let's roll!"

The officials boarded two brand-new red streetcars. The media and other guests clustered along the curb, while some of the cameramen crouched on the track. The front car began to move, Landrieu pulled on a bell, and the new streetcar line was born. As the cars rolled out of the station and onto Loyola Avenue, I noticed Ronal Serpas in plainclothes on the sidewalk, a woman by his side. The police chief didn't follow the rest of us as we walked behind the red boxes on the pathway to prosperity.

In their purple uniforms and knightly gold helmets, the St. Augustine High School Marching 100 kept pace with the streetcars, filling Loyola with thunderous, imperial sound. For a band used to Mardi Gras parades, the .8-mile route to Canal Street was a breeze. At Julia Street, I noticed the advertisements on the side of the station shelter. "New Jersey: A State of Resilience" referred to October's devastating Hurricane Sandy. The ads were part of a campaign paid for by Choose New Jersey, an initiative of the state's economic development agency, which sought to assure the nation—in this case, Super Bowl visitors—that New Jersey was still open for business. Ironically, New Jersey was the host of the following year's Super Bowl. Sports would play a role in another recovery.

We passed the post office and the Hyatt before pausing at Poydras. Police escorts halted traffic so the streetcars could pass. It was there that I noticed

Landrieu hop off the lead car and join the Marching 100 as they crossed Poydras. He threw his arm around a band director, shook hands and waved and then jogged across the neutral ground toward city hall. Photos of the moment ran with local and national coverage of the event. Energetic, embraceable and on the move—this was the image of the mayor as Super Bowl week began.

The week that followed brought more dramatic images and countless celebrations as the city swelled with football fans, cameras and celebrities. Amid the festivities, the conflicts that defined the previous ninety-four days failed to recede. As the new New Orleans took center stage, strange new settings popped up to highlight the contrasts amid the spotlights. The preceding weeks were ever more anxious, but now the world was here. I entered the fray to catch as much of the action as possible. It was a raucous experience.

The day after the streetcar unveiling, the White House announced Ray LaHood's resignation. "The bottom line is I've been in public service now for thirty-five years," LaHood said. "I believe in going out while they're applauding." An hour later, CNN announced that Carville and Matalin were leaving the network. "I was told that they wanted the contributors to be more available—essentially, closer to Washington. I'm not always available—I don't live there," Carville told Politico. "I'm totally cool with it." NOLA.com reported that Carville "hinted that Mayor Mitch Landrieu may have another project for him" after his host committee duties ended. Matalin e-mailed a Politico reporter: "Just saw your piece. In a whirling dervish of the best Super Bowl/Mardi Gras ever! Agree with everything James said. You didn't ask, so I am not sending my current projects. I loved my time in and out at CNN the many lifelong friendships made there. Hope you can make Jazz Fest this year. *Laissez les bon temps rouler.*"[155]

CHAPTER 13
JANUARY 29, 2013
(FIVE DAYS TO GO)

"WE'RE NOT LIVING IN A COMMERCIAL"

The headquarters of Occupy New Orleans was buried in an unmarked industrial space on Toulouse Street, next to a tire shop a few miles from city hall. The tire shop made its policy clear on a wooden sign: "NO REFUNDS, TIRES SOLD AS IS." I arrived at dusk as a strong wind began to sway the power lines. The block barely registered as a commercial area, much less the home base of someone who took on the NFL and won.

Inside, the space felt vast—maybe thirty yards long and ten yards wide. It was dimly lit and suitably ramshackle, full of bookshelves, worktables, old protest signs, pallets, tarps and couches. Along one wall, several small office spaces doubled as crash pads. In the center of the room was a circle of chairs lit from above by castoff traffic lights draped with Mardi Gras beads. Tonight, seven men and two women gathered for a general assembly. Three of the men appeared to be in their late twenties, while the other four were more grizzled. A pretty young woman with a vivid tattoo on her thigh served as note taker, occasionally leaning over to kiss one of the younger men. With the odd collection of chairs and battered rugs, the gathering resembled an open-mic poetry night or an AA meeting. I sat on a long bench and waited as the assembly plotted its strategy for a Super Bowl Sunday protest. They agreed to a theme, "Sponsored by Corporate Greed," but other details needed ironing out. The anarchists argued politely.

Occupy New Orleans had a unique history in the movement. Protesters marched in early October 2011 as part of the national wave of demonstrations inspired by Occupy Wall Street. The local contingent set up in Duncan Plaza, the park adjacent to city hall and where, in 2006 and 2007, homeless encampments brought attention to the plight of displaced New Orleanians. The plaza remained a magnet for transients, who soon mixed in with the protestors. But one month into the occupation, a man was found dead in a tent, apparently two days after he'd expired.[156] Along with three fatalities in other cities, the death gave traction to those who claimed the Occupy movement was derelict and unsafe. Landrieu was careful to avoid a visible conflict, even providing portable toilets for the protestors. But by early December, city officials had begun warning the occupiers that they'd need to move on. The police entered the square on December 6, and the removal was peaceful. "You can see from the way this was conducted it was very different from what happened around the country," said the mayor.[157]

Tonight at the Occupy headquarters, a plan emerged. The marchers would bear crucifixes emblazoned with "Super Bowl" as they made their way across the French Quarter en route to the Superdome. Someone mentioned a counter protest of the Westboro Baptist Church, the radical evangelical group known for its "God Hates Fags" messaging, reputedly planning to demonstrate on game day. There was general agreement that the Landrieu administration, the NFL and its sponsors were agents of the 1 percent who sought the further corporatization of America. With the whole world watching, Occupy could deliver a counterpoint to the fanfare.

When the assembly ended, one of the members, Tara Jill Ciccarone, greeted me. We had mutual friends, people she'd attended graduate school with when she arrived here in 1999 from Connecticut. She wanted to smoke, so we walked outside, where I reclined in an old car seat under a purplish sky to listen to Tara Jill's story.

News of the Clean Zone reached her in mid-December. "I was researching the taxi driver situation and them having to fix their cars, and then I saw something about the Clean Zone," she said. "I thought, 'Let me put this on my list of things to research.'" Tara Jill lived near the Fairgrounds and was familiar with the annual ban on itinerant vendors during Jazz Fest. As buzz about the Super Bowl built on Twitter, she downloaded the new ordinance. "When I saw the size of it—that it extended to Algiers—and the specific details about mobile signs, including signs attached to one's person, and that all signs had to be 60 percent NFL branding…I was really furious." For Tara Jill, the zone represented the very forces Occupy opposed: corporate interests that fleeced the public for their own gain to the detriment of employees and small businesses. It was movement orthodoxy, but her reaction included fears I'd heard elsewhere about both the game and the new New Orleans. "Right away, I saw it as Mitch Landrieu and the City of New Orleans and the Super Bowl host committee and these corporate sponsors trying really hard to show a certain version of New Orleans that will sell products. And that money is not really going to go into the pockets of the locals."

In December, they held a general assembly. Tara Jill explained, "I proposed that we do something about it. Justin [Warren, her boyfriend and fellow Occupy member] had the idea of making a stencil that looks like a sign that says, 'This Shirt Is Illegal,' because mobile signage, including signage attached to one's person, would've been illegal in the clean zone." She and Warren were regular attendees of the Music and Cultural Coalition of New Orleans (MACCNO) meetings held at musician Kermit Ruffins's restaurant during the "War on Music" controversy. At a December meeting, a representative from the ACLU noticed Tara Jill's "illegal" T-shirt and asked about Occupy's plans for the Super Bowl. "I said, 'I want to hold signs saying, Super Bowl XLVII: Sponsored by Greed, but I don't want to get arrested.'"

On January 24, the ACLU filed suit against Landrieu and Serpas on behalf of Tara Jill and a Bourbon Street preacher, Troy Bohn, who regularly donned T-shirts reading, "I Love Jesus" and "Ask Me How Jesus Changed My Life." Tara Jill stated that she intended to carry signs with messages like "Your Tax Dollars Working to Help the Rich Get Richer" and "New Orleans: Incarceration Capital of the World" but that she feared arrest. The suit alleged that the Clean Zone would "impose an unconstitutional time, place or manner restriction on First Amendment activity." In a statement, ACLU of Louisiana executive director Marjorie Esman put it plainly: "Even the Super Bowl isn't an excuse to suspend the First Amendment. The founders of our country didn't intend our rights to be suspended for a football game."[158]

Yesterday, the two sides agreed on a settlement. The Clean Zone "shall apply to commercial activity only and shall in no way be applied or enforced to encumber or burden noncommercial expressive activity." The agreement struck down the "60% Super Bowl/NFL branding requirement" and the "40% third-party commercial identification" restriction. The boundaries remained the same, but protests, Mardi Gras costumes and offensive signs could flourish therein. "I think the city crafted language that went further than they intended," said Esman. "I think that's why the city was so quick to reach a settlement."[159] In its statement, the city asserted that free speech was never the issue and that the Clean Zone was meant to bar illegal vending and protect residents from intrusive tents and temporary structures.

Tara Jill Ciccarone on Super Bowl Sunday, 2013. *Photo courtesy of Occupy the Stage.*

It seemed like a minor skirmish. In a city filled with independent spirits, small businesses and various forms of personal expression, the enforcement of the original Clean Zone was impossible and, most likely, never planned. The city simply agreed to the NFL's request. The league needed a receptive environment for official sponsors to take advantage of their agreements with the NFL to market their products unencumbered. As the city noted, there was nothing new about this concept. Complications arose because officials failed to take into account the many nuances, factions and circumstances that could form challenges to that agreement; perhaps the administration was preoccupied by its myriad challenges. In the rush to comply, no one brought up Mardi Gras costumes or the rights of Saints fans in the French Quarter to scrawl "Fuck Goodell" on their windows. The NFL demanded much from each city it occupied, but rarely did it tackle the question of a Bourbon Street preacher's right to proselytize.

Tara Jill put out her cigarette on the sole of a weathered cowboy boot. We repaired inside to a humid couch, where I asked if she was satisfied with the settlement. Yes, she said, but the game was larger than the Clean Zone. "I can't believe that Mitch Landrieu can say with a straight face that they want to show how far New Orleans has come with Verizon Super Bowl Boulevard and CBS in Jackson Square, calling it 'Super Bowl Park.' That is not showing an authentic New Orleans to the world. It's showing corporate sponsorship." The advertisements obscured the real issues. "The condition of the jail, the condition of the schools, the condition of the roads, the budget for the police…I've been a victim of burglaries before where I've had to wait hours for the police to come." At the very least, the settlement gave Occupy, too, a chance to take advantage of the Super Bowl spotlight.

"Now that we can hold these signs in this clean zone," she said, "hopefully it will raise awareness about these issues. People who come here to visit [and] people who watch TV will realize that it's not all perfect and pretty like an airport. I think this can get some media attention on these smaller local issues that are really important. I think that's a big win for anyone who wants to see change and who wants to see people wake up. Hopefully it will be inspiring for people who live here to realize, wow, we're not living in a commercial."

It sounded like a great theme for a protest. She called out to Warren.

"Hey Justin! We're not this city's commercial!"

CHAPTER 14
JANUARY 30, 2013
(FOUR DAYS TO GO)

RESIDUAL EFFECTS

At the New Orleans Morial Convention Center, the commercials were everywhere. Today marked the start of the "NFL Experience," the league's five-day "interactive theme park," which was officially "Driven by GMC." To experience the NFL, you first needed to express your preference in SUVs on touch screens mounted next to brand-new Yukons, Denalis and Acadias. In the multiple-choice questionnaire, I repeatedly selected the "crossover" Acadia as a tribute to the French Canadian exiles who settled in south Louisiana in the eighteenth century. The name was among the more subtle syntheses of product and culture on display this week.

The morning's cold rain defused the outdoor festivities, so I gladly accepted two free tickets and brought along Justin Micaroni from Handsome Willy's. Like millions of American boys, we'd both grown up on professional football. As we passed the twenty-foot purple banners at the entrance, childlike grins crossed our faces. Here, finally, was the Super Bowl circus. Music boomed from somewhere deep in the cavernous hall, spotlights roamed the walls and families strolled across freshly laid carpet. Giant cutouts of players dangled from the ceiling above life-sized, headless mannequins that allowed kids to stick their faces atop Troy Polamalu's body. We passed through a replica of an NFL locker room, perused a display of Super Bowl rings and watched the NFL Network's personalities record their show. Every fifteen minutes, a voice called out the names of current and former players available for autographs. Advertised by the league as a party for locals, the NFL Experience featured the Saintsations cheerleaders on the Entertainment Stage and various reminders of the 2010 championship. Apparently, we'd just missed the delivery of the Lombardi Trophy, ushered in by the St. Augustine Marching Band and former Saints running back Deuce McCallister. A line of fans waited to pose on stage next to a black-and-gold case containing the chrome figurine. Tickets were twenty-five dollars for adults and twenty dollars for kids, a relatively affordable way to join the Super Bowl magic.

The abundance of corporate logos was no surprise. The Super Bowl was as much an advertisement as it was a game, a premium opportunity for the NFL's sponsors to reach the biggest viewing audience. The NFL Experience provided an opportunity to align family fun with constant advertising. The interactive games included sprinting contests on a field sponsored by Under Armour and kicking contests by Visa. The premier brand in this fan's paradise was, of course, the league, which this year advertised its concerns. Visitors ran through tackling dummies provided by Play60, the NFL's anti-childhood obesity initiative. A Health & Safety display featured a timeline of rule changes, part of the league "Always Striving to Make the Game Safer." Along with photos of safer youth leagues were two video screens, on which former Cardinals quarterback Kurt Warner discussed the NFL's precautionary stance. Saints fans were likely to see the irony: Warner was one of the players allegedly targeted in 2009 by the Bountygate program.

Local iconography fused with the corporate sponsors in eclectic forms of product placement. Fans waited beneath a French Quarter–esque balcony for a run at the Drew Brees Quarterback Challenge, presented by Pepsi. The challenge: "Test your throwing skills to help Pepsi and the Brees Dream Foundation support music education in the City of New Orleans." Volunteers in teal Tostitos shirts gave instructions to a gaggle of kids who sat under a cartoonish backdrop of the city's skyline, including a jeweled Superdome, two flying Saints logos and a black-and-gold shotgun house. Numerous Tostitos banners promised that "We Kneaux How to Party." On the touch screen for a slot machine–like contest, the rolling symbols were the logos of Pepsi and Tostitos and a navy blue box simply labeled "JAZZ." There was no shortage of touch screens, all asking for your e-mail address, your Facebook or Twitter account and any other important pieces of information for advertisers. "Authorize Visa Super Bowl Make It Epic to Use Your Account?" asked one.

Visa oversaw the NFL Shop, an immense merchandise outlet in the convention center's Great Hall. Team jerseys ran in a seemingly endless rack down one wall, past racks of sweatshirts, water bottles and Mardi

ONE HUNDRED DAYS IN AMERICA'S COOLEST HOT SPOT

Scene from the 1984 World's Fair. *Photo courtesy of Creative Commons.*

Gras beads in team colors. Men and boys paced the aisles, many of them already swaddled in team gear. The NFL Experience lasted only a week; souvenirs were warranted. Camera phones came out to capture an eerie display near the cash registers. Positioned on wide, illuminated steps were muscular mannequins in helmets, pads and spikes, one for each of the thirty-two NFL franchises. Their arms were deep brown, their faces hidden behind facemasks and their pose suggested a collective pre-attack inhale. Here was a frozen army, a monument of professional football that doubled as a merchandise display. Not for the first time this week, I thought of the 1984 World's Fair. The commercial centurions stood on the fair's turf.

The 1984 World's Fair made the convention center possible and vice versa. Both served as visions for recharging the city's economy. Just as the Superdome promised the city a silver bullet to ride past Atlanta and Houston, the convention center was cast as an urgent weapon in the competition for New South superiority in the convention business. The new stadium was open less than two years when a veritable panic set in: New Orleans could not keep up. In 1976, the Georgia World Congress Center opened in Atlanta, with 350,000 square feet of exhibition space compared to the combined 250,000 in the Superdome and the Rivergate convention center, opened on Canal Street in 1968. By 1977, mayoral candidate Dutch Morial and his opponents were debating the means to fund a new facility. The state legislature created the New Orleans Exhibition Hall Authority the following year and tasked it with finding money and a location. Like its heirs in the 2010 Hospitality Task Force, the authority hired consultants, who confirmed the dire straits. Though New Orleans ranked fifth nationally in conventions attracted each year, the report by the Real Estate Research Corporation (RERC) pointed to new facilities in Atlanta and Dallas that already siphoned off business. Convention goers loved New Orleans, but its sites were problematic. "I consider the Superdome an excellent sports facility but a very poor convention facility," a representative from the World of Concrete Exposition told RERC. "The Rivergate is truly a fine exhibit facility but is too small." RERC calculated an economic impact of $300 million in the first year of a new 340,000-square-foot convention center. Inaction risked disaster. "If we don't do something, we'll be in the backwaters before you know it," said Ray Liuzza of the Hotel-Motel Association.[160]

Other voices joined the chorus. Lester Kabacoff was the developer of a new Hilton on the riverfront above Canal Street, then a forlorn neighborhood of dilapidated warehouses and old rail lines. A native New Yorker, Kabacoff looked at the riverfront and envisioned the next Soho or San Francisco's Fisherman's Wharf, where renovated industrial properties created vibrant residential and leisure spaces. He was a natural supporter of the convention center. "Rivergate should never have been built in the first place—it was too small for the city's needs before the cement on it was dry," Kabacoff argued in 1978. "If we're going to be the convention capital of the nation, we need this space." In fact, Kabacoff had just the space, a swath of riverfront property and the long-term leases for wharves that could accommodate the new facility and, if possible, a world's fair.[161]

In 1978, voters approved a hotel-motel tax to generate $15 million toward a new convention center. The following year, the city granted the Exhibition Hall Authority a $1-per-year lease on thirteen acres adjacent to Kabacoff's holdings on the river. The Morial administration also secured a $17 million grant from the U.S. Department of Housing and Urban Development, now led by former mayor Moon Landrieu. When the authority approached the state for a $30 million bond issue in 1980, Governor Dave Treen demanded that the new building serve as the Louisiana pavilion of the World's Fair. By 1981, the desperately needed convention center was on the horizon, thanks to new taxes, state bonds and federal grants. The hall would serve as the centerpiece of the World's Fair, whose organizers assured skeptics that the exposition would leave behind a signature capital project. The World's Fair needed the convention center, the convention center needed the World's Fair and, according to their backers, New Orleans needed them both.

When the organizers of the World's Fair flew to Paris in April 1981 to meet with the Bureau of International Expositions, they had no competition for the 1984 World's Fair. Knoxville had already secured the 1982 fair, Vancouver had 1986, Los Angeles would host the Olympics in 1984 and many thought such expositions were on the decline. The planners were undeterred. Their consultants predicted a $2 billion impact from a projected fifteen million visitors. The message to the world, according to the consultants' report, was "that New Orleans has ceased to slumber and is ready to be one of the world's great 21st-century cities."[162] The organizers were represented in Paris by fair general manger Petr Spurney, a veteran of the 1974 Expo in Spokane and the 1980 Winter Olympics in Lake Placid. Described by the *Times-Picayune* as a "highly paid exposition professional who goes from one international project to another," Spurney was emphatic in his self-regard and his faith in the fair's impact, telling the paper, "Let's make it significant! Let's make it go down in history! New Orleans is the place and 1984 is the time!"[163]

The federal government was not so sure. The fair needed the official blessing of the Reagan administration and a projected $25 million in federal funding, but after crunching the numbers, the Commerce Department expressed doubts. Presidential support was contingent on $26 million in private investment. Kabacoff and others reached out to Coke, Delta, Texaco and Louisiana's biggest companies, who agreed to back bank loans. The quick capital and Spurney's last-minute appeal won over the administration, but the commitment was capped at just $10 million. Unfazed, Spurney flew to Paris and received final approval for New Orleans.

Despite the spindly financing, the fair's construction budget quickly ballooned as the planners added more projects and attractions. Revenue failed to keep pace as corporate sponsors committed to the Summer Olympics, marketing efforts began late and season ticket sales lagged. By February 1984, with only three months before the scheduled opening, the organizers ran out of money. Kabacoff called newly elected governor Edwin Edwards to plead for a $10 million loan. "You've got to be kidding," Edwards responded.[164] The legislature approved the loan and eventually kicked in another $15 million, but the federal government was not so generous. Reagan's tepid support continued as official invites to other nations failed to go out on time, and in an unprecedented rebuff for a world's fair, the president decided not to attend the fair's opening day. On May 11, 1984, more than two thousand members of the national and local media arrived for a preview and found construction incomplete. The reviews were deadly. Though eighty-two thousand people came for opening day, fewer than thirty thousand arrived for day two. Within a week, the organizers realized something was wrong: the world wasn't interested in the fair. The fragile budget began to topple. Vendors and utility bills went unpaid, lawsuits bloomed and Spurney soon faced charges of nepotism and fraud.

The irony: locals loved the fair. Intended to attract tourists, the star-crossed expo delivered an outrageously overdone carnival enjoyed mostly by New Orleanians. For six months, every night ended in fireworks. Willie Nelson, Tom Jones and Julio Iglesias were among the performers at an amphitheater designed by Frank Gehry. The city's many Catholics toured a "Treasures of the Vatican" exhibit. There were synchronized swimmers, water rides and cheap souvenirs sold from the Chinese Pavilion. People partied at nightclubs, a German beer hall and the traditional jazz venue, Reunion Hall. And if they got too inebriated, a giant glowing heart called them to the first aid station. The Louisiana Folklife Pavilion brought the music and culture of Cajun Louisiana, with crafts displays and live bands. A giant exhibit of Louisiana artwork included studio space, where fairgoers could watch artists work. Reagan skipped out, but Bob Hope and Dick Cavett performed together, and David Letterman interviewed visitors at the gates. A gondola carried passengers high above the Mississippi to a landing in Algiers, while a monorail snaked through the fairgrounds. Plans to extend the monorail permanently to the Superdome and Armstrong Park were among the casualties of the finance crunch. Years later, most New Orleanians who attended the World's Fair still raved about the attractions.[165]

Poverty was cited when the organizers searched for clues to explain the silent turnstiles. Perhaps the fifteen-dollar tickets were too expensive in a city where one-fifth of the population lived in poverty. Some pointed to the fair's attempts to attract upscale visitors in big cities in the Northeast rather than middle-class tourists in neighboring states. A world's fair was meant for families, but families didn't typically visit New Orleans. "We are very slim on the station wagon tourist," said one analyst. The organizers rued the disastrous media cover from the *Wall Street Journal* and NBC News. Others blamed the summer heat. Management seemed to be the biggest issue. Red flags were ignored or answered with additional attractions or last-minute loans. "Each time," the urbane Spurney said later of the multiple crises, "we said, 'Ah, the magic of New Orleans will offset all this.'"[166]

Magic was not enough. In August, Spurney told reporters he hoped to keep the fair's losses to $50 million. In November, the fair declared bankruptcy, with $81 million in debt and investors' losses of $41 million. The final day was bittersweet. The largest crowds of the exposition horded souvenirs and memorabilia, watched a replica of a Viking ship sail down the river and witnessed fair officials greet counterparts from Vancouver and Japan at a ceremony to pass the "spirit of the fair." In the Louisiana pavilion, the last of that exhibit's three million total visitors boarded the *Louisiana Journey*, a boat ride through a "Disney-like swamp, bayou shack, and plantation house."[167]

The Louisiana pavilion was located inside the fair's Great Hall, which enjoyed better prospects than the fair's organizers: it became Hall A of the New Orleans Convention Center. On January 18, 1985, the facility opened its doors to welcome its first guests, the ten thousand delegates of the Helicopter Association International. Members of the city council were present to cut the ribbon on the $94 million project. "It's almost a miracle to see the place really functioning with a convention in here, after all the work done over the past seven years," said Frank Keevers, director of the Exhibition Hall Authority.[168]

Other pavilions had varying fates. Amid the wreckage of multiple lawsuits, the fair's bankruptcy allowed developers to buy up the leftover buildings on the cheap. The United States Pavilion, scorned by the Reagan administration, was built for $5 million and auctioned off for $130,000. The International Pavilion and China Pavilion, which cost $9 million to build, sold for $2.7 million to the company that developed them into the Riverwalk mall on land owned by Lester Kabacoff.[169] Kabacoff's son, Pres, began the redevelopment of the neighborhood near the fair site, turning the former German Beer Hall into the Fibre Mills, one of the first apartment buildings in what came to be known as the Warehouse District.

The Warehouse District was often cited as one of the fair's "residual effects." Lawsuits and investigations were still ongoing when, in May 1985, a group of supporters gathered to toast the fair's positive impact on the neighborhood. "Riverfront Development: A Catalyst for Recovery" headlined columnist Allan Katz's interview with the organizers. According to Katz, "The hopes of the early 1980s that New Orleans was about to take a permanent place as one of the leading economic centers of the Sun Belt have mostly faded, at least for the moment." But the Riverwalk and new residential developments were signs of new life. In the meantime, one of the party's organizers admitted, "I really have to grit my teeth when I hear some people say that New Orleans has become an economic disaster."[170]

In almost thirty years, with the exception of a fateful week in 2005, no one called the convention center a disaster. Today, the facility was the sixth largest in the United States. The Exhibition Hall Authority was flush with cash, as evidenced in its $20 million offer during the Hospitality District negotiations. During the 2011–12 fiscal year, the authority collected more than $24 million in hotel-motel taxes.[171] The NFL Shop marked the public unveiling of the Great Hall, reopened after a $52 million renovation funded by excess revenue originally dedicated for upriver expansion that stalled after Katrina.

The 2013 Super Bowl faced few of the risks that ensnared the 1984 World's Fair. The NFL was a powerful brand, able to attract its own fans and corporate sponsors, regardless of the location. There would be no surprises at the turnstiles. The host city needed to provide adequate facilities, either new or newly renovated; tax breaks and policing; and a willingness to satisfy the corporate sponsors. Carville and the host committee secured $6 million from the private sector, and the state gave up $6 million from Lieutenant Governor Dardenne's budget; even thirty years later, the numbers were small compared to the fair's budget. The Super Bowl was the safer bet.

New Orleans in 1984 was a tired, punched-out fighter, desperately launching haymakers. The oil bust and declining port left tourism as the city's brightest hope, a way to keep up with Atlanta and Houston. In the late 1970s, men like Lester Kabacoff provided a vision in a place largely absent of vision. Some ideas compounded the economic malaise, while others generated windfalls for investors like Kabacoff. Almost thirty years later, the new New Orleans overflowed with visionaries, from Landrieu to the hackathon contestants to Pres Kabacoff, who redeveloped housing projects and controlled large holdings in the gentrifying Bywater neighborhood. Initiatives like the Tourism Master Plan ensured a unified vocabulary and timeline for expressing those visions. However far the city had come post-Katrina, indeed since 1984, the Super Bowl was positioned as a crowning achievement, not a lifeboat. The World's Fair was an ill-defined scheme thrust on a staggered city; the Super Bowl symbolized a rebirth that, according to the mayor, was already here.

In the NFL Shop, I snapped my own photo of the mannequins and then made my way back to the attractions. Visa's kicking game was impressive. Contestants took their shots at a regulation goal post from twenty yards out. The set up was made beautiful by the bright green Astroturf and the transparent walls of plastic that hung around the field. Whenever a ball was kicked into these walls, the plastic shimmered like a digital body of water. The wall behind the goal post read, "Extra Points," which referred to the NFL Extra Points Visa credit card, available with any team's logo at nearby kiosks. The goal post stood next to the NFL Shop in the Great Hall. It was appropriate, I thought. The World's Fair site was once again in the business of debt.

CHAPTER 15
JANUARY 31, 2013
(THREE DAYS TO GO)

"THE GREEN STUFF"

If you're lazy, don't come do this. Don't say you don't want to pick up shit. You gotta pick it up! Whatever it takes, you gotta do it."

Lunch was over, and the night crowd wouldn't arrive for hours, so Paul Timphony had time to talk outside Hobnobber's, the bar he'd run for twenty-seven years on the 100 block of Carondelet. With a thick torso; dark, shaggy hair; and a jovial manner, he was the image of a New Orleans shopkeeper during almost any period in the city's history. Paul was glad to be here now.

"I'm all ready. Two hundred cases of beer on the second floor, ten kegs on hand, case of Crown, case of Jack. You gotta have it; you can't be running around like crazy—you won't make no money. It don't go bad. You gotta take the risk." It was the logic of a veteran who'd seen busy nights. The bar wasn't a dive, but there were few frills—just a long room with a pool table, beer signs and regulars who drifted in after shifts in the Quarter. He had a lunch counter in the rear that served plates of decent New Orleans food. On the 100 block of Carondelet, it was better to be dependable than unique.

"Place does some good business, man," Paul said. "The restaurant? I crank out eleven grand a week out of that kitchen back there. I got good food—there's no doubt about it. Look [he pointed to his scarred arms], I'm burned up for a reason. I'm in the kitchen. People say business is slow. Shiiit. I go get it." Having just turned fifty, Paul had grown up in the business and bought his own place on Dauphine Street when he was eighteen. He sold it after a year for three times what he paid and then bought the Hobnobber's lease from his brother in 1986. The

Paul Timphony outside Hobnobber's Restaurant and Bar at 139 Carondelet Street. *Photo by author.*

owner liked him, looked out for him when Domino's Pizza moved in next door and recently sold Paul the whole building, including several apartments upstairs. "He really blessed me, looked out for me. I'll never forget him, John Torre."

Only steps from the Quarter, the last block of Carondelet featured the Domino's, another nondescript bar, a restaurant that changed hands often, a tattoo parlor, a bike rental shop and a nail salon. When Paul's wife arrived, she looked across the street and wondered if the woman with a large handbag was a prostitute. Paul said the prostitutes got manicures, too. His wife handed him a cellphone to process credit cards in the drink booth they set up during big events. "Isn't it weird?" she laughed. "We're doing everything by phone!"

The Super Bowl already made one difference: this week the police presence had increased on the block, which could get a little seedy at night. "They ain't playing around," said Paul. The location was unbeatable, though, a block up from Bourbon and Canal, in striking distance of the Quarter and the Mardi Gras parades. The area bore no great attraction, no retail and nothing gourmet—just a cluster of scrappy businesses that lived off their proximity to the golden goose. Millions came each year to visit the Quarter, but the runoff dollars weren't enough to change this neighborhood.

Would the bar be full this weekend? "I tell you, I just don't know. But I'm prepared for it," Paul said. "I got five gallons of jambalaya already mixed—same thing with gumbo, same thing with red beans and rice. I got a hundred pounds of shrimp and six gallons of oysters—every day I refill it."

For the little kitchen, these were big amounts. New Orleans had countless versions of Hobnobber's, family-owned bars that plugged along because one individual refused to let up. Big events like the Super Bowl trickled down money to the less stylish watering holes, but a lot depended on geography. With his post locked down, Paul would make money and keep on hustling. The formula was simple: "I get here at 3:30 in the morning from Slidell, six days a week, and I ain't never missed a day's work since I've been here in twenty-seven years. You can't leave that green stuff for people to take."[172]

Club Metropolitan throbbed with heavy bass and the world-class testosterone of dozens of NFL players who laughed heartily over drinks. The *Moves* Magazine Party, hosted by football insider Jay Glazer and sponsored by Avion Tequila, was among the first exclusive parties of the week. According to the *Moves* website, the magazine was "devoted to covering and uncovering the exclusive, ever-changing, luxurious lifestyles of professional athletes."[173] The party appeared to reflect that lifestyle, as female servers in fishnet stockings navigated the crowd of snugly clothed women and immense men. The room was dim, but I recognized many faces, including sportscaster Joe Buck, ESPN host Stu Scott, Tom Benson's granddaughter Rita, Saints tight end Joey Graham and former players Eric Dickerson, Eddie George, Andre Reed, Rod Woodson and Merrill Hodge, along with assorted other vaguely familiar faces that swiveled on thick necks mounted on broad shoulders. At five foot five, I avoided elbows as I walked to the bar.

On the way, I passed Falcons wide receiver Roddy White, a talented player and, if you asked Saints fans, someone with a lot of nerve. Aside from Roger

Goodell, White was probably the most reviled visitor in New Orleans this week. "I don't like nothing about the Saints," White told the *Atlanta Journal Constitution* before the Falcons lost here in November. "The colors. The city. Nothing. But they've got some good food, though. Other than the food, nothing."[174] Immaculately dressed and chatting with a friend, he appeared to like the scene at Metropolitan just fine.

I waited to order my tequila and scanned the room. Due to their on-field helmets and equipment, it was more difficult to recognize football players in real life than it was basketball players. Coaches, though, were highly visible.

Sean Payton was at the bar with a blonde. She seemed steady, but he was in rough shape. Probably it was the hour, but I couldn't help but imagine the pain of this season in exile, when the popular coach was forced to steer clear of his team and the spotlight. Payton grew up a quarterback before becoming a coach; he was forty-nine and probably never spent more than a month away from football until this year. To make matters worse, he and his wife had filed for divorce in the summer. Now he hung on his date as they made their way across the room.

The players and media personalities appeared genuinely happy to see him as he stopped to accept hugs from the giants who filled the club. Congratulations were in order, too: on January 22, Goodell had officially reinstated Payton, putting an end to his forced remove. Glassy-eyed but smiling, Payton seemed glad to reach a booth, where the couple chatted and waited for the ladies in fishnet stockings.

The club's back room was normally used as a dance floor. Tonight, there were tables piled with memorabilia, leftovers from a silent auction for former Rams running back (and Lower Ninth Ward native) Marshall Faulk's charity. I'd attended that party this evening, too, and perused the oddly juxtaposed offerings. Autographed portraits of Prince rested next to autographed photos of Mickey Mantle and Ted Williams alongside a poster signed by the cast of *The Dark Knight Rises*. Similar arrangements grouped signed images of George Bush, Lionel Messi and Jerry Garcia. Next to the boxing gloves, guitars, cleats and soccer balls were clipboards where guests could place bids. Most of the clipboards were empty. Either the party planners brought too much product or the Super Bowl audience just wasn't the market for portraits of Bob Marley, Babe Ruth and Abbot and Costello.

Before I left Club Metropolitan, I watched Payton and his date walk to the back room. The coach who had saved New Orleans shuffled along with the blonde, both of them pointing at the random selection of autographs and artifacts. Somewhere in there, I imagined, was a photo of Payton at the 2010 Super Bowl. As the week's celebrity sightings went, this was my most memorable.

CHAPTER 16
FEBRUARY 1, 2013 (TWO DAYS TO GO)

DEMAND SPACE

At the foot of Canal Street, a young lady waited on the lawn of the World Trade Center, calling out cheerfully, "Would you like to try a free bike?" Next to her was a rack of bicycles and two couples who perused glossy brochures. The young lady's shirt bore the logo of the Downtown Development District, the organization tasked with fostering a healthy business environment downtown. The bikes and their ambassador stood on an appropriate spot, as this patch of land had a long tradition of welcoming guests and promoting economic development. As they strolled to Super Bowl Boulevard, today's visitors passed through the shadow of a monument to expired dreams and the locus for new ones.

The World Trade Center (WTC) emerged from the International Trade Mart and the International House, two organizations founded after World War II to promote the port. Designed by renowned modernist architect Edward Durell Stone, the tower opened in 1968 as part of the celebration of the city's 250th anniversary year. At the ribbon-cutting ceremony on April 30, 1968, Trade Mart president Lloyd Cobb told the audience, "Proudly we proclaim this the first great international center to be founded in the United States." Dock Board president J. Melton Garret said the thirty-three-story building was symbolic of "a new Louisiana."[175] In its heyday, the WTC housed foreign consulates, maritime law firms, shipping interests and trade organizations, as well as the headquarters of the World's Fair organizers; the adjacent, soon maligned Rivergate convention center offered meeting space for more than seventeen thousand guests.

The city leased the property to the WTC board for $1 a year. For a time, the tower was a premier business address, but occupancy waned with the oil bust, the rise of commercial space on Poydras Street and the decline of the port. Rivergate lost out to the Morial Convention Center and the new hotels and was eventually demolished in 1995 to make room for the Harrah's Casino. By the mid-1990s, half the WTC was empty. In 1997, the board announced plans to convert the majority of the 670,000 square feet of office space to hotel rooms. As the remaining consulates and other tenants moved out, plans stalled over financing and governance issues. By the time Landrieu took office, the most valuable—if cheaply rented—piece of land in downtown New Orleans was occupied by a vacant relic. In November 2011, several large chunks of concrete crumbled off the building and fell near the spot of the free bikes, startling but not striking pedestrians and affirming recent worries over the WTC's fate. In March 2012, the city bought out the WTC board's lease for $2.4 million. Landrieu saw the prime turf as central to a redeveloped riverfront. "I want to think about creating a space that is what we call a demand space, [a space] that makes people want to come down there. I want to create a space that's open," said the mayor. He was open to proposals for the WTC but admitted, "If it was up to me, I would tear it down."[176] In February 2013, the X-shaped tower's future remained uncertain, but the prospect of a giant Ferris wheel or public sculpture replacing a hive of international business seemed like a metaphor of the city's changed economy.

Along the river, police with assault rifles practiced an amphibious landing on the shoreline of Woldenberg Park. Their rubber boat bobbed in the muddy water against a small dock, where the men in body armor hopped off, crouched and then boarded the boat for another round. Behind Audubon Aquarium of the Americas, the TBC Brass Band mounted the "South End Zone" stage, one of four stages on the Verizon Super Bowl Boulevard. It was 10:30 a.m., and only a few people greeted the band, including two lone dancers with beer cans in hand. The scheduled forty-five-minute set stretched another half hour at the request of the organizers. The band walked off the stage for the last song, a less-than-inspired "When the Saints Go Marching In." Along with the extra time, the division between audience and performers seemed to bother them.

"It felt like work," said trombonist Joseph Maize. "We can't really get our point across because we're trying to have fun with the crowd, not y'all

ONE HUNDRED DAYS IN AMERICA'S COOLEST HOT SPOT

Super Bowl Boulevard in Woldenberg Park. *Photo by author.*

having fun and we playing for y'all."[177] Their audience was still mostly tourists, but the interactions that inspired the band on Bourbon Street were absent. The gig was work, though, and TBC had another show at 1:30 p.m. on the NFC Stage. They had released their CD two nights earlier with a party at Celebration Hall that was packed with members of the brass band community. TBC came on like a firestorm, the sort of statement younger players make when they know their peers and elders are in the club. Maybe the audience at today's second set would conjure a wisp of that gale.

I walked through the park to see the floating Super Bowl roman numerals, on view after their heralded arrival on a barge two nights earlier. Along the way were tents sponsored by Chevron, BASF, Steve Gleason's Team Gleason charity, Pepsi, the New Orleans Jazz & Heritage Festival and, of course, Verizon. Over the next hour, the crowd grew larger on the lawn near the NFL and AFC Stage, and when I swung back through in the early evening, the park was packed. Interestingly, Saints jerseys appeared to outnumber the Ravens and 49ers jerseys by at least a two-to-one ratio. Any lingering hostilities for the league and Roger Goodell were irrelevant when New Orleanians saw the lineup for the free concerts. The music was strong and homegrown, with bands like TBC, Lost Bayou Ramblers, Trombone Shorty, Walter "Wolfman" Washington and the Rebirth Brass Band. Food tents offered Louisiana fare from local restaurants, including Curtis Williams's Praline Connection, which sold crowder peas and okra. I didn't see Curtis, but I caught a glimpse of Quint Davis aboard a golf cart. He'd praised the NFL's vision when we talked last week, but Davis's incomparable talent was on full display. For four days, Jazz Fest staged a mini version of its annual festival under the eye of the national media and visiting football fans. As Davis said, there was no price you could put on that advertising.

My fellow volunteer could not understand why the "Jesus freak" on the other side of the street had chosen Pitbull as his theme music. Said fanatic nodded his head vigorously to a handheld radio blasting music that resembled the contemporary Miami sound of Pitbull, but, I assured my colleague, it was something else. A few minutes earlier, I had stood next to the man as he rapped along to praises for the singer's salvation, shout outs to other warriors and boasts of a battle for redemption. Up close, the proselytizer was even more off-kilter, with a fresh cut on his forehead and wild blue eyes. He held a large sign that quoted John 3:3: "Unless a Man Is Born Again He Can Not SEE the Kingdom of GOD." It was 8:00 p.m. outside the NFL Experience.

The windbreaker provided to volunteers by the host committee was nice but thin, and though I wore layers, I shivered through my shift on Convention Center Boulevard. At 5:00 p.m., I reported to the volunteer center set up in the Riverwalk Mall. I received a drawstring backpack, a map of the area and a bag of Zatarain's pens. A ranger from the Downtown Development District led me and five others to our spots. Along the way, we passed the three-thousand-seat Bud Light tent, where Pitbull himself would play later that night. My cohorts were three locals and a couple from out of town. The ranger left the couple closer to the Hilton but took the rest of us to join the state troopers milling about near the Great Hall entrance.

One of the state troopers told my fellow volunteer, whose name was Racquel, that the Jesus freak was harmless compared to some of the evangelists they had chased off earlier. "One guy was out here on a box, preaching," he said, "and we had to tone him down because he was starting to call people out, calling some of the women whores, calling guys out. There's a time and a place to preach. Friday in a family atmosphere, calling women whores and talking about masturbation and saying things, you're drawing attention to yourself and not God."

Based in Alexandria, the trooper was ready to get out of New Orleans. This day marked his fourth detail outside the convention center, where he answered tourist's questions, watched other cops direct traffic and received little help, he said, from the NOPD: "Good luck getting them to do anything." Behind us was the parking lot for passengers of the cruise ships that stopped every Saturday. He didn't want to, but the officer was forced to raise his voice this afternoon when a cruise ship employee insisted that the state police direct traffic when the ship arrived tomorrow. But the lodging was the worst part of this assignment. Unable to secure hotel rooms at a reasonable price, the State of Louisiana booked him and others at a convent in Metairie, where they returned after twelve- to fourteen-hour shifts to no television and meals prepared by the nuns. All in all, the officer didn't care if he ever saw New Orleans again.

The city spent hundreds of thousands of dollars on overtime for the NOPD, a force well versed in crowd control. The succeeding Mardi Gras-Super Bowl-Mardi Gras weekends were a unique challenge. "If we can, we'd like to give them some time down," Superintendent Serpas told CBS News. "But if we can't, they know it, and they'll stand up for it." During a period of troubled morale, Serpas was confident. As the mayor had reminded everyone at the press conference one hundred days earlier, the Super Bowl was a homeland security event. On Wednesday, Homeland Security secretary Janet Napolitano visited the city to review plans with the U.S. Coast Guard and Immigrations and Customs Enforcement (ICE), which scanned cargo shipments to the game. "There's no safer place to be than the city of New Orleans," said ICE special agent Raymond Parmer.[178]

Parmer's assurances were likely cold comfort for the families of those murdered in the city during Super Bowl week. Shots rang out at a Sunday night block party in the Iberville projects, leaving a twenty-one-year-old man dead. On Tuesday around 1:00 p.m., a bullet felled twenty-seven-year-old Keisha Love in Central City. That night, Steven Augustin, age twenty-three, was killed outside a home on Bunker Hill Road in New Orleans East. Wednesday afternoon, near Martin Behrman Elementary School in Algiers, someone inside a silver Pontiac Grand Prix shot and killed thirty-four-year-old Tyler Sims. Around 1:30 a.m., police found a fifty-five-year-old man dead of gunshot wounds inside a home in the 800 block of Jackson Avenue in the Lower Garden District. These were neighborhoods outside the focus of the increased police presence. By February 5, thirteen people had been victims of murder in New Orleans in 2013, down from twenty-six during the same period in 2012 and twenty in 2011. Perhaps the extra officers concentrated around the Superdome, convention center and French Quarter had an impact after all.

Much of the state troopers' work could hardly be called homeland security, though. An attractive woman interrupted to ask us where she could park her school bus. Where, she asked, was Lot F? The officer left to confer with his counterpart. When he returned, he told me he usually worked a nine-to-five shift in investigations. So, instead of working on cases for this week, a trained law enforcement officer was shipped to New Orleans to give directions and keep a lid on religious zealots. Along with at least one hundred officers from neighboring parishes, there were two hundred state police scheduled to arrive on Sunday for the game; many would remain for Mardi Gras. The trooper might complain, but the revenue generated by the state on the back of the big events in New Orleans more than justified the travel.

Another officer joined us. He hailed from Many, a town near the Texas border, and the contrast between the two men from the central part of the state and my partner Racquel from New Orleans was revealing. Both officers spoke with southern drawls and employed dry senses of humor in their storytelling, the one from Alexandria more talkative than his colleague. Short with dark features, Racquel was chatty, bragged of her days as a party girl and cursed not a few times. She resided in Jefferson Parish now and agreed with them that the city was no place to live. As far as he was concerned, said the officer from Alexandria, you could take everything east of the river and give it to Mississippi. We all laughed. Texas would snatch you guys up, I told him. "Good," he said with popped eyes. "I'll go!"

Near the entrance of the Great Hall, a clown twisted balloon animals for kids while a saxophonist played brief snippets of popular songs. People tipped them, so I knew their time was short. Sure enough, another state cop strode over to tell them that it was time to go. The duo stalled, the clown trying to please one final amazed child, but the officer returned with a sterner warning. The two artists headed off in the wrong direction, away from the hotels. "It's all about location, location, location," I heard the clown say. He left behind a collection of exploded balloon rubber on the sidewalk.

It was cold and getting colder. Racquel said she couldn't see what use there was in standing here until 10:30 p.m., when our shift ended. Between us, we had answered only a handful of questions. If they needed directions, most people asked the state police. Our DDD ranger returned. Did we know what happened to the other volunteers? We hadn't noticed them disappear. Oh well, he said, it was still better than last night, when the weather was worse and half the volunteers were gone within two hours. I asked how long he'd been with the DDD, and he said it had been more than a year. Before that, he had served two years with the NOPD but couldn't stand the way things operated. He wore diamonds in both ears.

With paid rangers and paid, disgruntled state police, there was no need for volunteers. I recalled the Disney Hospitality team leader's instructions on satisfied "wows" and the "extra inch." Indianapolis might need the extra help, but in New Orleans, crowd management was a year-round job handled by professionals who, however they were funded, did enough to keep people moving and informed. Cold, unnecessary and among a dwindling cohort, I resolved to abandon my post.

I told Racquel and the state policemen that I wanted to check out the line at the Bud Light tent. Across the street, the Jesus freak was gone. I looked for him outside the Pitbull show, but the line was very long, and he was nowhere to be found.

CHAPTER 17
FEBRUARY 2, 2013
(ONE DAY TO GO)

"I AM YOUR GREAT TIME"

Each metallic blue Bud Light bottle stood on its own tiny platform under the fountain's falling water. Like synchronized swimmers frozen in mid-routine, they encircled a large urn in a delicate display of product placement. The fountain sat in a shaded corner of a fully branded courtyard. Above the main doorway stood the letters "B," "L" and "H": Bud Light Hotel. Palm leaves caressed the top of my head as I sipped my coffee at a table next to the fountain. Saturday morning arrived balmy with a gentle breeze, the perfect weather for a lazy brunch at an exclusive location.

Entry to the Bud Light Hotel was restricted to guests with wristbands. Somehow I bypassed the security on Fulton Street with a focused nod, avoided the front desk and stepped into the courtyard of the former Wyndham Hotel. This was the fourth annual edition of the hotel for Bud Light, which, as the official beer sponsor of the NFL, had the league's blessing for maximum signage within the Clean Zone. A great wall of Bud Light–blue plywood blocked the hotel's main entrance on Convention Center Boulevard. Over the boulevard stretched a pedestrian walkway wrapped in Bud Light logos that delivered guests into the Bud Light music venue, where Pitbull had performed the night before. This night would bring Stevie Wonder and Paul McCartney to the Bud Light stage.

In the center of the courtyard stood a large flat screen tuned to the ESPN broadcast from Decatur Street. As the fountain gurgled, I pulled a Saturday edition of the *Advocate* from my backpack. The Baton Rouge–based paper

Inside the Bud Light Hotel. *Photo by author.*

had upped its distribution in the city since the *Times-Picayune* cuts, hired local writers and started home delivery in October. Unfolded in the idyllic Bud Light courtyard, today's front page bore signs of conflict.

Under the headline "Reaction Mixed to Consent Decree Deal," reporter Allen Powell outlined the latest developments in the battle between the mayor and the federal government. After the frustration expressed on the day of the Mardi Gras lottery, the mayor plotted legal action to prevent "catastrophic damage." On Thursday, the City Attorney's Office asked a federal judge to void the NOPD agreement, citing Justice Department misconduct, including failure to disclose costs of the prison consent decree, prejudiced prosecutors who left derogatory comments about Landrieu and Serpas in the NOLA.com comments section and an unresolved question about the reforms to the NOPD paid detail system. The mayor had declined comment since the filing, which was unsurprising, given the onset of Super Bowl commitments and the arrival of five thousand members of the media; let the conflict remain buried until Monday. The Justice Department, however, was not otherwise occupied. "Without these consent decrees the criminal justice system in New Orleans will remain broken, a fate neither the residents of New Orleans nor the hardworking members of the New Orleans Police Department deserve," wrote a department spokeswoman.

The headline's "mixed reaction" came from a Loyola University professor who felt certain the reforms would take root despite the legal battle. Others weren't so sure. "We said all along, 'It isn't the change we fear, it's the manner that it's being done,'" said Captain Michael Glasser of the Police Association of New Orleans. "I think we could have avoided all this from the beginning." Rafael Goyeneche of the watchdog Metropolitan Crime Commission lamented the city's "disingenuous" argument. "This is a lose-lose for the city on both fronts. I think both financially, and as well as the thing I think can't be overlooked, in the eyes of the public," Goyeneche said. "All this is doing is delaying the inevitable."[179]

In a separate article, Superintendent Serpas celebrated a 1 percent decline in crime for 2012 by declaring New Orleans safer than neighboring Jefferson Parish. The police chief pointed to a significant drop in overall crime during the final months of the year and an 18 percent decrease in homicides during the same period. "The safety level in New Orleans is getting better," Serpas said. "By and large, the city of New Orleans is on the right path." When adjusted for population, the article noted, the crime rate in New Orleans remained slightly higher than in Jefferson Parish.[180]

Taken together, the articles created a suitably ambivalent portrait of the criminal justice system in New Orleans. If any of the Bud Light Hotel guests bought today's paper, they learned that the city was at war with the federal government over crucial reforms to its police department, which was in turn encouraged by a 1 percent improvement over the previous year. This was hardly the image the administration desired during a high-profile weekend, but the morning sunshine and the excitement of Super Bowl eve were enough to distract most visitors. I finished my coffee, packed up my paper and climbed a set of stairs to a balcony above the courtyard, where a female bartender smiled at me as she poured a drink.

"I'm bored, Adam!"

"Adam, where's your three-piece suit? You look like shit!"

The hecklers were in their element behind the ESPN stage in the parking lot of the Jax Brewery on Decatur Street. Show host Mike Lupica turned to smirk, but the reaction only fired up his maligners. The backs of four studio commentators were targets for a running harangue from the crowd.

"Medium-starch!"

The parking lot provided a special place for white American males. They had open containers of booze, February sunshine and proximity to famous

The Bud Light Tent on Convention Center Boulevard. *Photo by author.*

sportswriters like Lupica and Mitch Albom, objects of scorn for their inflated egos and decades of moralizing analyses. Years of Deadspin and *College GameDay* poster humor blew forth from the young men. This afternoon in New Orleans was paradise for their demographic.

Fan Man was in a friendlier, if slightly imperious mood. "Great town, great venue. Walking distance. People are great," said the white-haired Ravens fan wrapped in a costume of bird feathers, stockings and a purple Santa hat. He handed me a card designating him as an NFL Hall of Fame fan, with a photo of him in front of the shrine in Canton and a list of appearances, including an engagement with Carson Daly and Jennifer Lopez at Super Bowl XXXV. According to www.theravenfanman.com, Fan Man was also the owner of something called the "FAN BUS," known for "its distinctive and daunting Raven eyes."

As a lifelong Pittsburgh Steelers fan who hated our division rival Baltimore, I'd braced myself for these interactions. "Saints fans have been phenomenal," said Fan Man's friend, who was more understated in his apparel. "We have a big rivalry with Pittsburgh"—I bit my tongue—"and [the Saints] are rivals with the 49ers. Everybody I talk to in New Orleans...gracious people—they've all been about us winning. The verbiage was, 'We want you to kick their ass.' I was like, damn! And that's pretty much what the Baltimore people would say if the Super Bowl were to be held in Baltimore."

"Y'know what? It's America."

It certainly felt that way. Above our heads, like the rabbit at a dog track, an ESPN camera slid along a zip cord the length of the parking lot. As it passed, people looked up and squealed. The crowds had arrived, the media was in place and this edge of the French Quarter was a playground where football fans could drink freely and scream at Mike Lupica.

Mardi Gras conditions reigned on Bourbon Street. Walking was possible, but no one moved quickly. Two young women in blue Bud Light spandex posed for photos with a group of Raven fans outside Club Razzoo. Next to me on the sidewalk appeared two small black boys, both in white shirts that read, "Brooklyn." The taller one tapped hesitantly on a snare drum that hung from his neck. "Can you dance?" asked a slender lady, but the boys played mute. They moved to the middle of the street, just behind the Bud Light girls, the older boy pulling the younger one along, both of them watchful as they cut through the crowd.

Amid the scrum of Super Bowl mania, the children slipped in to perform on Bourbon Street. They told me they were brothers and that the little one used to play harmonica but had lost it. "Now he's on probation," said the older brother. The probationer's stern face cracked slightly when I wondered if he was trouble. He was eight, two years younger than his brother, who said their mom usually dropped them off and picked them up. An uncle was a musician, and when he died, the older boy started to play the uncle's drums. What's the weirdest thing they'd seen on Bourbon?

"The man dressed like a lady," said the younger brother. "You don't have to be foolish to earn money," the older one added in agreement. I put ten dollars in the Pat O'Brien's hat they used for a tip jar and told the smaller one to watch himself. They trotted back to Bourbon, perhaps the two youngest members of the "back of the house," resolute in their commitment to making an economic impact.

Mena's Palace was open past its normal 3:00 p.m. closing time. The diner at the corner of Chartres and Bienville was one of the last of its kind in the Quarter and the first place my wife worked when she returned to New Orleans in December 2005. This afternoon, our friend Anne Marie greeted me from behind the bar. A native of Ireland, she moved to New Orleans twenty years ago and married her husband, Carl, from St. Bernard Parish, where they lost their house in Katrina. Carl was a contractor, Annie lived off tips and they believed in cash, so after the storm, Annie spent weeks gently airing out her money. Fortunately, they also believed in insurance, which enabled them to buy another, larger home in the parish. This afternoon, she slid me a Bud Light as I took a stool. Business had been OK this week, Annie said, nothing special. She echoed others who said these guests had pre-planned agendas that included restaurant reservations. Eight of Mena's ten tables were full, a normal Saturday—but they'd stay open awhile to see if the Super Bowl was worth it.

Next to me sat Will, an African American naval engineer currently stationed at the Poland Avenue wharf. Will grew up in New Orleans but traveled the world for his job and kept a house across the lake. He looked like a sailor, with his broad shoulders, granite face and an open smile. Back in town for a few weeks now, he enjoyed the walk from the boat through the Bywater and Marigny to the French Quarter. When Mr. Leo, the owner and head cook at Mena's, joined us, Will reminded him that he'd been a regular at the restaurant back in 1984, when Will worked as a commercial painter during the World's Fair buildup. Wrapped in an apron, his face still flush from the kitchen, Leo was a warhorse, a Greek immigrant in his sixties who'd run restaurants for decades. He'd done well, lived in Metairie and raised two daughters, but he stayed working.

Will and I agreed on another round. As the last customers left Mena's, the television above the bar showed the CBS evening news, broadcast live from Jackson Square, five blocks from our barstools. The thirty minutes included three New Orleans–related segments in honor of the Super Bowl. First was the Loyola streetcar line, accompanied with photos of the flooded city. The Katrina theme continued with a profile of Lieutenant General Russel Honoré, whose heroic service in the aftermath of the storm earned him Ray Nagin's praise as "a John Wayne dude" who "can get some stuff done." Musician Troy "Trombone Shorty" Andrews also received a profile for his immense talent and his new foundation. As summaries of New Orleans in 2013, the CBS segments were fuzzy appreciations of the city's resilience, well-suited advertisements for attracting future visitors. Heroes, musicians and the federal government received their due. I looked at Anne Marie and remembered long nights spent drinking beer outside her and Carl's FEMA trailer in St. Bernard.

The doors were locked now, but we were welcome to stay. With a light tap on the door and no other comment, the ATM service technician arrived to empty the machine of its cash. When the nightly news ended, I glanced out the window at Chartres Street to see large crowds on their way to Super

ONE HUNDRED DAYS IN AMERICA'S COOLEST HOT SPOT

Bowl Boulevard, Bourbon Street, wherever. I nudged Will, who agreed he'd never seen the street this packed, even on Mardi Gras. On the last evening before the Super Bowl, the French Quarter was finally full.

"Can we get your e-mail address?"

The trade was straightforward but delivered with a smile. The young ladies wore black dresses with ambitious necklines and wanted to take a picture with me. First, though, I needed to register for future offers. I complied, we posed and the pair moved along while I sipped the specialty cocktail from the party's official vodka sponsor. After four days of Super Bowl special events, the exchange was routine.

There were different tiers of access at the *GQ* party. Around 250 people with wristbands like mine mingled under a tent attached to the Elm's Mansion on St. Charles Avenue. Luckier guests had access to the mansion, which I imagined was warmer and more intimate than the tent. Networking and texting blossomed in the growing crowd of sharply dressed young professionals, everyone talking loudly at the same time. Here were the connected out-of-town visitors, the people who worked for the sponsors, brands and teams that made the week into a giant, if more glamorous convention. This was the last round for the big parties, and *GQ* had gone the extra mile: Lil Wayne was due on stage in a few minutes.

Standing next to a sleek new Mercedes, I met Mr. and Mrs. Mike Rubenstein of Rubenstein's, the famed clothing store opened in 1924 at the corner of St. Charles and Canal. They were invited to the *GQ* party, Mr. Rubenstein told me, because the store sold Lacoste, one of the night's brands. When their daughter called to ask how the party was, Mrs. Rubenstein moved further up in the crowd for a report, leaving Mr. Rubenstein and I there to converse and, I admit, for me to admire the gentleman's clothes. He was my height and wore a blue jacket over a green shirt, striped tie and dark pants, along with simple wire-rimmed glasses. Despite my envy, Mr. Rubenstein was such a regular guy that we easily fell into conversation.

Business on Canal Street, he said, suffered during the streetcar construction, no doubt. They had a busy week for the Super Bowl, a lot of people in the store. We compared neighborhoods we lived in or used to live in. Mr. Rubenstein knew that Lil Wayne emerged from a group of other local rappers, and I credited Wayne's industriousness and lyricism. Mr. Rubenstein said he used to see Fats Domino on Bourbon, along with Pete Fountain, Al Hirt and other local heroes; he even told me a dirty story about Pete Fountain. Surrounded by brands and out-of-town marketers, we talked as locals do, about legends and favorite corners.

Then the music grew loud, the DJ asked us yet again if we were ready and Lil Wayne burst forth to "If I Die Today," a song with all the metallic apocalypse of today's commercial rap. His verse closed with an updated version of the old "St. James Infirmary" request:

> *Load up the choppers like it's December 31ˢᵗ*
> *Roll up and cock it and hit them n—s where it hurts*
> *If I die today, remember me like John Lennon*
> *Buried in Louis* [Vuitton], *I'm talking all brown linen, huh*

When the track cut, he greeted us.

"How y'all doin' tonight? My name is Dwayne Carter. You can call me Lil Wayne or you can call me Tunechi. I am from this great place you are at right now, New Orleans, Lil-weezy-ana. If you're not from here, make some noise. If you're glad to be here, make some noise. What team you going for?" People called out names.

"Before I get started, I must let you know three important things about myself. One is I believe in God. Number two is, I ain't shit without you. And the most important is, I ain't shit without you, seriously. If you came to have a good time, say, 'Hell yeah.'" Hell yeah. "If you here to have a great fucking time, say, 'Hell yeah.'" Hell yeah. "Well, ladies and gentlemen, I am your great time. Let's go."

The *GQ* party turned into a forest of raised arms. No one pushed or danced. These were stylish adults with an open bar and connections, partygoers who could restrain their emotions. But Instagram the moment? Without a doubt. You couldn't play off being in the same room as Lil Wayne as no big deal. Lil Wayne, from New Orleans, was as A-list as they came in 2013.

Mr. Rubenstein and his wife were slightly amused and certainly not put off by all the cursing and bombast. They were New Orleanians, too, who ran a family business across Canal Street from Bourbon Street; they'd seen circuses before. When Wayne's set finished after thirty minutes, I wished them both well and stepped to the bar for a bottle of the newly debuted Beck's Sapphire.

It was almost 3:00 a.m. when I returned to the Quarter. Outside the Bienville Street entrance to the Olde N'awlins Cookery, a mountain range of garbage bags hugged the curb as cooks and dishwashers smoked cigarettes and watched the stumbling parade pass on Bourbon Street. Cups, beads and soggy cardboard filled the gutters along Bourbon. A young white man in a white sweatshirt stomped through a knee-deep patch of the filth, mumbling loudly that he was "a grown man." Aside from his troubadour-like determination, he stuck out because he was in the distinct minority: the crowd on Bourbon Street appeared at least three-quarters black. Teenage boys with ten-thousand-yard stares hugged girls who sucked on lollipops. Groups gathered amid the procession to flirt and share drinks, the famous street their own unsupervised mall. This was common in the early morning hours, when the street grew younger and, it seemed, more local. In the wee hours, the Super Bowl gave way to the status quo.

Confused but seemingly concerned, a bum with a long beard sat against the Sheraton and contemplated his hand. An EMS vehicle had parked in the middle of the 500 block. The friends of whoever was inside argued with the paramedics. "She's OK, she's OK," they insisted. Finally, a woman stepped down from the rear door on wobbly stilettos into the arms of her comrades. The navy blue EMS vehicle was not a traditional ambulance, but smaller, with a sleek cab. It looked like the perfect French Quarter rescue capsule.

In the hierarchy of tourist destinations—the Superdome, Jackson Square, the streetcars—everywhere else took second place to Bourbon Street. Bourbon Street was ensconced deep within the genes of the New Orleans brand. Master plans could plot new "demand spaces," but Bourbon was the city's Eiffel Tower, Millennium Park and Vegas Strip. Thousands worked there, millions visited and, in contemporary America, nothing truly compared to it. At 3:00 a.m. on the morning of the Super Bowl, Bourbon Street was filled with teenagers sipping vodka from the bottle and serviced by emergency vehicles that allowed injured patrons to walk out the back door. New Orleans had much to offer its visitors, but its most unique offering was a strip of land where you could drink in all-night bars or on the street until the sun came up. Conceivably, you could run into anyone from your past on Bourbon, your elementary school teachers, old flames or distant cousins—people from every level and locale passed through for a hand grenade or a hurricane. Wolves lurked on the side streets, ready to rob or proposition a boozy Minnesotan. The police stood sentry to make sure everything stayed on track, but they weren't sticking their hands in unless something was on fire; many times they were too late. People didn't get hit over the head inside Disney World, but on New Orleans' main tourist thoroughfare, you had to be careful.

At Rick's Saloon, John Amos had dancers on both stages. It was now 4:00 a.m. The room was packed with men and twice as many dancers as usual, some perched on men's laps, others who prowled back and forth. I took a stool at the front bar, where a short blonde soon joined me. She had grown up in St. Bernard Parish, but her family recently moved to Slidell, where, we joked, everyone was scared of the immigrants from the parish. The women working tonight were more beautiful than usual, she observed. They came in for the game.

An hour later, I walked off Bourbon. On St. Peter Street, a green garbage truck crawled from door to door. One worker grabbed a plastic bin with the company's name, Progressive, and slid it in front of the great maw in the truck's rear. A second worker positioned the bin on a lift attached to the truck and then guided the bin as the lift flipped it over, depositing its contents into the truck's teeth. As the bin tilted upside down, the second worker expertly dodged a rivulet of fluid. When all the trash was emptied, he pushed the bin back toward the curb, where the first man waited to trade him another bin of trash.

After one hundred days pondering the new New Orleans, I paused to watch the truck move along the poorly lit side street, methodically going about the upkeep of the golden goose. The cycle hadn't changed so much: New Orleans welcomed the big games, allowed the fans and corporate sponsors to run wild and then cleaned up the mess. Many different jobs existed within that cycle, with trash collector among the lowest and most crucial. The next party was impossible if tonight's garbage wasn't picked up, and in this new era, there were more parties than ever, so more trash collectors were needed. The supply chain of the new New Orleans might begin when a visitor arrived in a sparkling airport named after Louis Armstrong, but eventually it dwindled down to a couple men hoisting garbage cans into a truck labeled Progressive at 5:00 a.m.

For the first time in my life, I hailed a pedicab. The driver had shoulder-length hair and acne brushstrokes on either cheek. As we pulled away, he stood up to peddle, his beautiful head bobbing up and down against the pale sky. His name was Mitchell, he was nineteen and he had arrived from Chicago in September.

"What do you think?" I asked him.

"I love it," he said with wonder.

How else would he feel? He had cash in his pocket and a job in the French Quarter that allowed him to sleep in, only to reawaken in a city that encouraged him to remain poised at the edge of adulthood, meeting people who needed rides and told him things and asked him questions. I was once that age in another New Orleans, but I knew what he felt. No one should love New Orleans more than Mitchell. The question would always be: did New Orleans love him back?

He deposited me in the parking lot of my office building in the CBD. I leaned against my car to watch the sun rise on Super Bowl Sunday.

CHAPTER 18
FEBRUARY 3, 2013 (SUPER BOWL SUNDAY)

POWER

Each year before Carnival, a crew employed by the city would erect bleachers along the parade route between Lee Circle and Canal Street. They took their time, usually giving themselves a good six weeks to complete the job. Green, gold and purple plywood arrived in stacks; the men conversed along St. Charles Avenue; and slowly their work filled up the sidewalks. It was always a hopeful sign in the Central Business District, though—Mardi Gras was on its way.

You could buy tickets to sit in the bleachers on Lafayette Square across from Gallier Hall, a prime spot because each krewe's monarch stopped there to receive greetings from the mayor and enjoy a moment under the television cameras. Seats on the Gallier Hall side were reserved for people with connections—city hall employees, elected officials, family members and political operatives. Twice I've lucked into season tickets at Gallier Hall, and both times they were well worth the trip.

On this day, the bleachers were used for a different purpose, but no tickets were on sale. Ample space was available, but when I asked a sheriff's deputy on horseback if my wife and I could take a seat, he told me it wasn't possible. The registration table for media was unoccupied, so I had no recourse. Instead, we stood behind a chain-link fence as a group named the New Orleans Super Bowl Gospel Choir sang "When the Saints" from a stage set up on the Gallier Hall side. Over there, the bleachers were full. Mardi Gras masks and Super Bowl logos covered the bases of Gallier Hall's pillars, a twelve-foot-high Lombardi trophy loomed over the choir and a collection of very important people awaited the start of the "Handoff Ceremony." New Orleans was about to give up the ball; New York and New Jersey were set to run with it.

The stage presented a tableau of powerful people from Louisiana and New Jersey: Governor Jindal; Mayor Landrieu; Lieutenant Governor Dardenne; council members Clarkson, Latoya Cantrell, Susan Guidry and Cynthia Hedge Morrell; Greater New Orleans Sports Foundation CEO Jay Cicero; James Carville and Mary Matalin; Congressman Steve Scalise; Jefferson Parish president John Young; and Saints VP Rita Benson. New York sent representatives from the Cuomo and Bloomberg administrations. The owners of the New York Jets and Giants were on hand, along with perhaps the morning's brightest star: New Jersey governor Chris Christie. The aggregated political ambition on stage was impressive and intriguing.

Cicero began by recognizing Mississippi governor Phil Bryan and the members of the host committee, all present on the bleachers. Former NFL commissioner Paul Tagliabue received a hearty cheer, no doubt amplified by his services post-Katrina and as the Bountygate arbitrator. Cicero lauded the economic impact and free advertising generated by the game. "More importantly, 5,204 members of the media were here all week writing incredibly positive stories about our great city. You really can't put a value on that." Noise from a helicopter drowned out Cicero's description of the preparations for this historic week, which apparently did not include a no-fly zone over the Handoff Ceremony. He soldiered on as Landrieu searched the crowd for someone who could make the noise stop. When the chopper passed, Cicero introduced "our inspiration," Mayor Landrieu. Next to us behind the fence, a white man with thick, brown dreadlocks and neither shoes nor shirt let out a big whoop. Clutching a hand-rolled cigar, he danced off across Lafayette Square.

The mayor thanked Cicero. He touted the city's place at the top of many lists. The Super Bowl served as a catalyst for our ascent, as it could for next year's host city. "One of the things we did well here was use this game as an opportunity to rebuild the city to really think about how we were going to rebuild New Orleans back to better than she ever was, and I really think we succeeded in wonderful ways." New Jersey, the mayor knew, would respond with similar verve. "As fate would have it, it's going to go to the place that Mother Nature once again beat down, to our brothers and sisters in the Northeast. I can't think of a better place next year, to help that part of the country rebuild as well. I'm sure that they are going to do an incredible job."

ONE HUNDRED DAYS IN AMERICA'S COOLEST HOT SPOT

In one of his only appearances this week, Jindal echoed the mayor: "New Orleans is back and open for business." He made sure to mention his own contributions, the LSU medical center and education reform, and extended his remarks to take full advantage of the spotlight of an event he would not attend: on Friday, the governor's office announced that Jindal would watch the game at home in Baton Rouge. It was a fitting tribute to his relationship with New Orleans.

Jindal presented a ceremonial football to Christie, his would-be rival for the 2016 Republican presidential nomination. The difference between the two men was striking—Jindal, the ever-serious Indian American, barely filling out his sports coat, and Christie, rotund and charismatic in a royal blue shirt with an open collar. Christie began with a joke. "We're going to promise you weather just like this," he said to round laughter; the day arrived cloudless with temperatures in the low sixties. He thanked the New Orleans host committee for welcoming the Northeast contingent into its operation. In an interview after the ceremony, he told the *Newark Star-Ledger* of the strong bond forged between his state and Louisiana after Hurricane Sandy. "They have sent staff people up to New Jersey to help us work through all the problems with FEMA and the other issues," Christie said. "They're helping us with the Super Bowl, but more importantly, they're helping us get back on our feet up there."[181]

Carville wore a green-purple-gold rugby shirt for his valedictorian speech. On other stages filled with elected officials, I thought, Carville probably hung in the background, calculating the next move for his client. Today, he took the microphone and hit the final high notes of a week when, as much as anyone, James Carville owned the spotlight. In this journey, he said, everyone got along. He turned to Christie, who made waves among Republicans for his rebellious, bipartisan embrace of President Obama after Sandy.

"New Jersey and New Orleans may be 1,200 miles apart, but culturally, they're about this far apart," he assured us, his hands parted by mere inches. My wife wondered aloud about the New Jersey equivalent of the Mardi Gras Indians; I said their stadium was, after all, in a swamp.

Giants owner Jonathan Tisch, co-chair of the New Jersey–New York committee and head of the Loews Hotel Corporation, provided the day's clearest signal. An owner who fit the mold of today's ultra-wealthy NFL elite, Tisch lived in a $48 million co-op on Manhattan's Upper East Side. His father, Loews co-founder Robert Tisch, had purchased the Giants in 1991. The younger Tisch grew up in the hospitality industry and served as chair of New York City's tourism bureau from 2002 to 2007, when post-9/11

Manhattan became a mecca for Americans. Tisch was fluent in the language of the new New Orleans.

"We are currently dealing with challenges that are wrought by Mother Nature," he told the crowd. "The power of travel and tourism, the power of sports, can make it all better," said Tisch. His colleagues on stage applauded.

Cicero closed the ceremony with a presentation of helmets bearing logos from the 2013 and 2014 Super Bowls. The dignitaries struggled unsuccessfully to don the gifts, chuckling as they helped one another. Finally, everyone resolved to hold the silver helmets against their chests as the photographer captured one last beaming portrait of cooperation and triumph. As we walked toward Poydras Street, sirens rang out from the motorcades prepared to usher Jindal, Christie and the host committees to destinations near and far.

The river-bound lanes of Poydras remained open to traffic, but the Dome-bound lanes served as a pedestrian way. It was now 2:00 p.m., and people swarmed the former Park Avenue of the South. At the corner of Loyola Avenue, a sign outside the Lil Gem Saloon listed a $50 cover price that—if the crowd on the balcony was any indication—seemed reasonable. Scalpers mixed in among the Ravens and 49ers fans. During the week, the cheapest tickets I'd seen were around $1,200.

And I never bought one. I was exhausted by the many events leading up to the game, so I chose to work. The money I got as a DJ was helpful, I wanted to be around my friends and, I told myself, the story of the Super Bowl was complete. The Handoff Ceremony provided fitting punctuation for my coverage. Now there was only the game, which might feature some New Orleans flourishes during the pre-game and halftime shows, which I could watch on YouTube next week. I would read the economic impact reports when they came out; why spend money on a ticket when I could be part of that impact?

We turned down Loyola past city hall, where two young black men paced the sidewalk selling mixtape CDs. One salesman introduced himself as Eric from Los Angeles and told us he was only in town for the Super Bowl. I gave him three dollars for *Legend City*, a CD by a rapper named Yung Legend, and told him to come by Handsome Willy's for the game. *Legend City* seemed like an alias for the new New Orleans.

In front of Duncan Plaza, the members of the Westboro Baptist Church staged their silent protest against the day's events, the national media and, most of all, homosexuals. Among the handful of church members were two adolescent boys. One kid's shirt read,

ONE HUNDRED DAYS IN AMERICA'S COOLEST HOT SPOT

"GODHATESTHEMEDIADOTCOM"; he clutched a yellow "Thank God for Dead Soldiers" sign in one hand and a "You Hate God" sign in the other. The second boy was chubbier, his eyes hidden by sunglasses. He was armed with placards reading, "GOD H8S FAGS" and "'Christians' Caused Fag Marriage." They stood at the former home of Occupy New Orleans; I wondered if the two groups would meet here on Chep Morrison's plaza.

The sun was bright, so we stopped at the Walgreen's on Tulane Avenue, where my wife looked for a new pair of sunglasses; the racks were empty, a positive sign. Outside, two more mixtape salesmen prowled the curb. This CD's cover showed a plume of fireworks above a city skyline, with the Lombardi Trophy and Super Bowl XLVII logo among the buildings. I needed one last souvenir, so I paid five dollars before noticing that the skyline belonged to Manhattan. The group's name: Ambitious Grind World Wide. Later, I listened to the first track, a southern-style anthem about the perils of dropping out of school in Detroit. Apparently, word was out among the nation's mixtape industry: New Orleans was the place to be this weekend.

The parking lots around Willy's were packed, which surprised me. I figured fans of both teams would fly in and that foot traffic from the Quarter would mostly miss the bar. Instead, things looked promising as we waded through the cars.

Inside, the bar wasn't as robust as the parking lots suggested. We'd had that problem in recent years: the rise of Champions Square and competitors like Walk On's meant that people parked here but partied closer to the game. Our regular game-day staff was already in place. On the patio, assistant manager Pat White worked the grill while co-owner Jarret Lofstead tended bar. Victoria Treadaway and Elise Chalatain, Justin Micaroni's partner, served drinks inside. Justin Brunell manned the mobile sidewalk bar used on Sundays while bar backs Julio Ruiz and Will Woods tapped kegs, carried ice and took orders from Micaroni. Someone got the idea that we should flier the crowds near the Dome, so my wife headed back toward Poydras. It was a normal day, and I was glad to be home.

But I forgot something. I was still in a daze after my late night in the Quarter when I packed my equipment. The mixer I used was powered through my laptop. Now, as I switched on the computer, it hit me—I hadn't packed my power cord.

Nobody had brought his or her MacBook Pro to the bar. I sent texts, tried to think of someone who lived close by and told myself not to panic. With many of the streets in the neighborhood blocked off for the game, I couldn't ask anyone to drive home and back. I had enough power for maybe thirty minutes with the mixer plugged in. Finally, I posted to Facebook and Twitter: "If anyone is near Handsome Willy's Bar & Lounge and can bring me a MacBook power cord, that would make all this much more fun!" After twenty minutes, I got a reply from a friend, Marie Lovejoy: "Did you get one? I was headed out to paint faces; if I bring you a cord at Handsome Willy's, do you think I could paint there?" Sold. Thirty minutes later, Marie showed up. We embraced.

"I love this," I told her.

Justin moved one of the bar's picnic tables to the sidewalk so Marie could set up her paints and a tip jar. I plugged in my laptop, connected the mixer and cued up "Waterfalls" by TLC.

My wife's flyers brought in around forty Baltimore fans and maybe a dozen people who rooted for San Francisco. By the time Alicia Keyes sat down at the piano inside the Superdome to perform the national anthem, the place was packed. I switched off my mixer and took a lap through the crowd. At the bar, black women in purple Ravens jerseys sang "The Star-Spangled Banner" next to white women wrapped in red 49ers boas. On the patio sat a limousine driver in a black suit and gold tie. The staff paused for cigarettes. As Keys hit the "home of the brave" crescendo, I walked out to the parking lot. Along a fence, green, purple and gold tinsel blew in the breeze. The vacant Charity Hospital glowed in the fading sunlight.

The game was finally here.

And then…

EPILOGUE
FEBRUARY 8, 2013
(FIVE DAYS LATER)

RELAY MISOPERATION

The seats in the New Orleans City Council chambers were surprisingly comfortable, with ample legroom on a slightly sloped floor reminiscent of an old movie theater—you could really settle in. Dramatic moments took place there, too, amid the technicalities and extended public comments. I was present in December 2007, when the council voted unanimously to demolish the city's "Big Four" housing projects. Before the vote, police put stun guns to two protestors on the floor of the chamber and fired tear gas amid a near-riot outside city hall. It was a sad day for everyone involved.

This day's proceedings were much gentler, the stakes exponentially lower, but still a conflict bubbled up. Council vice-president Jackie Clarkson repeated her request. "I just think we've told the public we're going to have an outside inspection by a third party, and I think we have an obligation," Clarkson said. The gentlemen sitting before her were nonplussed. They'd already done an inspection; they would leave the chamber without committing to another.

The partial blackout during the third quarter of Super Bowl XLVII had led Councilwoman Cynthia Hedge-Morrell to call this Emergency Fact Finding meeting of the council's Utility Committee. The purpose wasn't to cast blame, Hedge-Morrell assured us. "We need to know that the lights will stay on for Endymion tomorrow," she said, referring to the Carnival parade that would conclude in the Superdome the following night.

Testifying before the council today were the men responsible for keeping the lights on inside the Superdome: Entergy of New Orleans CEO Charles Rice and the utility company's vice-president of customer service, Dennis

EPILOGUE

Dawsey; SMG's Doug Thornton, the top executive at the Superdome; and LSED chair Ron Forman. Together they explained their findings.

"[T]o provide a newer, more advanced type of protection for the Superdome," said Dawsey, Entergy installed an electrical relay device to monitor the stadium's three power lines.[182] If it detected an abnormality in one of lines, the relay would shut off that line, causing a brief blackout but preventing a longer, more widespread power outage by rerouting power through the other two lines. The system was tested without issue before the demanding run of Sugar Bowl, final Saints game and Super Bowl. On Sunday, the switchgear wrongly identified a problem, Thornton said, thus unnecessarily shutting off one power supply, triggering the blackout.

"The equipment did not function properly," Rice said. "At this particular time, based upon our analysis, we cannot say definitively that there was a defect in design." Hours later, the Chicago-based relay manufacturers denied blame, suggesting that Entergy had improperly installed the device. Inside the chamber, Clarkson suggested an outside opinion. Rice didn't think that was necessary—the company could handle it in-house. "We'll work closely with SMG, and if there is a need for a third-party investigation, we will do that," he said. As committee chair, Hedge-Morrell had the last word.

"I think we still maybe need to have this report and maybe get the forensic audit to make sure any outlining concerns are addressed," said Hedge-Morrell.[183]

A week later, Entergy hired an outside consultant.

In his surprisingly readable report of March 21, 2013, John A. Palmer, PhD, PE, CFEI, essentially confirmed the gentlemen's original assessment: "Tripping of the relay in the absence of any fault or undesirable operating condition constitutes a relay misoperation. Thus a relay misoperation was the cause of the partial power outage."[184]

The phrase "relay misoperation" triggered a memory of an earlier report about connections. The BCG master plan emphasized the many stages of the visitor experience, what airport director Iftikhar Ahmad referred to as the tourism economy's "supply chain." Ideally, a succession of linked components would work in concert to improve the economy and way of life in the region. If bathrooms were better, went the logic, then the business environment would improve, which meant more tax revenue for safer neighborhoods. The "relay misoperation" proved the opposite was also true: if a piece of equipment, ordered and installed with the best intentions, proved defective, it would misdiagnose an issue with the Superdome's power supply, triggering a partial blackout that lasted thirty minutes, and Twitter would achieve a new record for traffic during a televised event. Each piece was vital.

EPILOGUE

In fact, the blackout was demonstrably no more important than the tiles in the men's room of Armstrong International. The tweets and guffaws died quickly, and most every observer complimented the hospitality and beauty of the host city. Commissioner Goodell assured us that New Orleans remained a viable candidate for future Super Bowls. Life and tourism continued.

The host committee and the University of New Orleans released their economic impact report in April. Total net economic impact for the game was $480 million, with $21 million in state tax revenue and $13.9 million for the city. The totals surpassed UNO's 2009 forecast of $434.9 million, $15 million and $11.3 million. Of the visitors surveyed, 50 percent earned at least $100,000 annually, 74 percent were white, 65 percent were male and 40 percent were between thirty-five and forty-nine years old. The numbers suggested the game was a demand generator for the younger, more affluent demographic targeted by the tourism industry.[185]

The study failed to note the tax breaks provided to the NFL as part of the league's agreement with the city. In September, The Lens reported more than $514,000 in refunds from city government, the Orleans Parish school board, the New Orleans Tourism Marketing Corporation and the Regional Transit Authority to the nonprofit NFL.[186]

AUGUST 15, 2014
556 DAYS LATER

As Morley Safer observed to Mitch Landrieu, New Orleans continues to punch above its weight in the category of Most News Stories Generated. Here are a handful of events from the one hundred days that preceded the completion of this manuscript on August 15, 2014:

On May 5, Mayor Landrieu took the oath of office for a second term, secured in a February landslide.

On May 20, Minneapolis was awarded the 2018 Super Bowl, beating out the other finalists, Indianapolis and New Orleans. Several local media outlets noted that this was the city's first failed bid for the game, apparently forgetting Mayor Schiro's disappointment in 1968.

On June 12, Governor Jindal announced that Louisiana would withdraw from the federal government's Common Core education initiative. Formerly a supporter of the new curriculum model, Jindal now said he objected to the Obama administration's intrusion into local schools.

EPILOGUE

At a June 25 breakfast hosted by the Bureau of Governmental Research, Mayor Landrieu said the State of Louisiana had "robbed the city blind for years." Accounting for services, the City of New Orleans made a net profit of $500,000 from the Super Bowl. "People were asking how the city would spend its Super Bowl windfall," Landrieu said. "Most of the money went to the state."

On June 29, shots rang out on Bourbon Street. Bullets fired by two gunmen struck eleven people, two fatally. As of this writing, police have not located the second shooter. Mayor Landrieu requested one hundred state troopers to support the NOPD during the upcoming Essence Festival and through Labor Day; the Jindal administration sent fifty.

On July 9, Judge Ginger Berrigan sentenced former mayor Ray Nagin to ten years in federal prison on July 9. In September, Nagin will become the first New Orleans mayor to serve time for public corruption.

On July 26, readers of *Travel & Leisure* magazine named New Orleans the tenth-best city in the world, the city's highest ranking since 1996.[187]

On August 2, the court-appointed monitor for the prison consent decree blasted Sheriff Gusman for the slow pace of reforms. "This is an in-your-face, happening, bad, everyday thing going on in the jail," she said.[188]

On August 11, New Orleans public schoolchildren returned to class.

At his second inauguration, the mayor outlined the plethora of challenges facing the city, including the costs of the two consent decrees. "We are at a crossroads," he admitted. But forever undaunted, Mitch Landrieu looked beyond the 2018 tricentennial to a future New Orleans: "Three hundred years from now when historians look back, they will remember how we, the people of New Orleans—in this moment, in this time—came together to do what was hard for the sake of doing what was right and gave light and freedom, goodness and life to those generations we do not yet know."[189]

Time will tell. The one hundred days before Super Bowl XLVII included equal measures of goodness and light but also hostility and shadow. Three centuries from now, future generations may remember a people who lived at the crossroads of hard choices and extravagant celebrations. When they ask, "How was New Orleans doing?" historians will have better answers. The lights of the Superdome and the lights of police cruisers will illuminate their search. The Super Bowl and the rhetoric of the new New Orleans may come to represent this time, either as indicators of coming progress or as unfortunate overstatements. As the New Orleans philosopher James Carroll Booker III noted in his response to the dilemma of "put up or shut up," the best answer is maybe a little bit of both.[190]

NOTES

INTRODUCTION

1. Thomas Beller, "Exploring the New New Orleans," *Travel & Leisure*, November 2010.
2. Jessica Stillman, "New Orleans and Young Entrepreneurs: Nurturing Each Other," Inc.com, January 23, 2012, http://www.inc.com/jessica-stillman/new-orleans-and-young-entrepreneurs-nurturing-each-other.html.

CHAPTER 1

3. City of New Orleans (press release), "Transforming the Taxicab Experience in New Orleans: A Roadmap for Reform," http://thelensnola.org/wp-content/uploads/2012/03/taxi-laws.pdf.
4. YouTube, "Mayor Landrieu and Super Bowl Host Committee on 100-Day Countdown to Super Bowl XLVII," https://www.youtube.com/watch?v=APoZexusqX8.
5. Monroe Coleman, interviewed with the author, December 13, 2012.
6. John Simerman, "Feds, City Deliver Tough Talk to New Orleans Convicts in Closed-Door Meeting," *Times-Picayune*, October 25, 2012.
7. Brendan McCarthy, "The Finalists for New Orleans Police Chief: Native Ronal Serpas," *Times-Picayune*, April 30, 2010.

8. Katie Moore, "Serpas Sworn in as Chief," WWLTV.com, http://www.wwltv.com/news/crime/Serpassworninasnopdchief-93458704.html.
9. Martha Carr, "Ronal Serpas Sworn in as New Orleans Police Chief," *Times-Picayune*, May 11, 2010.
10. City of New Orleans (press release), "Mayor Landrieu, Justice Department Announce Details of Consent Decree to Oversee Transformation of New Orleans Police Department," July 24, 2012.
11. Richard Campanella, "'So Unsavory a Smell': Managing Streets, Utilities, and Municipal Services in Historic New Orleans, Part I: The Colonial Era," *Preservation in Print*, November 2012.

CHAPTER 2

12. Buddy Diliberto, "Protest by Negro Gridders Cancels N.O. All-Star Game," *Times-Picayune*, January 11, 1965.
13. Victor Jones, "Mr. Dixon's Imagination Probably Correct," *Boston Globe*, January 18, 1965. Quoted in Mark Souther, *New Orleans on Parade: Tourism and the Transformation of the Crescent City* (Baton Rouge: Louisiana State University Press, 2006).
14. Matthew B. Higgins, "A House Divided: The Evolution of the Louisiana Superdome from a Divisive Concept into a Symbol of New Orleans and the Surrounding Areas," *University of New Orleans Theses and Dissertations*, 2009.
15. Dave Dixon, *Saints, the Superdome and the Scandal* (Gretna, LA: Pelican Publishing, 2008).
16. Greg Easterbrook, "How the NFL Fleeces Taxpayers," *The Atlantic*, October 2013.
17. Richard Sandomir, "Congress's Team: Deal for Merger Included Saints," *New York Times*, January 26, 2010.
18. Bob Roesler, "New Orleans Loses Super Bowl Tug-of-War to Miami: Florida City Gets Encore," *Times-Picayune*, May 15, 1968.
19. Ibid., "Behind the Sports Scene: A $5 Million Setback," *Times-Picayune*, May 15, 1968.
20. *Times-Picayune*, "Super-Bowl Host," March 20, 1969.
21. Bob Roesler, "Super Ducat Plan to be Formulated: Demand Already Shown in New Orleans," *Times-Picayune*, March 21, 1969.
22. *Times-Picayune*, "Rhoden Lauds Healy's Effort: Plans Being Made for Super Bowl Game," March 21, 1969.

23. James H. Gillis, "Half-Mill Tax Hike Approved: Specifications for Street Paving also Amended," *Times-Picayune*, December 10, 1969.
24. Ibid., "Mayor Signs Access Law: Ordinance Becomes Effective on January 1, 1970," *Times-Picayune*, December 24, 1969.
25. Dave Dixon, letter to the editor, *Times-Picayune*, January 1, 1970.
26. Paul Atkinson, "Super Bowl Tax Exemption OK'd: City Councilmen Assure Welfare Assistance," *Times-Picayune*, June 6, 1969.
27. Bob Roesler, "Behind the Sports Scene: The Commissioner's View," *Times-Picayune*, November 9, 1969.
28. *Times-Picayune*, "Best Foot Forward for Super Bowl Fans," January 6, 1970.
29. Wesley Jackson, "Norsemen, Chiefs Grapple amid Resplendent Setting: Mighty Drama Unfolds at Tulane Stadium: N.O. Has Good Case for '71 Bowl—Schiro," *Times-Picayune*, January 12, 1970.
30. *Times-Picayune*, "Super Bowl Lesson: Promote Tourism," January 13, 1970.
31. Ed Anderson, "McKeithen: Dome Mired in Politics," *Times-Picayune*, March 30, 1975.
32. Larry Dickinson, "Edwards Offers 2 Plans to Bail Out Superdome," *State Times Advocate*, February 4, 1976.
33. J. Douglas Murphy, "Dixon Predicts Dome Financial Disaster," *Times-Picayune*, November 7, 1975.
34. Jimmy Smith, "Saints Torch Is Passed from Mecom to Benson," *Times Picayune*, June 4, 1985.
35. John McQuaid, "Saints: Inside the Sale," *Times Picayune*, May 26, 1985.
36. Mike Freeman, "Tagliabue's Hand in Saving Saints Aided New Orleans' Katrina Rally," CBSSports.com, January 27, 2013, http://www.cbssports.com/nfl/story/21619371/tagliabue-didnt-save-new-orleans-by-himself-but-was-major-player.
37. Skip Bayless, "Benson Should Say Good-Bye," ESPN.com, November 4, 2005, http://sports.espn.go.com/espn/page2/story?page=bayless/051104.
38. Peter Finney, "For the Good of the State, the Saints and Their Fans, Tom Benson Should Cut His Ties to the Franchise," *Times-Picayune*, November 04, 2005.
39. Associated Press, "Benson Vows 'I Will Not Return to Baton Rouge,'" November 3, 2005.
40. Jeff Duncan, "NFL Commissioner Roger Goodell Can Take Pride in Helping Bring New Orleans Saints Home," *Times-Picayune*, August 3, 2010.
41. Aaron Kuriloff and Darrell Preston, "Subsidies for Saints Owner Open New Orleans to Super Bowl," Bloomberg, January 31, 2013, http://www.bloomberg.com/news/2013-02-01/subsidies-for-saints-owner-open-new-orleans-to-super-bowl.html.

42. Ibid.
43. Associated Press, "Goodell, Tagliabue Praise 'Human Spirit' in New Orleans," September 26, 2006.
44. Keith Peneguy, "New Orleans Saints and Louisiana Work Out a Deal for Team to Stay at Superdome through 2025," *Times-Picayune*, April 29, 2009.
45. Jennifer Armstrong, "Tom Benson Tops List of the *Times-Picayune*'s 25 Most Influential New Orleans Sports Figures," *Times-Picayune*, July 19, 2009.

CHAPTER 3

46. New Orleans Regional Transit Authority (press release), "Streetcar Tracks Leading to Development Along Loyola Corridor," June 11, 2011.
47. Susan Buchanan, "Mayor Landrieu Warns the City's 2013 Budget Will Be Tight," *Louisiana Weekly*, August 20, 2012.
48. *Time*, "New Orleans Mayor deLesseps Morrison: He Closed Some Doors and Opened a Gateway," November 24, 1947.
49. Edward Haas, *DeLesseps S. Morrison and the Image of Reform: New Orleans Politics, 1946–1961* (Baton Rouge: Louisiana State University Press, 1974).
50. *Times-Picayune*, "History Making Day Monday: Bolivar Statue Event Sunday," May 5, 1957.
51. Ibid., "Troy Henry Concedes, Says Landrieu 'Is Going to Be Fantastic Mayor,'" February 6, 2010.
52. Frank Donze and Michelle Krupam, "Mitch Landrieu Claims New Orleans Mayor's Office in a Landslide," *Times-Picayune*, February 6, 2010.
53. Ibid.
54. Frank L. Schneider, "Poydras Pattern of Change," *Times-Picayune*, February 1, 1976.
55. Lettice Stuart, "'82 Recession Couldn't Halt Boom Shaping a New N.O. Streetscape: Developers Putting Faith in N.O. Future," *Times-Picayune*, January 1, 1983.
56. *State-Times* (Baton Rouge, LA), "LA's Boom-to-Bust Economy Dominates Headlines for Most of Decade," January 2, 1990.
57. Nicholas Lemann, "Hard Times in the Big Easy," *Atlantic Monthly*, August 1, 1987, http://www.theatlantic.com/magazine/archive/1987/08/hard-times-in-the-big-easy/304364/?single_page=true.
58. WDSU.com, "Hyatt Regency Reopens after 6 Years of Renovation," October 19, 2011, http://www.wdsu.com/Hyatt-Regency-Reopens-After-6-Years-Of-Renovation/10976702#!bAUYM4.

CHAPTER 4

59. Michelle Krupa, "French Quarter Streets Stand to Get Bulk of Convention Center Money for Tourism Upgrades," *Times-Picayune*, May 16, 2012, http://www.nola.com/politics/index.ssf/2012/05/french_quarter_streets_stand_t.html.
60. Luna Nola, "Storming the Castle re: LA SB 573: Game-Changing Amendments Added!" NOLAFemmes.com, May 18, 2012, http://nolafemmes.com/2012/05/18/storming-castle-sb-573.
61. Bill Barrow, "Latest Version of 'Hospitality Zone' Clears Senate Committee," *Times-Picayune*, May 17, 2012, http://www.nola.com/politics/index.ssf/2012/05/latest_version_of_hospitality.html.
62. American Zombie, "New Orleans Hospitality Zone—Senate Committee Hearing—Sen. Karen Carter Peterson Explains Amendments," May 22, 2012, http://www.theamericanzombie.com/2012/05/non-starters.html.
63. Ibid.
64. Ibid.
65. Kevin Allman, "NOLA Tourism Leaders Call for Hospitality Zone Legislation to be Pulled," *Gambit*, May 22, 2012.

CHAPTER 5

66. John Guidroz, "Area Lawmakers: Jindal Has Shown More Aggressive Side This Term," American Press, July 2, 2012, http://www.americanpress.com/Area-lawmakers-Jindal-has-shown-more-aggressive-side-this-term.
67. Charlotte Stanley, "Governor Jindal Announces Agreement with BP for Seafood Safety, Coastal Restoration," Examiner.com (Lake Charles), November 1, 2010, http://www.examiner.com/article/governor-jindal-announces-agreement-with-bp-for-seafood-safety-coastal-restorat.
68. Charles Maldonado, "The New Orleans Hotel/Motel Tax: Charles Maldonado on the 13 Percent Tax Levied on Hotel Rooms, and Where That Money Goes," *Gambit*, November 20, 2012, http://www.bestofneworleans.com/gambit/the-new-orleans-hotelmotel-tax/Content?oid=2102931.
69. *USA Today*, "Lt. Gov. Kathleen Blanco Wins Louisiana Governor's Race," November 16, 2003, http://usatoday30.usatoday.com/news/politicselections/state/2003-11-15-la-gov_x.htm.
70. Adam Nossiter, "New Louisiana Governor Pierces Brazen Style of Business as Usual," *New York Times*, February 28, 2008.

71. Jeff Adelson, "Jindal Administration to Announce $129 Million in Cuts; Colleges and Healthcare Expected to Take Big Hits," *Times-Picayune*, December 13, 2012, http://www.nola.com/politics/index.ssf/2012/12/jindal_administration_to_annou.html.
72. Jay Dardenne, interview with the author, December 18, 2012.
73. Edward F. Haas, "The Time of the Kingfish, 1924–1935," in *Louisiana: A History*, edited by Bennett H. Wall (Wheeling, IL: Harlan Davidson, 2002).
74. Alan Brinkley, *Voices of Protest: Huey Long, Father Coughlin, and the Great Depression* (New York: Alfred A. Knopf, 1982), 56.

CHAPTER 6

75. *60 Minutes*, "Outcry after NOLA's Daily Paper Cuts Back," January 6, 2012, http://www.cbsnews.com/news/outcry-after-nolas-daily-paper-cuts-back.
76. Kevin Allman, "After the News: Today at the *Times-Picayune*," *Gambit*, May 24, 2012, http://www.bestofneworleans.com/blogofneworleans/archives/2012/05/24/after-the-news-today-at-the-times-picayune.
77. *60 Minutes*, "Outcry after NOLA's Daily Paper Cuts Back," January 6, 2012, http://www.cbsnews.com/news/outcry-after-nolas-daily-paper-cuts-back.
78. Jed Horne, "Opinion: Changes at TP Were Necessary, But Are They the Right Ones?" The Lens, May 24, 2012, http://thelensnola.org/2012/05/24/opinon-on-tp-changes.
79. Nakia Hogan, "Saints Owner Benson Urges That Newspaper Remain Daily," *Times-Picayune*, May 29, 2012, http://www.nola.com/saints/index.ssf/2012/05/saints_owner_benson_urges_that.html.
80. Mike Hoss and Dominic Massa, "Benson Offers to Buy *Times-Picayune*: Paper Not for Sale Say Advance Officials," WWL-TV, July 26, 2012, http://www.wwltv.com/news/Benson-Times-Picayune-163863846.html.
81. Michelle Krupa, "New Orleans Mayor Ray Nagin Still Trying to Land Super Bowl Tickets," *Times-Picayune*, January 28, 2010, http://www.nola.com/politics/index.ssf/2010/01/new_orleans_mayor_ray_nagin_st.html.
82. Paul Spindt and Toni Weiss, *The Economic Impact of Mardi Gras Season on the New Orleans Economy and the Net Fiscal Benefit of Staging Mardi Gras for the City of New Orleans*, 2009, http://www.rexorganization.com/Downloads/2009/MardiGrasStudy.pdf.

83. Michael Patrick Welch, "How the Super Bowl Screws New Orleans," Vice.com, January 21, 2013, http://www.vice.com/read/how-the-super-bowl-screws-new-orleans.
84. ACLU.org, "Abandoned and Abused: Executive Summary and Recommendations," August 9, 2006, https://www.aclu.org/prisoners-rights/abandoned-abused-executive-summary-and-recommendations#notes, citing Richard Webster, "Jail Tales: Sheriff Gusman, Prisoners Differ on Storm Evacuation Success," *City Business*, February 20, 2006.
85. *Jones v. Gusman*, filed April 2, 2012, United States District Court, Eastern District of Louisiana, 2:12-cv-00859, http://www.splcenter.org/get-informed/case-docket/orleans-parish-prison-safety.
86. Tom Gogola, "Angry Council Member Declares $7M for Decree Monitor a 'Ripoff'," The Lens, November 14, 2012, http://thelensnola.org/2012/11/14/council-faults-consent-decree-budget.
87. Charles Maldonado, "Budget 2013: 'We Can't Host Our Way Out of a Budget Crisis,'" *Gambit*, November 1, 2012, http://www.bestofneworleans.com/blogofneworleans/archives/2012/11/01/budget-2013-we-cant-host-our-way-out-of-a-budget-crisis.
88. Bruce Eggler, "New Orleans City Council Makes Few Changes to Mayor's 2013 Budget," *Times-Picayune*, November 30, 2012.
89. John Simerman, "Mayor Landrieu Fails in Bid to Halt Pending NOPD Reform Deal," *Times-Picayune*, January 11, 2013, http://www.nola.com/crime/index.ssf/2013/01/mayor_landrieu_calls_halt_to_p.html.
90. Ibid.

CHAPTER 7

91. Ariana Lopez, "When Hackathons Meet Super Bowls: A New Orleans Entrepreneur Spurs a New Trend," Forbes.com, January 16, 2013.
92. *Gambit*, "2012 New Orleanian of the Year: Mary Matalin," January 1, 2013, http://www.bestofneworleans.com/gambit/2012-new-orleanian-of-the-year-mary-matalin/Content?oid=2122387.
93. Clancy DuBos, "2012 New Orleanian of the Year: James Carville," *Gambit*, January 1, 2013, http://www.bestofneworleans.com/gambit/2012-new-orleanians-of-the-year-james-carville/Content?oid=2122383.
94. Ibid.
95. Jennifer Armstrong, "James Carville, Mary Matalin to Co-Chair Super Bowl XLVII Committee," *Times-Picayune*, September 2, 2009,

http://www.nola.com/saints/index.ssf/2009/09/james_carville_mary_matalin_to.html.
96. Ibid.
97. Ibid.
98. Ibid.
99. Michelle Krupa, "Will Newcomers Stay?" *Times-Picayune*, August 30, 2008, http://www.nola.com/hurricane/index.ssf/2008/08/will_newcomers_stay.html.
100. Ibid.
101. Martha Carr, "Political Odd Couple to Call N.O. Home, *Times-Picayune*, March 28, 2008, http://www.nola.com/news/index.ssf/2008/03/political_odd_couple_to_call_n.html.
102. Ian McNulty, "Mapping the Political Landscape," MyNewOrleans.com, http://www.myneworleans.com/New-Orleans-Magazine/July-2009/Mapping-the-political-landscape.
103. Laura Bassett, "James Carville Takes on Obama on Oil Spill: He's 'Risking Everything' to 'Go Along with BP Strategy,'" Huffington Post, May 21, 2010, http://www.huffingtonpost.com/2010/05/21/obama-faces-new-wave-of-c_n_585620.html.
104. Anne E. Kornblut, "Democratic Strategist James Carville Upset about Oil Spill: White House Pushes Back," *Washington Post*, May 28, 2010, http://www.washingtonpost.com/wp-dyn/content/article/2010/05/27/AR2010052704545.html.
105. CNN, "The Situation Room with Wolf Blitzer," June 5, 2010, http://transcripts.cnn.com/TRANSCRIPTS/1006/05/sitroom.01.html.
106. Ibid., "Carville Bumps into BP CEO," June 2, 2010, http://politicalticker.blogs.cnn.com/2010/06/02/carville-bumps-into-bp-ceo.
107. Ariana Lopez, "When Hackathons Meet Super Bowls: A New Orleans Entrepreneur Spurs a New Trend," Forbes.com, January 16, 2013, http://www.forbes.com/sites/adrianalopez/2013/01/16/when-hackathons-meet-super-bowls-a-new-orleans-entrepreneur-spurs-a-new-trend.

CHAPTER 8

108. Lenny Vangilder, "Mayou [*sic*] Landrieu: Super Bowl Is NOLA's 'Time to Shine,'" SportsNOLA.com, January 16, 2013, http://sportsnola.com/mayou-landrieu-super-bowl-is-nolas-time-to-shine.
109. Ibid.

110. Edward Jackson, Devin Vance, Joseph Maize and Darryl Parlow, February 5, 2013 interview.
111. Mary Foster, "16 Shot, 2 Fatally, on Halloween in New Orleans," Huffington Post, November 1, 2011, http://www.huffingtonpost.com/2011/11/01/new-orleans-halloween-shooting_n_1070305.html.
112. Scott Hutcheson, interview with the author, January 14, 2013.
113. Matt Sakakeeny, "The Band Is Always There and It Is Always Playing," *Louisiana Cultural Vistas* (Spring 2013), http://www.nxtbook.com/leh/lcvspring2013/lcvspring2013/index.php#/38.
114. Owen Courreges, "The Latest Weapon in the War on Live Music," Uptown Messenger, August 6, 2012, http://uptownmessenger.com/2012/08/owen-courreges-the-latest-weapon-in-the-war-on-live-music/#more-22713.
115. Claire Galofaro, "Live Music Permit Crackdown Unplugs Entertainment at Two Popular New Orleans Bars," *Times-Picayune*, August 7, 2012, http://www.nola.com/politics/index.ssf/2012/08/live_music_permit_problems.html.
116. Alex Rawls, "The War Isn't Over; It Never Started," MySpiltMilk.com, August 16, 2012, http://myspiltmilk.com/war-isnt-over-it-never-started.
117. Ibid., "Dealing with City Hall: The Short Form," MySpiltMilk.com, September 11, 2012, http://myspiltmilk.com/dealing-city-hall-short-form.
118. Mitchell J. Landrieu, *2012 New Orleans Cultural Economy Snapshot*, http://www.nola.gov/getattachment/eb6a244f-4b51-49d9-8265-6dba5789da84/cultural_economy_2012.pdf.
119. Jocelyn Ninneman, "By the Numbers: Sweet Home New Orleans Releases 2012 State of the New Orleans Music Community Report," *Offbeat*, May 1, 2013, http://www.offbeat.com/2013/05/01/sweet-home-new-orleans-releases-2012-state-new-orleans-music-community-report/.
120. Gregory Rattler Jr. and Petrice Sams-Abioudun, "Recognizing the Underutilized Economic Potential of African American Men in New Orleans," Lindy Boggs National Center for Community Literacy, June 14, 2013.

CHAPTER 9

121. Alan Sayre, "Mercedes Benz Buys Naming Rights for Superdome," Yahoo.com, http://sports.yahoo.com/nfl/news?slug=txsuperdomenamingright.

122. Nakia Hogan, "New Orleans Saints Rev up Mercedes-Benz Moniker for the Superdome," NOLA.com, October 5, 2011, http://www.nola.com/saints/index.ssf/2011/10/new_orleans_saints_rev_up_new.html.
123. Les Carpenter, "After a Super Bowl Triumph, Joyous New Orleans Swings to the Rhythm of the Saints," *Washington Post*, February 8, 2010.
124. Rich Cimini, "New Orleans Saints Quarterback Drew Brees Says Super Bowl Win Was a 'Responsibility' to Fans," *New York Daily News*, February 8, 2010.
125. Mike Sando, "Tapes a Knockout Blow for Williams," ESPN.com, April 5, 2012, http://espn.go.com/blog/nfcwest/post/_/id/62434/tapes-a-knockout-blow-for-gregg-williams.
126. David Roth, "What's Eating Roger Goodell," TheClassical.org, February 1, 2013, http://theclassical.org/articles/whats-eating-roger-goodell.
127. David Hammer, "In Depth: Former N.O. Mayor Ray Nagin Indicted on Federal Corruption Charges," WWLTV.com, January 19, 2013, http://www.wwltv.com/news/nagin-indictment/Nagin-story-guts-182242111.html.
128. Gordon Russell, "Former Mayor Ray Nagin's First Court Appearance Pushed Back," *Times-Picayune*, January 23, 2013.
129. Rob Curwitt, "Creole Crackdown," Governing.com, October 2002, http://www.governing.com/topics/politics/Ray-Nagin-Creole-Crackdown.html
130. Recording, WBOK-FM, January 19, 2013.

CHAPTER 10

131. Alan Powell, "Airport Delays Cab Change," *The Advocate*, December 23, 2012, http://theadvocate.com/news/4734185-123/airport-delays-cab-change.
132. Ibid., "Kenner Cabbies Ready to Protest During Super Bowl over Required Upgrades," *The Advocate*, January 21, 2013.
133. City of New Orleans (press release), "Mayor Landrieu and Airport Officials Unveil Armstrong International Airport Improvements," January 15, 2013.
134. David Hammer, "New Orleans Aviation Director's Post Offered to Veteran Ohio Administrator," *Times-Picayune*, February 22, 2013.
135. Lee Zurik, "OIG Calls Armstrong Airport 'Pit of Corruption,'" Fox8live.com, March 30, 2012.
136. Iftikhar Ahmad, interview with the author, December 17, 2012.

137. Curtis Williams, interview with the author, January 24, 2013.
138. David Hammer, "Pampy's Surrenders New Orleans Airport Concessions in Court Settlement," *Times-Picayune*, December 5, 2011.
139. Mary Foster, "Owners Approve Hornets' Move to New Orleans," Associated Press, May 10, 2002.
140. Bill Simmons, "The Sixth Day of NBA Christmas," ESPN.com, December 15, 2011.
141. ESPN.com, "Saints Owner Agrees to Buy Hornets," April 14, 2012.
142. Jimmy Smith, "NBA Commissioner David Stern Says New Orleans Was in the All-Star Plans without New Hornets Ownership; Says Jazz Nickname Stays in Utah," NOLA.com, April 16, 2012.
143. Ibid., "NBA to Award 2014 All-Star Game to New Orleans Today," NOLA.com, April 16, 2012.
144. To be fair, I would add Cosimo Mattassa's J&M Studios into this debate.
145. Quint Davis, interview, January 24, 2013.

CHAPTER 11

146. Karl Dequine, "Jackson Square Artists, Businesses Upset at NFL's Concert Plans," *Times-Picayune*, September 4, 2010.
147. Frank Donze, "Jackson Square Rules Are Proposed by Panel of Residents," *Times-Picayune*, January 23, 2011.
148. Naomi Martin, "NOPD: 5 People Shot in Central City Where Martin Luther King Day Parade Had Passed Earlier," NOLA.com, January 21, 2013.
149. Tania Dall, "Proposed Jackson Square Ordinance Sparks Controversy," WWLTV.com, November 23, 2011, http://www.wwltv.com/news/local/orleans/Proposed-Jackson-Square-Ordinance-Sparks-Controversy-180652251.html.
150. Ibid.
151. Charles Maldanado, "The Evolution of the Super Bowl Clean Zone," BestofNewOrleans.com, January 29, 2013, http://www.bestofneworleans.com/blogofneworleans/archives/2013/01/29/the-evolution-of-the-super-bowl-clean-zone.

CHAPTER 12

152. Warren Bell, interview with the author, January 28, 2013.
153. Ariella Cohen, "Against Long Odds, RTA Seeks Federal Funds to Extend Streetcar Line to Poland Avenue," The Lens, September 14, 2011, http://thelensnola.org/2011/09/14/poland-streetcar-extension-encouraged/.
154. Michelle Krupa, "Official with Nonprofit Loan Program Got Loans Herself," *Times-Picayune*, August 14, 2011.
155. Dylan Byers, "James Carville, Mary Matalin Leaving CNN," Politco.com, January 29, 2013.

CHAPTER 13

156. Leslie Williams, "Man Found Dead in Occupy New Orleans Encampment," *Times-Picayune*, November 8, 2011.
157. Associated Press, "Police Clear Out Occupy New Orleans Camp," December 6, 2011.
158. ACLU.org, "ACLU Sues City of New Orleans over Super Bowl 'Clean Zone' Ordinance," January 25, 2013.
159. Charles Maldonado, "ACLU Reaches Agreement with City on Clean Zone Lawsuit," blogofneworleans.com, January 28, 2013.

CHAPTER 14

160. Paul Atkins, "NO Losing Out," *Times-Picayune*, October 26, 1978.
161. Dan Even, "Need for Exhibition Hall in N.O. Argued," *Times-Picayune*, May 19, 1978.
162. Alan Katz, "Consultant: World's Fair to Showcase N.O.," *Times-Picayune*, January 17, 1981.
163. Joan Kent, "Hard Hitter: Organizer for World's Fair Talks a Tough Game," *Times-Picayune*, January 4, 1981.
164. Bridget O'Brian and Dean Bacquet, "Going Broke: Troubled Story of World's Fair," *Times-Picayune* November 11, 1984.
165. Peggy Scott Laborde and Steven Tyler, *A World's Fair to Remember*, WYES-TV, 2003.
166. O'Brian and Bacquet, "Going Broke."

167. Nan Perales, "Fair Ready for Final Celebration," *Times-Picayune*, November 11, 1984.
168. John McQuid, "Helicopter Gathering Opens Era," *Times-Picayune*, January 18, 1985.
169. Nan Perales, "Fair Lost $6.3 Million in Rouse Deal," *Times-Picayune*, May 1, 1985.
170. Alan Katz, "Riverfront Development: A Catalyst for Recovery," *Times-Picayune*, May 5, 1985.
171. Louisiana Department of Revenue, "2011/2012 Annual Tax Collection Report," http://www.revenue.louisiana.gov/forms/publications/LDR_Annual_Report(11%2012).pdf.

CHAPTER 15

172. Paul Timphony, interview, February 1, 2013.
173. *Moves* Magazine, "About Us," http://www.movesmagazine.com.
174. D. Orlando Ledbetter, "Roddy White Goes on a Rant About Saints, New Orleans," *Atlanta Journal Constitution*, November 10, 2012, http://blogs.ajc.com/atlanta-falcons-blog/2012/11/10/roddy-white-goes-on-a-rant-about-saints-new-orleans/?cxntfid=blogs_atlanta_falcons_blog.

CHAPTER 16

175. Lanny Thomas, "Echavarria Sounds Plea to Hike U.S.-Latin Trade," *Times-Picayune*, May 1, 1968.
176. Christopher Tidmore, "Landrieu Poised to Tear Down World Trade Center Building," *Louisiana Weekly*, March 26, 2012
177. TBC interview, February 5, 2013.
178. CBSNews.com, "New Orleans' Challenge: Policing 2 Huge Parties," January 30, 2013.

CHAPTER 17

179. Allen Powell, "Reaction Mixed to Decree Deal," *The Advocate*, February 2, 2013.
180. Ibid., "Overall Crime in N.O. Drops Slightly in 2012," *The Advocate*, February 2, 2013.

CHAPTER 18

181. Jenny Vrentas, "Gov. Chris Christie Hopes 2014 Super Bowl Will Help 'Turn the Page' from Hurricane Sandy," NJ.com, February 3, 2013.

EPILOGUE

182. Michael Kunzleman, "Super Bowl Blackout Was Caused by Electrical Relay," Associated Press, February 8, 2013.
183. Paul Murphy, "Entergy Admits Super Bowl Power Outage Was a Problem on Its End," WWLTV.com, February 8, 2013.
184. John A. Palmer, "Superdome Partial Power Outage: Report Prepared for Entergy New Orleans, Inc., SMG, Louisiana Stadium and Exposition District," Palmer Engineering & Forensics, March 21, 2013.
185. The New Orleans Super Bowl Host Committee and the University of New Orleans Division of Economic and Business Research, "2013 Super Bowl Visitor Study & Economic Impact," April 2013, http://media.nola.com/business_impact/other/Super%20Bowl%20XLVII%20Economic%20Impact%20Study%20UNO.PDF.
186. Charles Maldanado, "Local Tax Rebate to NFL for Super Bowl Tops $500,000—But Well Below Cap," The Lens, September 25, 2014. http://thelensnola.org/2013/09/25/local-tax-rebate-to-nfl-for-super-bowl-2013-tops-500g-well-below-negotiated-cap.
187. Timothy Boone, "N.O. Ranks 10th on *Travel & Leisure* Best Cities List," http://www.theneworleansadvocate.com/opinion/9739362-171/no-ranks-10th-on-travel, July 26, 2014.
188. Jim Mustian, "Jail Monitor Blasts Gusman for Lack of Progress at OPP," *New Orleans Advocate*, August 2, 2014.
189. Mitch Landrieu, "City of New Orleans Inauguration," May 5, 2014.
190. James Carroll Booker III, "Classified," *A Taste of Honey*, 1977.

INDEX

A

Acme Oyster House 70, 125
Ahmad, Iftikhar 18, 126
Alexandria 178, 180
Algiers Point 142
Allen, Thad 97
American Civil Liberties Union (ACLU) 146, 159
American Football League (AFL) 28, 29, 32
Amos, John 148, 191
Andrews, Troy 178, 188
Angelle, Scott 70
Armstrong Park 19, 168
Askiel 41, 42, 43
Atlantic Monthly, The 30, 49
Audubon Aquarium 176
Augustine, Justin 17, 152
avenues
    Claiborne 105
    Loyola 11, 17, 41, 42, 43, 44, 50, 54, 84, 151, 155, 196
    North Claiborne 11, 20
    St. Bernard 105
    St. Charles 17, 81, 189, 193
    Tulane 23, 28, 44, 197

B

Bacardi 115
Bajoie, Diana 72
Barrea, Marlo 142
Barre, Stan "Pampy" 131
BASF 177
Baton Rouge 36, 62, 109, 114, 126, 183, 195
Baton Rouge Press Club 72
Bayless, Skip 37
Bayou Classic 140
Beaulieu, Paul 122
Beller, Thomas 9
Bell, Warren 151, 153
Benson Boogie 36, 135
Benson, Gayle 25, 113, 135
Benson, Rita. *See* LeBlanc, Rita Benson
Benson, Tom 25, 36, 39, 82, 93, 114, 132, 173
Berni, Ryan 92, 96, 108
Berrigan, Ginger 202
Blanco, Kathleen 37, 73
Boggs, Whip Hale 30
Booker James, Carroll, III 202
Boston Consulting Group 59
Bountygate 123, 135, 164, 194
BP 70, 96, 97

INDEX

Brees, Drew 22, 38, 114, 164
Brother Martin High School 26
Brown, Christy 79
Bryan, Phil 194
Buck, Joe 173
Bud Light 178, 181, 183, 184, 185, 187, 188
Bywater 95, 146, 170, 188

C

Café Envie 142
Cajun Louisiana 168
Calliope 11
Campanella, Richard 23
Cannizaro, Leon 21
Cantrell, Latoya 194
Capitol Annex 69
Carondelet 171, 172
Carr, David 81
Carter, Dwayne 190
Carville, James 38, 91, 153, 154, 194, 195
CBS 139, 141, 144, 161, 179, 188
Celebration Hall 105, 111, 177
Central Business District 11, 17, 43, 100, 108, 146, 193
Certificate of Public Necessity and Convenience (CPNC) 13, 20
Champion Square 135
Charity Hospital 33, 44, 117, 198
Charlotte Hornets 19, 81, 132, 133, 134
Chevron 177
"Chocolate City" speech 123
Cicero, Jay 93, 194
Circle Bar 108, 109
Clarkson, Jackie 72, 87, 154, 199
Club Metropolitan 173, 174
CNN 96, 156
CODEMKRS 91
Coleman, Monroe 15, 16
Congo Square and Municipal Auditorium 136
Convention Center Boulevard 18, 178, 183
Copeland's Cheesecake Bistro 129
Copelin, Sherman 35
Cortez, Page 63
Cosentino, John 139
Creole Kitchen 129

D

Dardenne, Jay 69
Davis, Arthur 136
Davis, Quint 103, 109, 135, 178
Deepwater Horizon 70, 96, 110, 118, 133, 134
Delaware North 130, 131
Dickerson, Eric 173
Disney Institute Super Bowl Fans First Team 113
Dixon, Dave 29, 31, 32, 132, 135
DJ Action Jackson 105
Dooky Chase 129
Downtown Development District 175, 178
Duncan Plaza 44, 46, 158, 196

E

Easterbrook, Gregg 30
Edwards, Edwin 35, 133, 167
Elk Place 43
Elm's Mansion 189
Elysian Fields 11, 19
Entergy of New Orleans 199
Ernest M. Morial Convention Center 18, 59, 60, 163, 176
Esman, Marjorie 146, 159
Essence Music Festival 108

F

Faulk, Marshall 174
Federal Aviation Administration 131
federal corruption 121
Federal District Court 89
Federal Emergency Management Agency (FEMA) 38
federal funding 67, 167
Federal Highway Administration 55
federal indictment 122
federal levees 10, 36
Finney, Peter 37
Fontainebleau Motor Hotel 28
French Market 19
French Quarter 11, 17, 28, 66, 67, 103, 125, 139, 158, 179

INDEX

G

Gallier Hall 79, 83, 193
Gambit Weekly 72, 87, 92, 146
Garret, Melton J. 175
George, Eddie 173
Glazer, Jay 173
Gleason, Steve 38, 119, 177
Goodell, Roger 37, 76, 118, 119, 121, 123, 174, 177
GQ 189, 190
Graham, Joey 173
Grant, Cedric 17
Greater New Orleans Data Center 97
Greater New Orleans Sports Foundation 93, 194
Guidry, Susan 194
Gusman, Marlin 21, 86, 87

H

Hall, Gallier 22
Hammer, David 11, 121
Handsome Willy's 116, 120, 142, 163
Harrah's Casino 18, 59, 176
Hayward, Tony 97
HBO 110
Healy, George 31
Hedge-Morrel, Cynthia 87, 199
Helicopter Association International 169
Hirt, Al 31, 34, 189
Hodge, Merrill 173
Holder, Eric 21, 87
Home for Colored Waifs 44
House of Blues 103
Hull, Malachi 15
Hutcheson, Scott 18, 107

I

Idea Village 95, 97, 98
Inc. magazine 97
Initiative 4 French Quarter 61
International Trade Mart 175
Interstate 10 69

J

Jackson, Edward 105
Jackson Square 19, 67, 139, 141, 144, 145, 154, 161, 188, 191
Jefferson Parish 55, 180, 185, 194
Jernigan, Mark 57
Jindal administration 39, 44, 202
Jindal, Bobby 39, 70, 73, 74, 77
Johnson, Troy 21
Juvenile (rapper) 101

K

Kabacoff, Lester 166, 169, 170
Kaigler, Cecil 130
Katzs, Allan 169
Keevers, Frank 169
Kenner City Council 126
Kingfish. *See* Long, Huey
Kopplin, Andy 62
krewes
  Krewe du Vieux 120, 121, 142
  Krewe of Ponchartrain 85
  Rex 79
  Zulu 79, 83
Krupa, Michelle 94
Krygowski, Walter 126

L

LaHood, Ray 153, 156
Lake Maurepas 69
Lake Ponchartrain 45, 69
Landrieu administration 15, 58, 62, 87, 129, 145, 146, 158
Landrieu, Maurice "Moon" 32, 35, 46, 166
Landrieu, Mitch 13, 21, 22, 42, 62, 84, 103, 126, 134, 153, 176, 194
Laurendine, Travis 91
LeBlanc, Rita Benson 82, 93, 194
Letten, Jim 21, 131
Lieb, Ernst 115
Lil Wayne. *See* Carter, Dwayne
Lindy Boggs National Center for Community Literacy 111

INDEX

Little Gem Saloon 49, 100
Lloyd, Cobb 175
Lofstead, Jarret 117, 197
Long, Huey 76
Long, Russell 30
Loomis, Mickey 119
Lost Bayou Ramblers 178
Louis Armstrong International Airport 18, 130
Louisiana Department of Children and Family Services 74
Louisiana Department of Culture, Recreation and Tourism 59, 70
Louisiana Department of Health and Hospitals 73, 74
Louisiana Department of Natural Resources 70
Louisiana Department of Transportation 55
Louisiana Folklife Pavilion 166, 168, 169
Louisiana Lottery 125
Louisiana Office of Community Development 154
Louisiana Sports and Entertainment District 30
Louisiana Sports and Exposition District 134
Louisiana State Exposition District 39, 60
Love, Keisha 179
Lower Ninth Ward 45, 174

M

Major, Barbara 154
Maldonado, Charles 146
Marigny 62, 63, 95, 108, 120, 139, 188
Martin Behrman Elementary School 179
Matalin, Mary 91, 101, 103, 153, 154, 194
Mayer, Peter 91, 92, 98, 100
McCallister, Deuce 164
McKeithen, John 29
Mena's Palace 187
Men of Unity 105
Mercedes-Benz 114, 115
Meyers, Joel 134
Micaroni, Justin 116, 163, 197
Mid City 41

Miner, Allison 136
Mitchell, Ralph M. 88
Molly Marine statue 43
Moore, Curtis 130, 132
Morgan, Susie 89
Morial administration 131, 166
Morial, Dutch 166
Morial, Marc 86, 122, 131
Morrison, deLesseps "Chep" 45, 49, 86, 155, 197
Moses, Robert 67
Moves Magazine Party 173
Multi Cultural Tourism Network 63
municipal code 85
Murray, Edwin 62
Music and Cultural Coalition of New Orleans (MACCNO) 159

N

Nagin administration 94, 154
Nagin, Ray 37, 46, 83, 96, 121, 122, 123, 132, 188, 202
N'awlins Cookery 190
Nelson, Rock 86
Newhouse, Steven 82
New Orleans Brass 132
New Orleans City Council 13, 32, 33, 61, 62, 63, 87, 154, 169, 199
New Orleans City Hall 11, 22, 44, 84, 121, 141, 156, 193
New Orleans City Park 23, 25
New Orleans Convention and Visitors Bureau (NOCVB) 32, 60, 61, 62, 63, 64, 106
New Orleans Country Club 29
New Orleans Department of Cultural Economy 110
New Orleans Department of Economic Development 71
New Orleans Department of Parks and Parkways 141
New Orleans Department of Public Works 57
New Orleans Department of Sanitation 141
New Orleans East 55, 89, 179

INDEX

New Orleans Exhibition Hall Authority 166
New Orleans Jazz & Heritage Festival 135, 177
New Orleans Pelicans 134, 135
New Orleans Police Department (NOPD) 21, 83, 106, 122, 179
New Orleans Regional Planning Commission 55
New Orleans Regional Transit Authority 17, 42, 151
New Orleans Saints 28, 31, 35, 36, 38, 39, 47, 70, 113, 114, 116, 117, 118, 119, 129, 136, 143, 164
New Orleans Strategic Hospitality Task Force 59
New Orleans Super Bowl Host Committee 71
New Orleans Tourism Marketing Corporation (NOTMC) 60, 61, 122
New York Times 30, 74, 81
NFL Experience, the 163, 164, 165, 178
Ninth Ward 55
NOLA Brewery 100
NOLA.com 81
"NOLA for Life" 21
Nola, Luna 60, 62
NOLA Parks 100

O

Ocala 144
Occupy New Orleans 157, 197
Old U.S. Mint 120
OPEC 48
Orleans Parish 9, 21, 94, 97
Orleans Parish Civil Courthouse 84
Orleans Parish Criminal District Court 21
Orleans Parish Prison (OPP) 86
Orleans Parish Sheriff's Office 85

P

Palmer, Gisleson 141, 145, 146
Palmer, John A. 200
Palmer, Kristen Giselson 60
Pampy's Inc. 131

Pan-American Life Insurance 115
Parlow, Darryl 106
Parmer, Raymond 179
Partners-N-Crime 100
Paul, Chris 132
Payton, Sean 38, 119, 174
Pecoul, John 32
Pennington, Richard 122
Pepsi 164, 177
Perlis Cajun Clothing 129
Perry, James 22
Perry, Stephen 62, 106
Persia, Mike 26
post-Katrina era 10, 39, 59
Powell, Allen 184
Praline Connection 130, 178
Preservation Resource Center 23

Q

Quatrevaux, Ed 128

R

Rawls, Alex 108
Real Estate Research Corporation (RERC) 166
Rebirth Brass Band 178
Reunion Hall 168
Rhoden, Robert 32
Rice, Charles 199
Richardson, Rodney 135
Rick's Cabaret 125
Rick's Saloon 147, 191
Ritz Carlton Davenport Lounge 125
Riverfront Expressway 67
Riverwalk mall 169
roads
  Bunker Hill 179
Rock-n-Sake 86
Rodrigue, Melvin 63
Roesler, Bob 31
Romig, Mark 83, 92, 103, 122
Roosevelt Hotel 29
Rosenberg, Stanley 27
Rubenstein, Mike 189, 190
Rubenstein's 189

INDEX

S

Saenger Theater 42
Sakakeeny, Matt 107
San Diego Chargers 29
Save the *Times-Picayune*! 81
Scalise, Steve 194
Scandaliato, Sam 85
Schiro, Victor 29
Scott, Stu 173
Senate Bill 573 62
Serpas, Ronal 19, 22, 83, 127, 144, 155, 179
Seventh Ward 26, 36, 62, 63, 82, 105, 135, 146
Sherman, Mike 96
Shinn, George 132
Siberia 108, 109
Sigel, Gertrude 66
Simmons, Bill 133
Slade, John 122
Slidell 173, 191
Sorrento 69
Spurney, August 168
stadiums
  City Park 29
  Superdome 29, 31, 34, 38, 113, 132, 165, 200
  Tad Gormley 25, 28, 40
  Tiger 36, 37, 39, 134
  Tulane 28, 29, 31
St. Aloysius High School 26, 27
State Capitol Park 76
St. Augustine High School 155
St. Bernard Parish 140, 187, 191
Stern, David 133
Stewart, Naaman 79
St. James Infirmary 190
St. Louis Cathedral 139
streets
  Basin 42
  Bienville 187, 190
  Bourbon 11, 28, 42, 104, 125, 142, 159, 173, 191
  Canal 18, 29, 41, 42, 55, 85, 152, 173, 189
  Chartres 144, 187, 188
  Dauphine 19, 171
  Decatur 120, 139, 141, 142, 183, 185
  Frenchmen 130
  Julia 155
  Magazine 119
  North Rampart 26
  Poyrdras 13, 16, 17, 47, 49, 100, 155, 176, 196, 197
  Royal 23, 42, 55, 64, 65, 66
  Toulouse 157
Super Bowl Hackathon 91, 92, 93, 97, 101, 103, 170
Super Bowl IV 31
Super Bowl LII 19, 201
Super Bowl Park 161
Super Bowl Super Challenge. *See* Super Bowl Hackathon
Super Bowl Super Hole XLVAG 121
Super Bowl Task Force, 1970 31
Super Bowl XLIV 47, 117
Super Bowl XLVII 10, 23, 39, 59, 80, 103, 122, 146, 159, 197
Super Bowl XXVI 85
Super Bowl XXXV 186
Superdome Services Inc. (SSI) 35
Swigart, Frances 56, 66

T

Tagliabue, Paul 37, 194
Tanner 64, 65, 66
Tarver, Greg 63
taxicab bureau 15, 142
taxicab drivers 126, 129, 132
TBC Brass Band 103, 176
Team Crawfinder 93
Thomas, Irma 42
Thomas, Michelle 18
Thornton, Doug 200
Tiger Grant 42, 152, 154
Times-Picayune 21, 29, 47, 80, 167, 184, 213
Timphony, Paul 171
ToBeContinued. *See* TBC Brass Band
Tremé 62, 63, 110

INDEX

Tunechi. *See* Carter, Dwayne
1201 Canal 42
2Chainz 105

U

Undefeated Gents 105
Union Passenger Terminal 42, 45, 51, 151
United Cab Company 61
universities
   Loyola 27, 111, 185
   Tulane 23, 28, 95, 107, 136, 197
   University of New Orleans 201
U.S. Department of Health and Human Services 73
U.S. Department of Housing and Urban Development 166
U.S. Department of Justice 22, 88
U.S. Department of Transportation 42

V

Verizon Super Bowl Boulevard 103, 161, 176
Vieux Carre 55, 57, 120
Vieux Carre Property and Residents Association (VCPORA) 57
Vitt, Joe 119
Voodoo Festival 23
Voting Rights Act, 1965 30

W

Warehouse District 86, 169
Warlick, Ernie 28
Washington Artillery Park 141
Washington, Delores 16
Washington Post 118
Washington-Ranson, Addie 126
Washington, Walter "Wolfman" 178
WBOK 84, 122
Wein, George 136
Westboro Baptist Church 158, 196
Westmoreland, Dick 29
White, Roddy 173
Williams, Curtis 178
Williams, Gregg 119

Woodson, Rod 173
Woolridge, Ray 132
World's Fair, 1984 49, 165, 175
World Trade Center 175
WWL-TV 37, 82

Y

Young, John 194

Z

Zapp's chips 129
Zatairain's Kitchen 129
zones
   Clean 139, 146, 158, 159, 160, 161, 183
   Constitution Free 146
   Hospitality 17, 18, 62, 63, 64, 65, 66, 83, 146
Zurik, Lee 128

ABOUT THE AUTHOR

Brian W. Boyles is a native of Pittsburgh and a graduate of Tulane University. Since 2007, he has directed public programming at the Louisiana Humanities Center in New Orleans, including oral history projects with local brass bands, piano players and politicians. A founding member of East Village Radio, he was named to *Gambit Weekly*'s "40 Under 40" list in 2011. He serves as creative director for www.thepeoplesayproject.org, a website about culture and money. His work has appeared in *Oxford American*, Vice.com, The Classical, *Offbeat*, The Lens, *The Brooklyn Rail* and *SLAM*. Boyles lives in New Orleans' Thirteenth Ward with his wife and son.